The Parent Backpack for
Kindergarten through Grade 5

THE
PARENT BACKPACK
for Kindergarten
through Grade 5

*How to Support Your Child's
Education, End Homework Meltdowns,
and Build Parent-Teacher Connections*

ML NICHOLS

TEN SPEED PRESS
Berkeley

IN MEMORY OF

Sandy Wade, my mom, to whom I promised a finished book;
Sandy, the hurricane, which dared to hit the day my first
draft was due; and the Sandy Hook Elementary children
and teachers we will never forget.

Published in the United States by Ten Speed Press, an imprint of the
Crown Publishing Group, a division of Random House, Inc., New York.
www.crownpublishing.com
www.tenspeed.com

Ten Speed Press and the Ten Speed Press colophon are registered
trademarks of Random House, Inc.

The Parent Backpack is a registered trademark of Marylisa Nichols.

Library of Congress Cataloging-in-Publication Data
Nichols, Marylisa.
  The parent backpack for kindergarten through grade 5 : how to support your
child's education, end homework meltdowns, and build parent-teacher connections /
Marylisa Nichols.
      pages cm
  Includes bibliographical references and index.
1. Education, Elementary—Parent participation—United States—Handbooks,
manuals, etc. 2. Parent-teacher relationships—United States—Handbooks, manuals,
etc. 3. Home and school—United States—Handbooks, manuals, etc. I. Title.
  LB1048.5.N54 2013
  371.19'2—dc23
                                    2012050585

Trade Paperback ISBN: 978-1-60774-474-0
eBook ISBN: 978-1-60774-475-7

Printed in the United States of America

Design by Chloe Rawlins
Front cover photograph © KidStock
Interior notebook paper photograph © subjub

10 9 8 7 6 5 4 3 2 1

First Edition

Contents

PART THREE
Supporting Your Child's Learning at Home

Acknowledgments

I always thought I would have three children. What I didn't know is that the third would be a 300-page, nine-month labor of love, made possible through the generosity of many educators, parents, and writers. I am lucky and eternally grateful.

To the school administrators I've worked with over the past decade from whom I've learned so much: Candy Weiler, whose insight and encouragement shines through every chapter; Wayne Ogden, my wise coach who keeps me on course; Ed Walsh and Debbi Zetterberg, always there with answers and perspective; Suzanne Billingham, Gail Callahan, Kevin Clark, Bruce Cole, Blake Dalton, Andrew Stephens, Ann Taylor, Christopher Trombly, Karen Whitaker, and my three superintendents: Dr. Eileen Williams, Susan Skeiber, and Dr. Ben Tantillo, thank you for your support, your candor, and the many opportunities you've given me.

To my amazing teacher readers, Nancy Fenstemacher and Betsy McCarthy, who offered invaluable feedback on an endless stream of chapters. To the more than sixty brilliant psychologists, educators, and parenting experts I've hosted through my nonprofit, The Parent Connection. To the excellent educators who have shaped my thoughts on teaching, learning, and family involvement: Sheila Arpe, Missy Bateman, Britta Bodine, Lisa Buchholz, Jay Craft, Chris Delano, Peggy Germain, Michele Glynne, Tom Gotsil, Dianne Hearn, Anne Henderson, Carol Jankowski, Meg Jordan, Ann Kalous, Kathleen Kedzeirski, Denise Lamare, Renee Lewin, Carole Love, Sara Madigan, Chris Maiorano, Karen Mapp, Kitty Marrone, Chris Naton, LeeAnn Nash, Stu Peskin, Susan Riser, Rachel Stadelmann, Nancy Stearns, Pat Tarantino, Michelle Taylor, and Liz Woollacott, thank you for all you've taught me. And to every devoted librarian, teacher, school nurse, counselor, office assistant, and custodian out there, thank you for putting children first.

To the parents who have helped me, especially Jamie Therrien, my sounding board, my brakes, my chief reader, and confidante who made this book possible. My co-founders on The Parent Connection—Sally Runci, Laura Smith, and Carrie Couto—and all the past and present board members whose contributions humble me daily. To the parents who read a chapter, provided input, or offered a shoulder: Maryann Aubrey, Kate Brewer, Marilyn Burnham, Mary Lynne Carson, Barb Desai, Robin Elliott, Anne Fleming, Mark Germain, Kim Hunt, Cari Kent, Christine Leonard, Brooke McDonough, Lynn O'Neil, Jen Quinlan, Patty Roberts, Gay Shanahan, Jen Sullivan, Scottie Summerlin, Marci Teah, Selden Tearse, Michael Trottman, Anne Ward, Kristin Zaniboni, and Elena Zongrone. To the many other parents who participated in focus groups or workshops, shared their stories, or asked for my help somewhere along their child's journey. To my fellow moms on *Parenting* magazine's Mom Congress on Learning and Education, thank you for all you've given me.

To my editor Julie Bennett, who understood and championed this book from day one. Your acumen for knowing just what a paragraph or a sentence needs—and communicating that perfectly—amazes me every time. And to the terrific team at Ten Speed Press who brought this book to life: Michele Crim, Kara Van De Water, Ashley Matuszak, and Chloe Rawlins, and to copy editor Jean Blomquist and proofreader Molly Woodward, thank you.

To my agent and teacher, Mollie Glick of Foundry Media, whose vision and enthusiasm for *The Parent Backpack* never waned. Thank you for pushing me. To Katie Hamblin, who proved to be a stellar substitute. To Grub Street in Boston, Eve Bridburg, Lynne Griffin, and Katrin Schumann, who helped me find, shape, and launch this book, along with my fellow Launch Labbers, thank you for your inspiration and community.

Finally, to my family. For your unconditional love, encouragement, and tolerance of no matching socks throughout this journey. To my dad, Frank Germain, for your love and support at every turn. To Barry and Sara Nichols, for my Cape room-with-a-view and home-cooked dinners. To Emily, my oldest daughter and title creator, for all of your understanding of "the book." To Olivia, my junior editor and bundle of love, for whom I will delete half my dashes. To Evi, my Fresh Air Fund "daughter" who will go to college. And to my devoted husband, Tom, my toughest editor, a fabulous dad, and launderer extraordinaire, I am forever indebted.

Introduction:
What I Wish I Knew Then

We need a revolution in this country when it comes to parenting around education. —THOMAS FRIEDMAN, *The World Is Flat*

When my forty-two-pound, forty-two-inch, five-year-old Emily hoisted herself onto that big yellow bus to begin her journey through elementary school, I had a few questions. I was, admittedly, not one of those trusting "just send her to school, she'll be fine" kind of parents. I was nervous, curious, and, yes, a little intimidated. What really goes on behind those big walls? How has school changed since I went? How do I support my child's learning? When do I talk to the teacher? What can I do to make sure my daughter—both my daughters—get the best education possible?

Besides having a baby, one of the biggest milestones in this parenting journey is sending our children off to school. I devoured parenting books on what to expect when my kids were little. But as I watched my oldest head off to kindergarten over a decade ago, my nightstand sat empty. I had no trusted resource to guide me through those emotional and important elementary years, no book to coach me on how to be involved in my kids' education or what to expect. I did find lots of books on education—the problems with it, what makes effective teaching, urban-suburban performance gaps, the perils of standards-based testing—all written by educators, for educators. And I found books on parenting related to education—the child with behavioral issues, what to do when your child doesn't like to read, and grade-by-grade curriculum books.

But where was the book to help me navigate the vast and intimidating world of schools so I could better understand my role as a parent in my kids' education? I scoured the library, spent hours in bookstores, and searched online, but found nothing that gave me the insight I was seeking. And it didn't take me long to discover that elementary school is a winding, and sometimes frustrating, journey—unless you understand the system. But it takes a few years to figure that out and when you do, it's often too late, or you find yourself dealing with your next child who has completely different needs. I needed to know what I didn't know.

So while other moms became soccer, swim, and scout moms (and I thank them all for doing that for my kids), I raised my hand to volunteer in the schools. And one position led to another. By the end of my two daughters' six-year journeys through elementary school, I had served in just about every role possible, from PTA president and school council cochair to classroom parent (seven times) and grants chair for an education foundation. I cleaned chick cages for science and spent hours talking with teachers. I was a crusader for causes like smaller class size and a school-wide directory, a member of numerous district-wide committees that changed policies, renovated schools, and searched for new administrators and superintendents. I became a "school mom," and in the process, I learned a few things about schools and education. Some considered me the lowest paid employee in the district; others thought of me as a persistent change agent challenging the status quo. And now that I've been through those elementary years, I want to share what I've learned with you so you don't have to figure it all out on your own.

I came to understand the ins and the outs of schools, what goes on behind the scenes, what's working—and not working—in our complex, overburdened, bureaucratic system. I also began to see how parents and educators often work toward the same goal, but don't always connect. I frequently see the need for more education for parents and better communication from schools. To help bridge this gap, I cofounded a nonprofit in 2006, a parent education organization on the South Shore of Boston (www.theparentconnection.org) to connect parents, teachers, and kids. As director of this group, I've worked with more than sixty parenting and education professionals and presided over parent education events on topics ranging from bullying and raising resilient kids, to the importance of play and the future of schools. I've read well over a hundred parenting books and mounds of research on parenting and education. When I started working with parents and educators one on one, I discovered how important parent involvement is to a child's education, what it takes to turn kids on to learning, what motivates and frustrates teachers, and what motivates and frustrates parents.

Through my insatiable need to know and understand, I became the go-to parent on schools and education in my community and beyond. Nearly every day I get specific questions from parents on everything from who to talk to about what, classroom situations, conflicts with teachers, dealing with homework, getting more academic support, and social issues on the playground to general questions about schools, testing, and education. I also help administrators connect to or communicate with the community on various issues. Not long ago, while I was working with a group of parents and educators, a teacher jokingly said to me, "ML, whose side are you on, anyway?" The truth is, I'm not on any side. Part of the problem in education today is that people see sides. Let's not forget, in the end, this is about the kids: no sides, no blame. The blame game must be the enemy. Parents and educators need each other if we're serious about giving our children the best education possible. We need to work together. But most importantly, we need to respect each other.

How This Book Came to Be

One day about four years ago, I was coaching parents on a technique I call the Power of P3—showing them how to talk to their son's teacher so she could hear their concerns rather than their anger (more on this in chapter 5). At the end of our conversation, the dad said, "Thank you. You've helped us a lot. Have you ever thought about writing a book on schools?" A lightbulb went on. Maybe I could write that book I never found. Friends, family, and educators encouraged me. The final motivation came while reading Thomas Friedman's *The World Is Flat*. When I read his words "We need a revolution in this country when it comes to parenting around education," I knew what I wanted—what I needed—to do. I closed that book and wrote the outline for this book.

Five years and many focus groups, workshops, and interviews later, I've written the book I needed but couldn't find when my oldest daughter started school over a decade ago. I've written it for busy parents who don't have time to figure out the system or read lots of books on parenting or education, for parents who know the basics but aren't sure how to put them into practice or how to advocate appropriately in each situation. I've written it to give you what it took me years to figure out: knowledge of and insight into schools and education, with all their social, emotional, and academic parts. This book gives you the perspective and tools you need to be involved with your kids' education in meaningful ways. It offers guidance on how to support your children throughout their journeys, especially during these elementary years, the years when their foundation for learning is built. It teaches you how and when to talk to teachers, how to deal with bullying, guide homework without meltdowns, and connect to what your kids are learning. It helps you discover how to build the confidence and competency of your kids, create bridges with schools, and move past the proverbial conversation of "How was school today?" "Fine" to make sure your kids do have the most successful elementary school experience possible.

Most parents instinctually know it's important to connect to their children's education, both at home and at school. But schools can be funny places. On the one hand, they say they want parents involved and encourage them to become partners. On the other, despite well-intentioned efforts to become welcoming, responsive institutions, some schools continue to be unfriendly, alien bureaucracies. And on the parent end, the fears we harbor, or the approaches we take, often undermine our best intentions. As parents, we're concerned because our children's futures are at stake. But too much, too little, or misguided involvement can negatively affect a child's appetite for learning and a school's culture as well.

How to Use This Book

The Parent Backpack for Kindergarten through Grade 5 is divided into three parts. Part one provides you with the big picture—the insights and perspective you need to be involved in your kid's education in the right ways. These first four chapters give you a solid foundation for understanding your child's journey, where education stands today, the important role you play as a parent, how to get involved, and what to expect. Part two gives you the background, practical tips, and tools you'll need to navigate the many different phases you'll discover as a parent of an elementary student—from learning to read to managing the social-emotional journey and communicating with teachers. Part three provides you with everything you need to know to support your children's learning at home, including how to fuel little brains and bodies, end homework battles, and coach your kids on advocating for themselves.

If you're feeling eager to jump ahead to a chapter that deals specifically with an issue that you need help with now, by all means, do that. This book can be read from beginning to end or by skipping around to relevant chapters. Be sure to read the first few chapters so you gain an understanding of the system, where it's been, where it's headed, and why your role in your child's educational journey is so crucial. It's important to understand where things stand and what to watch out for so you can be an effective advocate for your child.

Throughout the book, I share stories about real kids, real parents, and real teachers who have grappled with the same questions and situations that you might be experiencing. The names have been changed, but all of these stories are based on situations that I either experienced or heard about in consultations, interviews, or focus groups. Each chapter also ends with a list of Top Ten Takeaways. These are key summary points from each chapter: what to consider, to avoid, and to do. You can refer back to these takeaways after you've read the book. They are the reminders that we all need—that I still need—no matter how hard we try to parent well around education. It's not always easy to do, especially in this busy, activity-crazed world we live in, but it is doable.

Getting involved in your child's education today is tricky. No matter what zip code you live in or what school your child attends, there has never been more controversy about how we educate our children. Most of our schools struggle with test-driven mandates, higher expectations, underfunded budgets, and teachers who need more support. Add to this our hypercompetitive culture, and it all adds up to growing tension and fear among parents, teachers, and kids. Tension that trickles down even to our kindergarten classrooms. Expectations for student achievement turn some reasonable, levelheaded parents into unreasonable watchdogs, who often watch the wrong things, while other parents run the other way and hope for the best.

Our world is changing faster than our schools. Connecting to our children's learning has never been more challenging—or more important.

Our system has become so overburdened that in most schools, we parents have to advocate for our children more than ever before. But how we do that makes all the difference. The more parents we have who support education and advocate for their kids' needs in effective ways, the better our schools will be. It's up to parents and teachers to work together so that our children do get the best education possible.

I hope that *The Parent Backpack* helps to bridge the gap between parents and teachers. I hope it inspires you to support, encourage, and guide your children to do the best they can, knowing that their best will look different every day, and to cherish those questions that keep your kids' curiosity alive. I hope the tools in each chapter help you advocate effectively for what your child needs. Most of all, I hope *The Parent Backpack* helps you discover and celebrate the joy within your child's journey.

PART ONE

Education Today: Insights and Perspective

CHAPTER 1

Understanding Your Child's Journey

A love of learning has a lot to do with learning that we're loved.
—MISTER ROGERS

Think back for a moment to your child's first and most influential teacher. The one your child connected with early on—that caring person who made a difference. Who was that person? A day-care provider, a preschool teacher, a kindergarten teacher?

The answer is . . . none of the above.

Your child's very first teacher is *you*. As the parent—mom, dad, or primary caregiver—you are and always will be your child's first and most influential teacher. You guide, coach, train, nurture, or instruct your child on what *not* to do, what to do, or how to do it, every day. There is no person more influential in your child's journey than you. You celebrated her first step, taught him that first word, and showed her how to ride a bike. You know his strengths. You understand her quirks. This innate, primal love and connection to your child marks the beginning of your journey together. It's the "gut" that guides you through the years. It's the "mama bear" or "papa bear" instincts within you, guarding, protecting, and nurturing your baby.

For most of us, "parent as teacher" is a learned concept. But learn it we must, because it takes three things to make sure our children get the best education possible: parent involvement, great teachers, and high expectations. The most important part of this equation is parent involvement, and the most important teacher in that mix is you. And it *stays* you long after you send your kids to kindergarten.

The role you play in your children's education—both formal (in school) and informal (what happens around family and outside of school)—is huge. Much bigger than most of us realize. Did you know that the average eight-year-old spends 1,170 hours a year in school versus 3,500 waking hours at home? That's more than three times as many hours at home than at school. When you take into account weekends, holidays, and summertime, children spend 14 percent of their time at school, 33 percent sleeping, and 53 percent at home or in the community. What you say and do—or don't do—regarding school, teachers, and education influences your child's attitudes and behaviors around learning in significant ways.

Your Child's Mind: The Difference You Make

Your role in shaping your child's mind, especially through the early elementary years, is crucial. The fact that you're reading this book means you already realize the important role you play in your child's schooling. The key is how you use that influence at home with your children and at school with their teachers. The level of education you have doesn't matter as much as your attitude, the quality of time you spend with your kids around learning, and how effectively you advocate for their needs at school. This is far more important than having a college degree or knowing the right answers on their homework. It's about attitude and making a commitment to be involved in your child's education in meaningful ways.

Why You Need This Book

The Parent Backpack will equip you with the skills, perspective, and strategies you need as a parent to connect to your children's learning and their teachers so your kids can thrive. This first chapter will walk you through what you can expect along your child's elementary journey with all its social, emotional, and academic parts. It also gives you a framework to understand and appreciate your child's uniqueness. In chapter 2, I'll give you some big-picture perspective and insights on the state of education today and the impact that has on your child. In the remaining chapters I'll discuss each aspect of your child's education from reading and extra support to homework and technology.

I've divided chapter 1 into three parts. First, I'll talk about your child's journey, the importance of reading, and the social-emotional issues that come into play. Next, we'll look at the classroom, the importance of play, and the typical milestones your child will hit from kindergarten through grade five. Finally, I'll share the different temperaments kids are born with, the different ways children learn, and how to identify your child's learning style.

The Winding Journey

Will jumps up from the table to show his dad the story he worked so hard on. Proud of his five-sentence paragraph, he waves the three-hole punched paper inches from his dad's face. "Dad . . . Dad, read my story!"

Will's father glances at his eager son, adjusts his glasses, and begins to read. He stumbles on the second sentence about a boy's dog. "Geez," he wonders. "Why is Will still making backward b's and d's at the beginning of second grade?" He continues to read until he notices another letter reversal—a backward p. He remembers that Becca, his older daughter, never did that.

Concerned that Will is regressing, he points at the mistake. "William, is this a b or a d? You're old enough now to get these letters right."

Will's face falls. "But Dad, my teacher says it's okay if we still mix up b's and d's. Did you like my story?"

It's every parent's fear. Your child isn't keeping up with other kids, or worse yet, may have something "wrong" with him. As much as we try not to stress about where our kids stand or compare them to other children—cousins, siblings, friends, or neighbors—it's inevitable that we'll do both. It's human nature. Because every child's journey from kindergarten through grade five looks so different, it's easy to get tangled up in details, like backward *b*'s and *d*'s. It's easy to lose sight of what matters most.

Your child's journey through elementary school is like a winding river. Imagine viewing this river from above as it twists and turns from one grade to the next. Each child's river looks unique as it ebbs and flows from kindergarten through grade five. Some kids stop at every interesting point, others glide right through the bends and curves, while still others need a buoy to help them stay afloat. Even sibling rivers differ in remarkable ways. Our role as parents is to accept our child's winding river, to be on the bank, offering support, a guiding hand, comforting words of encouragement, and an occasional nudge. This is not always easy to do, because we're often tempted to push or pull them through. As you look down on this river, another teacher on the opposite bank instructs, engages, and inspires your child. For the next six years, you'll share your child with these other teachers. That's why making connections and building a bridge to that other bank will make your child's elementary education the best it can be.

This river of learning is as social and emotional as it is academic. At times, the water is calm; other times, it's rough. Friends and classmates will begin to influence your child's thoughts and behaviors from kindergarten on. This shift from family to friends will follow a natural progression to independence, but it won't always be easy. Some teachers along this journey will inspire your child to create, invent, think, and dream. Other teachers will strengthen your child's resilience and test coping skills you never knew your child—or you—had. And there will also be an abundance of screens, activities, and homework vying for your kid's attention.

There will be highs and lows throughout this journey, and about a foot of growth to show for it all, give or take an inch or two. Your children will learn to read and write—some early, some later on. They will learn how to work with others. They will learn how to learn. With the right mix of support and learning at home and at school, a five-year-old's natural curiosity will blossom into a fifth grader's love of learning. There will be tears. There will be joy. There will be challenges. There will be moments you'll treasure, days that you'd like to forget, and weeks that you'll never forget. You'll experience good years and hoping-next-year-will-be-better years. But I hope there is mostly joy. I've learned that if you guide your child's journey from the bank rather than push or pull him through his river, you are much more likely to experience that joy.

By the end of this chapter, I hope you will visualize your child's winding river and smile—without wishing it were a straighter, more "perfect" journey like that of the neighbor down the street. I hope you can picture yourself on the banks of that river, guiding, reading, and supporting your child throughout her winding journey while building a bridge to the teacher on the other bank.

Getting Ready to Read: A Waterfall of Words

The current that carries your child through this river is reading. During the elementary years, reading, writing, and listening are known as *literacy*—or *emergent literacy*. Just as every river begins with a source, your child's educational journey began with the words and language he's been exposed to from birth.

I think of this source as a waterfall of words: language that you shower your child with every day. The richer and deeper the words, books, and experiences are that make up this language, the sooner your child will begin to read and move confidently along her journey. The conversations, language, and books your child is exposed to from birth to age ten shape the student she will become. The more time you spend talking with your children, explaining what you're doing as you do it, trying new experiences, reading *with* them (not just to them) in a fun and engaged way, and sharing stories, the better start they'll have in kindergarten and the easier they will learn to read and move from grade to grade.

Curiosity and reading, combined with some discipline, provide the foundation for learning and a successful journey through school. So the more you interact with your child in a positive way, at any age, about what they're reading, what they're seeing, and what they're thinking, the more likely they are to become a reader, a critical thinker, and a student who loves to learn.

If you're experiencing pangs of guilt wondering if you've done enough reading or started early enough, you're not alone. All parents look back and question what they did and didn't do. But know that it's never too early or too late to read with your child regularly, to talk to your child about what you're doing, to try new experiences, and to ask questions along the way. I'll talk more about the different stages of reading and how to spark a love of reading in your child in chapter 6, but the point to remember is this: the waterfall of words that you create, the source of language, experiences, and stories, provides the current for your child's river and keeps it flowing forward. Just fifteen minutes a day makes a difference—a very powerful difference.

The Social-Emotional Waters

It was a tough day for eight-year-old Jeremy. He started out the day anxious about riding the bus to school for the first time. Every day for the first month, his mom had driven him to school. Sitting alone on the bus made this new experience even scarier. Then, later at lunch, a new kid joined the boys' lunch table and Jeremy felt excluded from his buddies. When he returned to class after lunch, he found a substitute continuing the math lesson he didn't understand the first time around. That's a lot for a more reserved child like Jeremy. When he got home, Jeremy realized he forgot to write down his math homework, which meant he'd receive an "oops" sticker tomorrow. Jeremy hit his wall. Lucky for him, his mom was there to empathize with his flood of feelings and accept that his twenty-minute meltdown needed to happen. His mom knew this wasn't just about homework and the "oops" sticker. Eventually, Jeremy bounced back, now a little more resilient for having survived a rough day.

A critical part of your child's school day is the social-emotional journey. Understandably, some parents overlook or discount its importance because when report cards come and portals report grades, we tend not to pay as much attention to areas that aren't quantified or measured. On a typical school day, your child is one of hundreds of children funneled from one activity to another, from one group to another. These transitions are made multiple times a day. Dozens of five- to eleven-year-olds move from bus to classroom, from recess to lunch, from literacy to math, and then to a different classroom for science. They head down to the gym for physical education, return to the classroom, and then back to the bus again—every day. And along the way—in hallways, at tables, on the playground, and in classrooms—kids jockey for position, friends come and go, and feelings get hurt. Kids don't learn in a vacuum; they have emotions and feelings that play a big role in what and how they learn.

It's a daily schedule charged with emotions, stress, and social encounters that would send many adults into a tailspin, let alone a child still learning to navigate these social-emotional waters. Your child worries about making mistakes, being ridiculed or left out, and not meeting expectations—yours or the teacher's. Our children's social-emotional challenges are sometimes hard for parents too, because they can cause us to reexperience our own childhood school years, or bring to light what we're seeing versus what we had hoped to see.

WHAT'S UNDER THESE WATERS?

Your child's social-emotional learning is rooted in three areas: getting along in a group setting, making and keeping friendships, and being able to exercise some self-control. Let's take a closer look at each of these areas.

The first area of social and emotional development is how your child gets along in a group setting. This is not a playgroup-size crowd or the neighborhood clan or even twelve to fifteen soccer players. Instead, this group setting involves two dozen children with wide ranges of temperaments, personalities, and learning styles that form a class. Some may have learning disorders or disabilities. In this diverse setting, children begin to learn more about themselves. They begin to understand who they are in relation to others. Does your child empathize with how others feel? Does he share? Does she use words when she's mad? Does he stand back and observe or jump right in and play? Most teachers agree that a child's demeanor looks and feels quite different in a classroom setting than it does in a smaller size group.

The second area is your child's ability to make and keep relationships with friends. Are there one or two children your child connects with? Are these relationships that you can help nurture? Though childhood friendships will ebb and flow, they are still an important component of your child's day. Having at least one school friend and feeling connected in a positive way helps keep a child motivated to learn and more confident about navigating the social-emotional waters.

The third area of your child's social-emotional world is her ability to exercise self-control, that is, to self-regulate. Does he use words to express his feelings? Does she know how to ask for what she needs? Because a child's ability to follow directions and make good decisions often predicts future success in school, let's take a closer look at the area of self-control, also known as self-discipline.

The Role of Self-Control
(aka Social-Emotional Intelligence)

In the 1960s, a researcher at Stanford University conducted a now-famous longitudinal study called the "marshmallow test." Walter Mischel put four-year-old children in front of a marshmallow. He told each of the children that they could have one marshmallow now, or if they waited fifteen minutes, they could have two. One-third of the kids (the "nondelayers") ate the marshmallow within thirty seconds. Another third waited as long as they could before eating it. The final third ("the delayers") were able to wait the full fifteen minutes and received two marshmallows.

Mischel then tracked these kids through high school and into their forties. In 2011, he reported that the delayers group scored on average 210 points higher on their SAT tests and had fewer behavioral issues in school. This experiment showed us that kids who could control their impulses and imagine the marshmallow as something other than good to eat (a few turned it into a cloud) realized greater success in school and life. The kids who ate the marshmallow immediately ended up having difficulty paying attention, solving problems, and maintaining friendships. So the ability to control impulses at an early age and follow directions ends up being among the most critical skills your child can develop in life.

Your child's ability to calm herself, understand emotions, and communicate feelings are skills that, alongside reading and math, are needed to succeed in school. A child who is impulsive, anxious, or angry will likely have difficulty learning no matter how skilled the teacher is. Impulse control and decision-making abilities are formed in the frontal cortex of our brains—an area that continues to develop through the early twenties. Some school districts now provide social-emotional skills training, but many do not. It's our role as parents to nurture these qualities in our children and work on them every day. Given the astonishing statistics showing how much more successful children are when they are able to delay gratification, exercise self-control, and then follow directions, it's clearly important that we as parents figure out how to help them develop these fundamental skills.

The most important thing we can do as parents to help our children in this area is to model the behavior we want to see in them. That's easier said than done, I know, with our busy, stressful schedules. Especially when kids push our buttons—or, rather, when we allow them to do this. Children's inborn temperaments also contribute to their behavior and that's important to understand. (We'll talk more about children's temperaments on page 20.) One example of where we can help our children learn self-control is with their homework. Guiding children in learning how to break down their homework or project into smaller tasks so they don't get overwhelmed or frustrated helps them control their emotions and navigate expectations successfully. We'll talk about homework and organization in chapters 12 and 14. We'll also explore the social and emotional world of kindergartners in chapter 4, how to ensure your kids are confident and connected in chapter 8, and how to deal with bullying in chapter 10. Lots of areas touch on children's social-emotional learning throughout elementary school because it's a critical part of their journey. For now, let's turn to academics.

Higher Expectations and Child Development

The expectations for kids in elementary school today are higher than ever. While this is generally a good thing, it comes with a cautionary note. As children progress from one grade to the next, they become more independent thinkers. They learn to read fiction, nonfiction, and poetry with fluency and insight. They learn to write with voice and persuasion. They become masters of numbers, from addition to geometry to algebra. Kids reason and process information in a more logical way as they make their way toward middle school. By fifth grade, as they enter the world of preadolescence, they think in more abstract, hypothetical ways. But in the attempt to raise the bar on academics in elementary school, we—parents and teachers—cannot forget the important role that play provides in a child's development.

Letting Our Kids Play to Learn

A well-respected twentieth-century child psychologist, Jean Piaget, discovered that children are born with a natural desire to learn. They are innately curious about objects, people, and life around them. They possess a deep-seated, intrinsic motivation to explore and to understand. And with that motivation comes a natural ability to act out what they see, hear, and learn in order to make sense of it all. This is why kids play house, school, doctor, farm, gas station and dress-up. As they try on different roles, navigate social situations, and attempt to solve problems, they are processing and learning about life—through play. Unstructured play is a child's work, both at school and home.

Kids don't have to learn to play—they naturally play to learn. Through open-ended, simple toys—like blocks, Play-Doh, LEGO bricks, chalk, farm animals, trucks, dolls, and puzzles—children explore and discover what works and what doesn't work through their own trial and error. Children learn by controlling the toys, rather than voices or buttons directing them on what to do next. Children are also naturally wired to conquer a concept. That's why they love I SPY games, computer games, and the *Highlights* Hidden Pictures. Kids thrive on repetition, which explains why they want to read the same book again and again or watch the same scene of a movie fifty-seven times. They want to master the words, the action, and the characters. They practice what they've learned, feel competent, and then eventually move on to something harder. This internal motivation is also what naturally drives kids to explore electronics: just like a book, they want to discover what lurks beneath the buttons and screens, to learn it, master it, and then—when they're ready—move on to something else.

To a child, the heartbeat of learning is play. The more children learn through play, the more their natural motivation to learn will thrive throughout the elementary years. But today there's a significant issue with learning and problem solving through play: kids don't do enough of it. Too much of their out-of-school time is structured—just like it is in school—with sports and activities. Kids learn best through unstructured play because it fuels their curiosity and imagination, builds problem-solving abilities and competencies, and fosters their social-emotional skills. Our kids are desperately seeking good old-fashioned play and it's up to parents to carve out time to make that happen.

Free time for unstructured play—without adults directing—makes kids more resourceful, optimistic, and self-motivated. It also helps them discover what they like and don't like, where their strengths lie, and the kind of kids they work best with. This is why project-based learning is an effective practice in education today and why it is integrated into the Common Core standards (I'll explain these further in chapter 2). Project-based learning—hands-on, experiential learning—is all about problem solving. Kids are given a question that must be answered. They are excited to figure it out and engage in the learning.

I had the pleasure of hearing Dr. Kathy Hirsh-Pasek, author of *Einstein Never Used Flashcards: How Our Children Really Learn and Why They Need to Play More and Memorize Less*, give a talk when my nonprofit organization hosted her a few years ago. Dr. Hirsh-Pasek suggests we have three goals as parents when it comes to supporting our children's play: (1) making sure there is enough downtime in our busy family schedules so kids can engage in unstructured play; (2) joining in our children's play—*but only when invited*—so you contribute to their world, guide them, and ask more questions; and (3), exposing them to a limited number of simple, open-ended toys—those without buttons and prescribed directions that dictate how to play. I find that organizing toys on shelves instead of piling them inside toy boxes also helps promote play. Rotating toys in and out of circulation keeps kids excited to see and use them again.

Children's natural curiosity and need to understand the world around them begins to wane by third grade—the age when social issues start to mean more than learning. Giving your children a strong foundation of play early in the elementary years helps to instill a love of learning and a motivation to keep on learning, the pillars of success for students. Enriching your children's learning through activities, music, play, and conversations keeps you connected to your kids, what they're doing in school, and their desire to learn beyond workbooks and study guides. As you encourage and support your children's play and learning, you'll find it helpful to know more about what to expect at each grade level for your child. So let's take a look at the specific milestones your child will reach along his elementary journey.

Grade-Level Expectations for Your Child

First, a word of caution: remember that each child's river of learning is unique. Each month, each week, and each grade will look different for all children, even if they're in the same class. Oftentimes, children take a few steps back before they make a big leap, just as they do when they jump off a diving board. These are general benchmarks based on the current Common Core standards for literacy and math. I have included social-emotional expectations and organized all skills by two-year increments because some children will meet them sooner while others will meet them later. Expectations for organizational skills are discussed in chapter 14. Remember, our role as parents is to be on that riverbank to encourage, support, and nudge when necessary rather than to push or pull them along. All children will hit these milestones in their own way, in their own time.

THOSE BACKWARD *B*'S AND *D*'S

Many kids reverse the letters *b* and *d*, *p* and *q*. This trait is expected in kindergarten and first grade and often continues into grades two and three. Some kids even write entire words upside down or backward. While reversing letters could be a sign of dyslexia (discussed in chapter 9), it's most likely a developmental phase that a child will outgrow. If your child still reverses letters toward the middle of third grade and there are other signs of reading issues, bring this to the teacher's attention, if it hasn't been flagged already.

If your child recognizes the letter mix-up and wants to "fix it," reinforce that it's natural to make this mistake so he doesn't get anxious over it. One way to help with the confusion is to use the "bed" method. With the *b* as the headboard on the left and *d* as footboard, the letters form the ends of a bed. Another way to distinguish between *b*'s and *d*'s is to make two "thumbs up" and then turn your fists in toward each other to form a *b* on the left (because it comes first) and a *d* on the right. Try it yourself.

But remember, on its own, mixing up these letters is developmentally appropriate and nothing to worry about until third grade. It's their journey, remember, full of twists and turns. It's our job to be patient—to encourage and guide them and offer support from the banks.

WHERE DID KINDERGARTEN GO?

Despite the importance of play to a child's development, kindergarten curriculum is now more academic than ever before—with half-day programs squeezing as much as possible into two and a half hours. Understanding whether your child is developmentally prepared for kindergarten—socially and emotionally—and what type of experience you want for your kindergartner are important issues that deserve a chapter of their own. We'll explore these and other aspects of kindergarten in chapter 4.

FIRST THROUGH SECOND GRADE

During these pivotal years, most children learn to read fluently. Toward the end of second grade, as their fluency and comprehension improves, they are reading to learn. First and second graders also develop a sense of numbers—addition and subtraction, basic geometry—and gain an understanding of themselves in relation to their community. By the end of second grade, your child will likely master the following knowledge or skills:

Social-Emotional

- Sit in a circle, listen for thirty minutes, and comprehend two-step directions
- Recognize and identify feelings in oneself and others
- Identify and practice cooperative skills like sharing or empathizing
- Express anger in appropriate ways, most of the time
- Work together in a group in class or at recess without conflict, most of the time
- Understand that the desire to win, be right, and be first won't always be realized

Literacy (Reading and Writing)

- Read sentences fluently with expression and comprehension
- Use decoding strategies for difficult words

- Know up to two hundred sight words (high-recognition words that don't follow typical sounding out rules)
- Make connections between ideas and begin to expand vocabulary
- Use strategies for comprehension and begin to use a dictionary
- Write complete paragraphs with capitalization, punctuation, inventive spelling

Math

- Count and recognize numbers up to one thousand
- Know addition and subtraction math facts through twelve
- Add and subtract up to one thousand; compare and contrast numbers
- Start to tell time to the hour and half hour
- Count change
- Know how to use different coins to make ten cents, twenty-five cents, and one dollar
- Master two-digit addition and subtraction

Science and Social Studies

- Understand living things and their environments—oceans, human body, matter
- Experiment with concepts of electricity, magnetism, sound, temperature
- Report on scientists and their discoveries
- Participate in a science fair
- Understand oneself in relation to family, boys, girls, and community

THIRD THROUGH FOURTH GRADES

This is when children become students. They read and analyze more complicated texts, including nonfiction and poetry, and they write longer and more persuasive documents. In math, they master multiplication and division and begin working with fractions and decimals, and they begin to understand the scientific method. By the end of fourth grade, your child will likely master the following knowledge or skills:

Social-Emotional

- Understand cause and effect; realize that choices have consequences
- Want to be part of a group or clique; become more competitive with peers
- Recognize discrimination, exclusivity, not treating others fairly in a group
- Want immediate rewards; can be cooperative and empathetic
- Worry about competencies

Literacy (Reading and Writing)

- Read independently and comprehend longer chapter books
- Use strategies to infer meaning in a story
- Understand nonfiction, poetry, and fiction
- Write longer compositions with structured paragraphs and proper language use
- Think more critically and independently
- Write persuasively with evidence-based arguments

Math

- Know multiplication and division facts up to twelve
- Multiply and divide two digit numbers
- Add and subtract three-digit numbers
- Understand basic fractions; add and subtract decimals
- Start estimating and reasoning
- Complete long division
- Tell time; make change up to ten dollars
- Begin to understand geometry and two-dimensional shapes

Science and Social Studies

- Understand electricity, energy, and matter
- Recognize historical figures of the United States
- Learn about other world cultures
- Know the state capitals, geography, and how to read maps
- Classify organisms

FIFTH THROUGH SIXTH GRADE

As fifth and sixth graders become more independent and able to advocate for themselves, they continue to strengthen their reading fluency and comprehension. They sharpen their critical thinking and analytical skills through writing and research, and progress to more advanced math concepts, including prime numbers and algebraic order of operations. They also study earth science, American history, government, and health. By the end of fifth or sixth grade, your child will likely master the following knowledge or skills:

Social-Emotional

- Show much more independence; test limits
- Become more dependable and trustworthy; monitor homework assignments
- Begin to accept responsibilities for mistakes and failures; understand "fairness"
- Show more interest in peers, music, clothing, and socializing
- Struggle to balance heavier workload in school with activities and friends

Literacy (Reading and Writing)

- Analyze characters, plot, and structure of books
- Read newspapers and current events and write or present opinions on events
- Learn phases of outlining, writing, revising, editing

- Write research reports with several sources, Internet, and reference books
- Continue to read more challenging fiction and nonfiction books
- Increase vocabulary

Math

- Learn about prime numbers
- Learn basics of statistics: mean, mode, median, and range
- Add, subtract, and multiply fractions
- Calculate perimeters and areas of triangles, rectangles, and other shapes
- Become skilled at mental math
- Learn order of operations in algebra

Science and Social Studies

- Study American history, Constitution, Bill of Rights
- Understand branches of government
- Identify landmarks around the world
- Learn about the human body: cardiovascular, skeletal, and reproductive systems
- Begin basic chemistry and physics
- Understand our solar system and planets
- Learn about ecosystems, global warming, and other environmental phenomena

Kindergarten through grade five are your children's formative years—the time period when your children develop the values, beliefs, and behaviors that you want to instill. The social-emotional and academic skills that your children acquire during these key years will serve them forever. Our role as parents—to guide, support, and nurture these values and skills as we walk along the bank of our children's river of learning—is critical.

A New Way of Teaching and Learning

If these milestones and expectations seem overwhelming to you, the structure of today's school day and the atmosphere in which our children learn will probably seem different to you as well.

Michelle and her first grade daughter, Emily, race to the corner to catch the school bus, just in time. Waving to her daughter, Michelle catches her breath and then turns to answer another mom's question about how her first day of volunteering in the classroom went yesterday. "Well, I was impressed with the teacher," said Michelle. "Lots of the kids aren't reading yet, but they still understood the story just from talking about the pictures. But the classroom seemed so, I don't know, lively, I guess. Kids were up and down, and in small reading groups, working from different word charts or big books. It seemed as if they were constantly talking and moving around. It's so different from when we went to school and the teacher just stood at the front of the class."

Your child's classroom looks quite different from what you remember twenty or thirty years ago. The days of desks lined up in rows with the teacher standing at the head of the class talking 90 percent of the time has given way to better practices. When you walk into an elementary classroom today, you're more likely to see tables with four to six chairs or desks pushed together to form table groups. After giving a twenty- to thirty-minute class lesson, often using some form of interactive technology (you'll learn about this in chapter 11), the teacher will usually break kids into groups or centers, check in on students' progress, reteach in different ways to connect with kids at different levels of understanding (called "differentiating instruction"), correct work, ask questions, and redirect behavior.

You'll hear kids discussing questions or working problems through on their own and conversing with classmates. A best practice today in kindergarten through grade two is small or close reading groups where students read—aloud, with a teacher, or silently—and work on decoding strategies, blending words, fluency, or comprehension. Project-based learning is also an effective way to prepare our children to function in our smaller but global world. Now, it's more about letting the learning unfold and be experienced versus filling a student's brain with information.

A typical school day in elementary school is divided into blocks of core academics and "specials," with recess and lunch sandwiched in between. Specials include art, music, physical education, and library (now referred to as a "media center" or "instructional media center" in some schools) and are typically held outside the classroom, rotating one per day. Blocks of academics usually last thirty-five to sixty minutes. Literacy subjects (reading and writing) and math are taught every day while social studies and science are taught less frequently. Literacy is often held twice a day. Some schools introduce a foreign language in the early elementary grades because research suggests this is the optimal time for a child's brain to learn another language. Core academics are usually taught in four- to six-week subject units or themes. Expecting your child to know what day of the week she goes to gym and needs to wear sneakers, when she goes to the library and needs to return her library book, or what day she needs her recorder or violin is a great way to encourage independence—and take the burden off you.

As project-based learning plays a bigger role in schools today (more on this in chapter 11), the academic divisions are blurring as instruction becomes more integrated. This means your children may read a biography on George Washington during literacy when they're studying the Revolutionary War in social studies. Similarly, spelling words are more likely to be part of this theme, giving kids multiple connections to the same subject.

Your Child's Temperament

Now that you understand the critical role of reading, the social-emotional parts of your child's journey, and grade-level expectations, let's turn our attention to your child's unique personality.

There's a widely held belief in child psychology—based on the research of psychiatrists Alexander Thomas and Stella Chess—that children are born with one of three different types of temperaments or dispositions. These temperaments are believed to be hardwired and play a significant role in your child's behavior. Some kids fall in between temperament types, but generally, your child will lean toward one of these three:

- The easy-to-raise child who is flexible, stays on course, listens well, and makes most parents and teachers look fabulous.

- The more cautious, slow-to-warm-up child who prefers to first observe a new situation, a new toy, a new food, or a new lesson.

- The spirited, strong-willed child, who may be more difficult, intense, and extrasensitive to noises, clothing tags, or visual details, and who tests parents or teachers on a good day.

In addition to these temperaments, children may be more social or more solitary in their quest to understand the world around them. You may also find that certain temperaments fit into your family's lifestyle easier than others. I was blessed with children who touch each temperament, so I'm forever morphing my words to motivate a different child in a different way, some days more successfully than others.

Accepting your child's unique temperament with all the good and the challenge that comes with it is the first step to supporting and encouraging your child's education. This is one of the hardest jobs we have as parents because we're so prone to comparing and labeling our children. Labeling our kids—beyond the basic understanding of their inborn temperament—can have damaging, long-term effects on their mindset and their self-esteem, especially in the early school-age years.

Children are more likely to learn how to navigate the social-emotional waters when Mom or Dad understands their unique temperament. When we empathize with our kids and help them identify how they're feeling, they are more likely to be able to handle the ups and downs that come their way. Whether it's frustration, disappointment, hurt, or anger, children need help in identifying and labeling their feelings. Showing ongoing support for your children's efforts and progress rather than criticizing outcomes helps, too. I'll talk more about this in chapter 8. Once you understand your child's temperament, it's also helpful to understand your child's learning style.

Getting to Know Your Child's Learning Style

Cara's and Abbey's moms stand on the lacrosse field talking about their girls' third grade teacher, Ms. Knight. "I like her personally, but Cara doesn't like the way she teaches," explains Cara's mom. "She uses those shapes and manipulatives, or whatever they're called, for math lessons—like little kids used in preschool. Cara just wants someone to explain the lesson, not show her how to do it with blocks."

"That's funny," responds Abbey's mom. "Abbey loves that she teaches like that—in a hands-on kind-of way where she can see it. She understands it better. I'm like that, too."

....

Just as each child's journey is unique and each child has an inborn temperament, each child learns differently, too. Understanding and honoring your child's learning style can make a big difference in his success, at school and at home. A learning style refers to how a person processes and best comprehends information. How a child learns also affects basic listening and comprehension skills as well as homework and studying skills. Showing kids how to tap their strengths as a learner is an insight they'll use for a lifetime. Three primary types of learning styles—visual-spatial, auditory-language, and kinesthetic-physical—are widely recognized. Most children (and adults) learn in a combination of ways but lean toward one style. Keep in mind your child's temperament will also influence her learning style. See if you can recognize your child—and yourself—in one or more of these learning styles.

THE VISUAL-SPATIAL LEARNING STYLE

Visual-spatial learners remember best through what they see. They visualize words as images and learn best through pictures, by creating an image or watching a video. They tend to like charts, diagrams, maps, and puzzles. Visual-spatial learners prefer to see—to draw pictures, write things down, and watch—rather than talk or act in class. They can be well organized and tend to like reading. They usually notice details. They may lose patience when oral explanations go on too long. They may daydream in class as they visualize what they hear or think. When you need to go somewhere, it's usually more effective to show young visual learners on the clock that you will leave when the big hand points to the six rather than telling them, "We're leaving in ten minutes."

Visual-spatial learners learn best by seeing concepts as images or words written down. They study best by flashcards, highlighting in colors, creating pictures in their mind or on paper, and making lists.

THE AUDITORY-LANGUAGE LEARNING STYLE

Auditory-language learners process by what they hear. They think in words and sounds and prefer to verbalize ideas. They still need to hear things more than once but are more apt to retain what they hear by repeating it to themselves. They're more likely to remember jokes and have an excellent memory for dates, names, faces, and trivia. Auditory learners usually like word games and prefer to listen to books while reading along. They can be heard talking to themselves, humming, or whispering while they read or process information. They participate in class discussions and often find noise distracting because they are processing it all. Auditory learners like to be quizzed on spelling words orally. But it's also a good idea to have them take a written pretest so they can adjust to writing down the words on class tests. Let them know it's okay to whisper the letters aloud as they write. They enjoy hearing facts and words in a rhythmic song or acronym so they can process them better.

THE KINESTHETIC-PHYSICAL LEARNING STYLE

Kinesthetic–physical learners learn best by what they do and experience. They like to move around and are not able to sit still for long. They tend to lose interest if they're not actively involved in doing something physical. They like to touch, feel, and use their hands to process information and learn best through experiential, hands–on activities. Kinesthetic learners often need physical stimulation like chewing gum, rocking, or walking around. They are sometimes labeled ADHD (even when they're not) and tend to be naturally athletic. Kinesthetic learners prefer books with action and may find the act of writing notes helpful during a lesson because it keeps them physically busy. They are more likely to get through homework with fewer battles if it's broken up into chunks—maybe ten to fifteen minutes before soccer practice and then another ten to fifteen minutes after. This may not be ideal for a parent who wants it done before the next activity, but it taps into the child's primary learning style.

An effective teacher will instruct students using a combination of styles. My oldest daughter is primarily a visual learner, with some auditory traits—give her a list or a quick picture and she gets it. Now a teen, she thrives on writing everything down on the whiteboard in her room and listening to light music while she studies. My younger daughter is more of a visual and kinesthetic learner. She looks at visuals first and likes to touch and feel what she is doing or learning. She rarely gets the summary of the day orally in one shot, but if I write it down once, it's embedded in her brain. Knowing how your kids process information helps both at home and at school.

If you're not sure you understand your child's learning style—or your own—check out the resources at www.theparentbackpack.com for a source that will help you identify it. Once you understand your child's learning style, share this information with your child when you think she's ready to comprehend it. The more self-aware a child is, the more able she will be to advocate for herself. Knowing her learning style and strengths will also help her become more resourceful at an earlier age. Share this information with your child's teachers, too, at the start of each year. Use examples to show how you've connected with your child's learning style or strategies that have worked. You can share this kind of feedback on the student information forms that the school sends out at the beginning of the year or in a separate note if your school does not use forms.

As your children get older, you may also notice that learning styles impact how they think and do homework. We'll talk more about this in chapters 8, 12, and 14.

Exciting, Yet Daunting

If all this information seems overwhelming, take heart. We've covered a lot of ground: how you can encourage, guide, and support your child; the social-emotional waves that come with each child's elementary journey; why reading and language is so important to success; academic milestones to be aware of; and ways to understand your child's temperament and learning style.

These six years will go by faster than you ever dreamed. By fifth grade, your role as parent will begin to take a backseat to friends, coaches, and teachers, which is why it's critical to connect with your child now.

The next chapter provides you with perspective on education today, the issues that impact your child, and ways you can ensure your child gets the best education possible.

TOP TEN TAKEAWAYS

TO CONSIDER

- Your child's journey through elementary school looks like a winding river that twists and turns; our role as parents is to be on the banks of that river, guiding, encouraging, and supporting this unique journey.

- Reading and talking with your child—the waterfall of words you shower your child with from birth throughout the elementary years—contributes significantly to your child's success through school.

- Your children's social-emotional skills play a critical role in their success at school.

- Classrooms and teaching look quite different today; expectations from kindergarten through grade five are higher than ever.

- Unstructured play is a child's work; it's critical so your child can process information and learn new skills.

TO AVOID

- Don't try to push or pull your children through their journey; it usually backfires. Respect your child's individuality and nudge gently when necessary.

- Don't stress about what milestones your child has or has not achieved; each child is on his own unique timetable. Kids feel your anxiety when you are stressed.

continued

TOP TEN TAKEAWAYS, *continued*

TO DO

- Read with and to your children every day in a way that helps them associate reading with pleasure. This is the single most important activity you can do to support your child's learning.

- Find time for your kids to play in an unstructured way with other children, so they can use their imaginations and work out problems together.

- Understand your child's temperament and learning style so you can connect with her; convey this information to your child's teacher, and to your child when the time is right.

CHAPTER 2

Your Role in a Changing System

Upon the subject of education, I can only say that I view it as the most important subject which we as a people may be engaged in. —ABRAHAM LINCOLN

The pace of technology in this information age moves so fast that we are educating our children today for jobs that don't yet exist. And we're doing that against a backdrop of many antiquated, narrowly focused, test-driven school systems that have little involvement with the skills our kids need to be successful. As a society, we marinate in facts, dates, data, people, places, and things every day—so much so that we can't begin to process even 10 percent of what we take in. Our children were born into this world. Information is literally at our fingertips—and no one accesses it faster than kids.

So why do our children need to memorize state capitals when they can access these simple facts in less than five seconds? Certainly students need to memorize basic math facts and formulas. They need to become strong, fluent readers and writers so they have a solid foundation for future learning. Memorizing some basic information is important and necessary for this to happen. But our educators and policy makers are writing standards now to catch up with the challenges and complexities of the information age—just in time for the next three decades, which some have dubbed the "age of innovation."

If you have kids under the age of twelve, you are likely part of generation X or generation Y, also known as the Millennials. Your generation is better educated, more ethnically diverse, and less trusting of institutions than any previous group of parents. You hold high expectations for your kids and want them to get the best education they can. Most of you are more involved in your children's schooling than your parents were. You're also more comfortable questioning the system. You ask questions: Why can't Jack read like his friends? When should we talk to the teacher about this? Is this the right school for Alex? Is Sara being challenged? What do these test scores mean? Is Will slipping through the cracks? Why do I feel unwelcome in my child's school? How do we get the "good" teachers? You ask these questions for good reason: they need to be asked. The fact that you're reading this book is a testament to your desire to support your child's learning at home and advocate effectively for your child's needs at school.

To educate our children effectively in this millennium, we need schools to teach and empower students on how to find, evaluate, and apply information. As parents we need to step up and connect to our kids' learning and challenge them to think on their own. We need to teach our kids *how* to think versus *what* to think. Even elementary students need to know how to organize, prioritize, and synthesize information so they can think about what they're learning. All students need to learn how to analyze, rationalize, and criticize facts and data. Once they master these skills, they can voice their opinion about information and bring their thinking to a higher level. Educators refer to this as "critical thinking" or "twenty-first-century" skills. While this higher level thinking plays a prominent role in the middle and high school years, the foundation for these skills is established in the elementary grades.

In its simplest form, our education system provides a service: the vital and indispensible service of teaching our youngest citizens. The end result of this service is learning: the knowledge and skills our children acquire that drives our future economy. A child's attitude also impacts this outcome, which is why social-emotional learning is so important. The system is not complete without parents, who have the daily, demanding responsibility of supervising their kids as they acquire knowledge and skills. Before we dive into more details and strategies for this important task, it's helpful to step back and understand a few issues about education today.

In many ways, more has changed in our schools in the last decade than in the last century. Some of that change is good, and some is not so good. And some big factors, like accountability and teachers' unions, are still changing. One of the pillars that America was built on was a quality education for every child—not just the rich and privileged. That assumption held true for well over a century. But it can no longer be taken for granted. This chapter discusses the state of education today and the impact that our complex, overburdened system has on our children. This information is important because when you understand the educational climate we're operating in, you'll be a better advocate for your child's education.

Issues that Challenge Your Child's Education

When pressure from outside forces (like higher standards and tougher competition) intersect with lower level stagnating systems (our school system infrastructure and student performance), a storm results. Our nations' education system has been spiraling through this perfect storm for three decades now. The days when parents sent their kids off to public school trusting that they would get a great education are gone. Yes, there are many great schools and teachers out there. Some are public, some are private, and some are charter. But they are harder and harder to find because they, too, are battling this storm on some level. This pressure from all sides—a struggling economy, federal mandates and incentives, state and local budget cuts, international competition, accountability, standardized testing, a world gone digital—touches every child and teacher in the classroom. This is why there's never been a more important time to equip yourself with the information and tools you need to support your child's journey from kindergarten through grade five.

LACKLUSTER PERFORMANCE

Way back when American education led the world, our school systems were revered. Our graduation rates were the highest. Our colleges were the best. In the postwar 1950s, the suburban sprawl and baby boom triggered construction of thousands of elementary schools. Many were put up fast and on the cheap. Women worked their way into teaching jobs, supported by unions that promised equal hiring standards and equal pay. Our schools continued to thrive into the late 1970s. Or so we thought.

In 1983, the Department of Education conducted a significant study on our education system. A shocking report, *A Nation at Risk*, revealed that U.S. schools suffered from low expectations at every level. Students spent less time in school and on homework than students in other developed nations and our test scores reflected this. Too many teachers were unqualified, underpaid, and came from the bottom quartile of graduating college students. The teacher tenure system often rewarded adults—without benefiting kids. Fifteen years and many policies later, the new millennium rang in the bipartisan No Child Left Behind (NCLB) initiative to fix these issues.

Sadly, thirty years after that first wake-up call in 1983—*three decades later*—education reformers and politicians are still tackling the same problems. Although standards have been raised, the resulting pressure and hyper focus on high-stakes standardized testing in many schools has compromised our children's education. A narrow focus on reading and math at the elementary level, at the expense of science, social studies, the arts, and even recess, is now a reality for many of our kindergarten through fifth grade students. Not surprisingly, frustration has been felt nationwide. In 1973, a Gallup poll suggested that 58 percent of Americans had a great deal of confidence in American schools. In the 1980s that number fell to 40 percent. In 2012, the number fell to an all-time low of 29 percent.

U.S. STUDENTS ARE AVERAGE

In a worldwide study called the Program for International Student Achievement (PISA), a set of tests assessing the knowledge and skills of students, the United States was ranked along with thirty-four other nations—some developed, some still developing. Over 400,000 fifteen-year-olds were tested in reading, math, and science—first in 2000, and then every three years after that.

The result: American students ranked mediocre, smack dab in the middle of thirty-four participating nations. American students scored average in reading and science, and in math they were statistically below average. On the latest PISA test results from 2012, the world's wealthiest and presumably smartest nation scored 14th in reading, 17th in science, and 25th in math, behind Poland, Iceland, and Estonia; the United

States wasn't even in the top ten. And America's most affluent students in high-performing districts fared only slightly better. Leading the pack were China, Korea, Finland, Singapore, and Canada.

Unlike our own states' standardized tests that measure skills and standards, PISA was created to understand how well students use and apply what they've learned in school. This test measures thinking, making inferences, and drawing conclusions, and shows where kids across the world stand relative to one another. This international test, along with our own longitudinal national test, the National Assessment of Education Progress (NAEP), casts a gloomy picture of the state of education in America. NAEP scores have been flat for the last decade, despite increases in standardized testing. Our SAT scores have also been flat for the past decade. Furthermore, two other international tests—the Trends in International Mathematics and Science Study (TIMSS) and the Progress in International Reading Literacy Study (PIRLS)—also show U.S. students struggling in the bottom to middle half of fifty-nine nations. Yikes.

MANY ARE UNPREPARED FOR COLLEGE

It's no surprise then, that 75 percent of American kids graduate from high school and only two-thirds of those enroll in a two- or four-year college. While this statistic is higher in suburban school districts, what is surprising—even shocking—is the percentage of our students who graduate from college. Among U.S. students who start college today, little more than 50 percent actually graduate. And that's based on a six-year timetable. Nearly half of American kids who begin college do not graduate. Many students—even those in higher performing suburban school districts— enter college unprepared and unable to compete with the new wave of international students. Indeed, the world is flat. These facts play a role in why so many American kids are no longer getting into top colleges.

Our Education System's Broken Infrastructure

Our nation's answer to these problems begins where it must—by fixing our system's infrastructure and striking the right balance in accountability. Let's look at the infrastructure problems first and then I'll discuss what you can do to impact your child's education.

Our school system infrastructure is comprised of the buildings, equipment, curriculum, and athletic fields that our teachers, administrators, and coaches use to educate our children. When we take a close look at each of these factors, we see why our schools and students are not performing as well as they could be.

THE DETERIORATING STATE OF SCHOOL BUILDINGS

Nearly half of our nation's 100,000 public schools were built forty to fifty years ago and now sit in bad to poor condition. Even schools in high-performing districts suffer from crumbling walls and leaking roofs, often the result of deferring capital or maintenance dollars in order to hire teachers to meet growing enrollment. Some communities have successfully raised their tax base enough to renovate or rebuild their schools, but in many districts students sit in run-down, deficient buildings. A good education is about more than bricks and mortar, but it's difficult for students to concentrate and learn (especially the littlest ones) when rain water drips into a bucket next to their desks, insufficient heating requires kids to wear jackets to stay warm, or a small storage room has been converted into their windowless classroom. What's worse is that we're in the middle of a digital revolution that nearly half of our schools cannot support. Installing wireless Internet access in old buildings crisscrossed with steel beams and multiple additions creates a patchwork of inconsistent service at best. Even our best schools are not equipped for the digital world our children thrive in. Keep in mind, too, that the best teachers are more likely to accept a job in a healthy, modern school environment versus one that is run down.

How can you impact all this? One way is to be aware of and support your school district's budgets. Participate in key school committee meetings and make your voice heard. Maintenance dollars and capital expenditures are often budgeted, then cut throughout the year to absorb operating expenses. If and when it comes time to vote for a tax override in your community for school renovations, make this investment in our kids' education. Encourage others to get out and vote to rebuild your schools. If you see a need for rebuilding but no action, consider taking the initiative to get things rolling. Get a group of like-minded parents together and form a committee. It takes leadership, some vision, and parents and teachers working together to keep your school system up to date. For more information on how to advocate for new or renovated schools, check out the resource section at www.theparentbackpack.com.

OUTDATED UNION REGULATIONS

Unions have served an important role in equal opportunity and due process in schools for many decades. But many people—teachers included—believe that traditional union regulations have surpassed their useful life. In many districts, a locked-in seniority system and "step pay"—where the longer teachers work and the more degrees they earn, the more money they make—still prevail, protecting ineffective educators in schools across the county. Because unions strive for equality and don't acknowledge differences between educators, great teachers can't be rewarded with higher pay. Even recognizing outstanding teachers raises eyebrows in some districts. In some union contracts, it takes over twenty steps to dismiss a teacher, a decision that is then subject to a *union grievance* (a legal term for a teacher filing a complaint against the school).

But good news is on the horizon for many states and school districts. Union regulations for teacher evaluations and accountability are beginning to change. This new and improved evaluation and training system is discussed further in chapter 7. It will take time to implement because contract negotiations typically operate on a three-year cycle and there is opposition from some unions, but this is a long-overdue improvement for our children, our teachers, and our schools.

SQUEEZED BUDGETS

Due to a poor economy and decreased tax revenue, most local, state, and federal budgets continue to shrink. Public schools are funded through local taxes, with varying amounts of state and federal dollars. So a poor economy impacts our children's education. Eighty percent of a school system's budget is made up of fixed, contracted salaries based on union negotiations; these dollars have already been negotiated and can't be touched. That means cuts have to be made in the other 20 percent—programs and nonunion personnel—or by laying teachers off, usually on a last-in, first-out basis. When this happens, your child is at risk because class size goes up, individual attention decreases, and fewer dollars remain for extra support. These cuts are realities that leave teachers juggling more than they can handle and some kids slipping through the cracks. Sadly, when budgets don't balance, the teachers and staff who are needed to provide kids with the extra supports they require are often less available. Our children, our teachers, and our schools suffer. When a budget deficit persists and enrollment increases, as has been the case for the past five to seven years in most towns, fewer teachers can be hired and class size goes up. This is a bigger problem for the early elementary grades where class size matters the most.

You can play a key role in the quality of your child's education by advocating for and voting on the school budget. School budgets are more than numbers on a spreadsheet. They reflect the values of your community. In some suburban towns, the school budget makes up more than half the town budget. Know when your school district budget is established each year; it's usually in winter or spring for the following school year. This information must be made available to the public before the final budget is voted on. Be sure you are registered to vote so you can voice your opinion. Get together with like-minded parents and advocate for what you want your child's educational experience to be. Your state's Department of Education website offers reams of interesting data organized by school district. You'll also find school budget resources at www.theparentbackpack.com.

GROWING SPECIAL EDUCATION BUDGETS

Another challenge for school budgets and teachers is the fact that 10 to 12 percent of students in a typical elementary school are now diagnosed with learning disabilities or emotional-behavioral disorders. And the numbers continue to grow: Autism, ADHD, Asperger's, and other disabilities are being diagnosed at all-time-high rates, putting teachers and aides in situations they are not always trained for.

A child with a learning or emotional challenge usually receives a special education plan known as an *Individualized Education Plan (IEP)* or accommodations known as a *504 Plan*. These are personalized plans created to help students successfully access the curriculum. (See more on special education in chapter 9.) Under federal laws passed in the late 1970s and 1990, children on an IEP must receive a "fair and appropriate public education—in the least restrictive environment." So it's up to schools—teachers, special education teachers, and aides—to implement these plans. A best practice in elementary education today is an inclusion classroom model. This means kids on IEPs are in regular classrooms so additional assistants, aides, or coteachers are needed. School budgets have increased significantly in the past twenty-five years to support these important special education needs and the kids who deserve them. These needs, sometimes called "unfunded mandates," are a reality for most public schools today.

Balancing Accountability with Quality Teaching and Learning

We desperately need a system that holds schools responsible for how effectively teachers teach and what kids learn. Accountability is needed and long overdue in our education system. Back when we went to elementary school, teachers taught more or less what they wanted based on loose curriculum requirements at the district or state level. No organization tracked how students fared year to year. Neither the Iowa Test of Basic Skills (ITBS), the California Achievement Test (CAT), nor NAEP tracked the same students year to year. Today all public schools in the country must publish a school report card every year based on how its third through tenth grade students perform on state standardized tests in math and reading, and more recently in science. Part of your school's federal and state funding is computed by a complicated and politicized system formerly called Adequate Yearly Progress or AYP, and now called Progress and Performance Index or PPI. This system ranks how well a school improves each year based on student scores on standardized tests. A full report of your school district's scores and how they trend and compare can be found on your state's Department of Education website.

The good news is that holding our schools accountable for what children learn and what teachers teach has propelled our education system forward in many ways. For one, it has generated higher standards and more consistent curriculum, much needed in many states. It has triggered a more comprehensive grading system at the elementary grade level, and recently refocused more time on science (hopefully social studies and the arts will follow). A more thorough and effective evaluation system for teachers is also in the works, as discussed on page 33. The best schools are beginning to integrate technology into the curriculum and focus more on higher level thinking and problem solving. All of this is good news that impacts what our kids are learning.

QUALITY OF CURRICULUM AND TESTS

For years, each of our states' education departments has operated under different curriculum standards. For the past decade, we've also administered fifty different standardized tests—all unique in expectations and difficulty. The fourth grade test Sarah takes in Massachusetts, for example, is much more rigorous than the test her fourth grade cousin, Jack, takes in California, reflecting the disparity in state standards. These variances also explain why Harry is converting fractions to decimals in third grade in Maryland, while in Florida, Sally doesn't do this until fifth grade. The differences make it difficult to compare students and schools across the country and can result in artificially inflated test scores in many states and school systems. All this reinforces why it takes more than one measurement tool to effectively judge schools, teachers, and students. (To see where your state ranks in a weighted education comparison, visit kidscount.org or dashboard.ed.gov/dashboard.aspx.)

A NEW CURRICULUM: THE COMMON CORE

For the first time in our nation's history, beginning with the 2013–2014 school year, more than 90 percent of our public schools will operate under the same learning standards for literacy and math. Forty-six out of fifty states (exceptions at this printing being Alaska, Nebraska, Texas, and Virginia) have adopted what's referred to as the Common Core State Standards (CCSS, or the Common Core). These standards define the knowledge and skills our children are expected to acquire in math and literacy from kindergarten through grade twelve to become "college and career ready."

I think of the Common Core as a huge cart of groceries for each grade level to consume by the end of the year. The recipes a school or teacher chooses to use with these ingredients will vary, but eight-year-olds like Teddy in New Jersey and Bridgette in Illinois will both be introduced to fractions in the second grade. The timing of what's taught when will differ within the year, but what teachers teach and what students learn, in theory, are now the same across most states. This coast-to-coast curriculum is not technically national because it has been adopted and is being implemented by the National Governors Association and State Education Leaders, but it provides much-needed continuity across states, districts, schools, and, most importantly, within each classroom at your child's grade level. This consistency makes moving from school to school in or out of state easier, eliminating gaps in your child's education. It also helps administrators assess how teachers are doing relative to the standards and their peers.

These expectations will translate into significant changes and more rigorous curricula in many states. In states where standards were already high, like Massachusetts, New Jersey, and Maryland, changes will be limited. But no matter where you live, the Common Core brings some changes to your child's school day. In math, you will see more spiraling curriculum with greater focus on understanding. (*Spiraling curriculum* refers to teaching the same subject at different depth levels from grade to grade.) For example, algebraic concepts will be introduced in grade two, and then repeated in grades three and four on a deeper level, before they are fully explored in grade five. Under the Common Core, your children will read more nonfiction in literacy from the earliest grades and be required to write more opinion paragraphs and essays using evidence to support their views.

In short, the Common Core requires higher standards and more thinking and understanding from our children. To make sure these standards are being met, the U.S. Department of Education incentivized states to administer one of two standardized tests that are aligned with the Common Core by 2015. Depending on what state you live in, your child will either take a test called PARCC or Smarter Balanced instead of the individual state tests now in place. This will help measure consistency from state to state. But because it is recommended that the tests be given multiple times a year (rather than once at the end of the year), this may fuel concerns among teachers and parents about overtesting and the quality of teaching and learning.

THE REALITIES OF TEACHING TO THE TEST

A key hurdle that undercuts accountability and higher standards is a hyperfocus on testing. Testing itself is not a bad thing; it's absolutely needed to measure where kids stand so they can move forward. But too many assessment points and benchmark tests that are tracked and reported can result in more data than teachers know what to do with and less time for higher quality instruction. In some schools, it means your child is taking a class test almost once a week in literacy and math. This practice results in teaching to the test, or placing too much emphasis on testing strategies and covering only material expected to be on the test. Excessive testing can lead to a narrowing of the curriculum and misleading rankings about how effective schools really are. The reality for most teachers is what is tested gets taught. While emphasizing reading and math is not a bad thing, it's often done at the expense of social studies, science, art, music, or recess. In some elementary schools, these subjects have been eliminated altogether.

Few educators will argue with the fact that social studies and science are important subjects that must be covered to educate students well. Most teachers don't want to spend extra time on testing at the expense of teaching and learning. But the desire to improve test scores (and in some cases teacher evaluations) chips away at valuable learning time across other subjects. School administrators feel pressure from state and federal mandates to improve tests scores because federal money is tied to school performance.

NEW STANDARDS FOR ENGLISH LANGUAGE LEARNERS (ELL)

Because more than 11 million kids (20 percent of kids in school) speak a language other than English at home (8 million speak Spanish), there are new federal mandates for teaching ELL students. In some urban districts, the percentage of ELL students is as high as 35 to 40 percent. In suburban and rural districts, the number is lower but growing significantly. To help these kids access the content and curriculum of the Common Core, no matter what their level of English proficiency, states must apply standards that help teachers adapt materials and engage and test ELL students. The program of choice used for these standards and professional training for teachers is called World Class Instructional Design and Assessment. Within a few years most school systems will adopt this (or a similar) program so ELL kids have equal opportunities in reading, writing, and speaking. Teachers will also have to be certified in these ELL standards within the next few years.

This often creates friction among teachers and administrators. In theory, skilled teachers plus strong curriculum plus a good test equals a great education. But when teacher evaluations, school funding, and federal incentives become tied to multiple-choice test scores, the waters get cloudy and political. While there are exceptions and schools that do maintain a healthy balance between subjects and test preparation, watch the priorities in your child's classroom and school. Pay attention to and advocate for making science, social studies, and the arts—or wherever you see gaps—priorities in your child's elementary school. That can be as simple as saying, "I'm concerned about the lack of focus on social studies (or science or the arts) this year. What can be done to get the balance back? What can I do to help?" Chapters 3 and 11 will give you more ideas on this issue and how to enrich your child's knowledge of these subjects.

A NEW GRADING SYSTEM

A standards-based grading system—grading against a specific set of goals or objectives—is now being implemented in most elementary schools. This grading system results in teachers and students who are very clear on teaching and learning expectations and the progress kids are making. It provides data to help teachers know what a student understands and when a child needs more support at multiple points during the year. Your child may have brought home a "rubric" or mentioned one that they need to follow. That's a fancy term for written expectations on what a student is supposed to learn from an assignment or a project. As my youngest says, "The rubric is the grader."

This system has triggered comprehensive standards-based report cards for elementary schools that reflect lots of "grades" for each standard. Some schools use B for beginning, D for developing, or P for proficient—to measure your child's progress in each strand, or area. Others use different letters or numbers denoting a similar scale from E for Exemplary to NI for Needs Improvement. While a dozen scores for each child in every subject area may be frustrating for elementary parents to absorb three times a year, this system, in theory, allows teachers and parents to track where children are and where they need to go. Because every child hits milestones at different times, standards-based grading is more in sync with a child's developmental journey and her natural readiness for skills and knowledge. It reminds us all that children need time and support to develop and practice a skill before they finally master it. Many schools hold information sessions to help parents understand these report cards. If your child's school does not, suggest to the principal or PTA/PTO that they consider doing so. Once kids move on to middle school, letter grades usually begin.

MORE FOCUS ON SCIENCE

Another piece of good news is that some districts are starting to ramp up science due to a national push to improve STEM (Science, Technology, Engineering, and Math) and the Common Core's focus on integrating curriculum. This means that literacy time today is more likely to include reading material related to science or social studies. And spelling word lists that are part of reading passages or books are becoming a best practice in elementary school curriculum. While this may seem like a common-sense approach, until recently most school subjects have been taught independent of one another and still are in some districts. Integrated learning opportunities are critical to successful schools and students because the more connections a child makes to a subject, the richer and more relevant the learning. Extending these connections at home is also crucial, as I discuss in chapter 3. This is easier to do now that most teachers create web pages that highlight current themes and projects.

TEACHING HOW TO THINK VERSUS WHAT TO THINK

Some schools are beginning to put a greater focus on understanding, thinking skills, and project-based learning that requires kids to reason and reflect. As your children's most influential teachers, you can help grow these skills by simply asking your children questions along the way. You don't need to have all the answers; part of the fun is watching them figure out the solution.

When you're helping your child study for a test (more on how to do that in chapters 12 and 14), stop and ask a "why?" question. If your second grader is learning grammar and proper sentence punctuation, ask why she thinks it's important to write well. Talk about how important writing and communication skills are for college classes and future jobs. Likewise, if your fifth grader is studying the mitosis in cell production, ask him broad questions: what are cells and why are they important to your body? Our kids are sometimes so caught up in the details of what's expected, they lack an understanding of the bigger picture. As parents, we can inspire them to understand on a deeper level by asking questions. In a culture that feeds on sports, social media, instant answers, and an eroding work ethic, this is not always easy to do. But it's never too early, or too late, to start asking why and what do you think. This intersection of technology, twenty-first-century skills, and thinking will be discussed in depth in chapter 11.

....

We've covered a lot of information in this chapter: the perfect storm our country has experienced in education for decades and the impact that has on our children, families, and teachers; the increase in international competition; the need to balance the good that accountability and higher expectations have created; measureable quality testing; and finally, what your children need to learn today to succeed in a world that will be very different in the future.

Now that you understand these bigger picture issues, you'll be a more informed parent and a more effective advocate for your child at home and at school. Chapter 3 will show you specific ways to build a bridge to your children's school and learning experience and why this is so important.

TOP TEN TAKEAWAYS

TO CONSIDER

- American students rank in the middle of the pack among developed nations worldwide in English and science, and even lower in math. Students in higher performing districts fare only slightly better.

- Accountability is leading to higher and more consistent standards in curriculum and teaching.

continued

TOP TEN TAKEAWAYS, *continued*

TO CONSIDER

- The key challenges that impact your child's schooling today are an education system that's falling behind the rest of the world, a broken infrastructure, and the need to balance accountability with quality teaching and learning.

- For the first time, our nation has consistent standards across most states. Balancing these Common Core standards with quality standardized tests, and not overtesting, will be key.

TO AVOID

- Don't let your child's school cut science, social studies, the arts, or even recess to make more time for literacy and math; all these subjects help create well-rounded kids.

- Don't judge a school system based only on its standardized test scores; this is one of many factors that should be taken into account.

- Don't relegate your child's education to teachers and schools; parents play a critical role in shaping a child's mind and supporting their learning.

TO DO

- Ask your children questions about what they're learning and doing in school that encourage them to think.

- Support budgets that keep schools up to date and keep class size lower at the elementary grades; this usually translates to more individualized attention for your child.

- Look for trends—where progress is made and where attention is needed—in your child's standards-based report cards; praise progress and effort made.

CHAPTER 3

Building Bridges to School and Learning

Setting an example is not the main means of influencing another; it is the only means. —ALBERT EINSTEIN

Wendy scanned the pile of printed emails and paperwork she vowed to get through before her daughter's first day of school. Working full-time with two young kids, she found it hard to get to that school pile. Besides health forms and signatures needed everywhere, there were endless requests: school supplies, PTA and PTO fundraisers, school councils looking for parents, directory forms, and classroom parents wanted. "It's overwhelming," she thought. "I need to figure out the best way for me to get involved with the little time I have."

Wendy thought about her siblings' advice—and their opposite approaches— to school involvement for the past few years. Her brother's let-the-schools-do-the- teaching style led to more than a few "needs improvement" on his kids' report cards. He also complained about public schools constantly. "One big bureaucratic web," he'd grumble. "Just stay away and hope for the best." Wendy's sister was a more involved parent, despite working full-time. Her sons' report cards touted more grades of "proficient" and "exemplary" than those of their cousins. "Maybe a coincidence," she thought. "Maybe not."

This chapter shows you why connecting to your kids' learning is important, the different ways you can get involved in your children's education, and how to build relationships with teachers. It also helps moms and dads recognize what type of parent they are when it comes to being involved in their children's education and what kind of parent they want to be.

Why Building Bridges Matters

For more than thirty years, educators and think tanks have researched parent involvement and its effect on student achievement. The studies are indisputable: parent involvement is the backbone of successful students. Seventy-seven studies link family involvement to better grades, higher test scores, improved graduation rates, and fewer behavior issues. It's well documented by outstanding educators and researchers from Johns Hopkins University, Harvard University, the Southwest Educational Development Laboratory, and numerous other educational organizations. All studies point to the same conclusion: regardless of race, nationality, income level, or educational background, children do better in school when their families get involved in their education.

But what exactly does "involved" mean? What does it look like to be involved in meaningful ways but not be overinvolved? With busy work and family schedules, how do you connect to your kids' education in productive ways? You know it's important to support your children's learning, or you wouldn't be reading this book. I've always been curious about what type of involvement influences a child's journey the most, so I was happy to find a number of recent studies that show what type of involvement has the greatest effect on learning.

PARENT INVOLVEMENT IN LEARNING
IS LINKED TO KIDS' SUCCESS

A key finding in the research is that when parent involvement is "logically linked to learning," it has a greater impact on student achievement. Furthermore, the more parents are involved at home, the more students feel it's important to perform well in school and achieve higher grades. So connecting with your child's learning, at home, plays a significant role in your child's motivation to succeed at school. Kids care when you care. Studies also show that communicating high expectations for your child's education, your knowledge of your child's homework, your perception of how engaged he is in his homework, and using reference materials at home (a dictionary, an atlas, the Internet) all influence a child's success in school more than other factors. This doesn't mean being involved in your child's school and classroom is not important. It simply means that being involved with your child's learning at home leads to greater success in school.

When it comes to parent involvement at school, the research suggests that teachers have higher expectations of students whose families show up at school. When parents are involved, the school as a whole improves, and students, families, and the community benefit. Children perform best when parents connect to and care about their education. This is especially true at the elementary level. Finally, when parents and teachers work as a team, children are more apt to thrive in their classroom environment. Getting involved in your child's education pays off, and there are three ways to do that.

Three Ways to Build Bridges

If we want our children to get the best education possible, we need to support our kids in their journey, connect to their learning, and create positive parent-teacher connections. We do this by building a strong bridge to our child's education, through relationships with our children and their teachers. Fostering a true and meaningful dialogue between home and school is a foundation for your bridge. And keeping your child at the center of that bridge is critical. What you say, write, and do around learning or education either strengthens or weakens this bridge, with each person you encounter, each grade, and each year. It also influences children far more than most parents realize. I talk in great detail about how to communicate effectively in chapter 5. In this chapter, we'll focus on how to be involved and build bridges to your child's education.

Beyond the basics of providing school supplies, making sure your kids get enough sleep, eat breakfast, and get to school on time (we'll discuss these topics in part three), there are three ways to be involved with your child's education: (1) connect to your child's learning outside of school;

(2) build a relationship with your child's teachers and support the classroom; and (3) get involved at the school level through events and organizations like school councils, parent-teacher groups, and policy committees. Let's take a close look at each of these bridge builders.

Bridge Builder #1: Connect to Your Kids' Learning at Home

When you reconnect with your child after school, you likely ask one of the infamous questions echoed by millions of parents every day: "How was school today?" or "What'd you do in school today?" Unless you're okay hearing "fine" or "nothing" 180 times a year, these kind of broad what or how interrogations usually don't work to connect to your child's day. Instead, make open-ended statements or ask specific questions. "Tell me about your day" sometimes works, or "Tell me about the best part of your day." If that doesn't work, try one of these: "Tell me what you worked on in math today." or "What games did you play at recess today?" or "Tell me about lunch." And don't shy away from "What was the worst part of your day?" Listen and empathize with your child's feelings and observations. Remember, school is a child's work. Try to find ways to connect with what they're doing or learning such as, "That's a fun way to learn multiplication," "I loved playing flag football when I was your age," "Passing out papers really helps the teacher," or "Sounds like you had a hard day." This type of interaction will inevitably lead to some connection you can make around your child's learning. Sometimes just having the conversation is all the connection you need.

As I touched on in chapter 1, providing your children with connections outside of school that relate to what they're doing in school is one of the strongest and most effective ways to support their learning. The more relevant and tangible the information and knowledge is to their world, the more excited and curious they become about the subject. The best kinds of connections are hands-on or experiential and come from activities like cooking, reading books, or playing games rather than doing worksheets from a study guide. Connections around reading, math, social studies, science, and art happen naturally because we're surrounded by them.

Your support at home is not meant to be another lesson; these are casual connections—as little as one example, a comment, a simple experience—that may relate to what your child is doing in school. Because most teachers write monthly newsletters or keep websites that summarize class events and upcoming curriculum themes, it's easier than ever to stay up to date. Your children's homework is another lens into what they're learning. If your child's teacher is communicating what students did last month instead of what's coming up, send a short email explaining that you'd like to make some connections at home to support your child's learning and ask for a preview of what's to come. Once you know that, think about ways to connect with what your child is learning in school. Here are some ways to do that.

READING CONNECTIONS

The most important way to support your child's education is to read to and with him throughout the elementary years. Even when they begin to read themselves, read to your kids and keep the experience fun and enjoyable. If you can consistently set aside fifteen to thirty minutes every night for reading, your child will have a more successful elementary education. Ask questions about what she's reading. Relate a story to your family experiences and her own life. Read a story that relates to a literacy theme. If your child is more interested in math or science than reading, read books about math and science with her. If he's focused on nothing but sports, read books about sports. Tap the children's librarians at your local library—they are usually very eager to help find a book or a series of books that matches your child's interests.

Because reading is so important, it needs its own chapter. In chapter 6, I will talk in depth about reading with your child, why it's so important, how kids learn to read, and how to create a reader.

SOCIAL STUDIES CONNECTIONS

When my daughter was in fourth grade, she struggled through a unit on the Revolutionary War. She just wasn't interested in King George and what all the different groups were fighting about. I read the material to her and reminded her of the Freedom Trail we had walked in Boston a couple years earlier, but her mind was blank. As a last-ditch effort, my history-loving husband pulled out some plastic army figures and created the Loyalists on the British side and the Patriots on the American side and reenacted a few of the battles. Suddenly, the Revolutionary War came to life for her. When we took her back to the Freedom Trail later that month, she spent over an hour in the cemetery, mesmerized by the graves carved with people's names she had just learned about. Creating a visual and a connection helped to make this subject more relevant and memorable to her. Think about ways that you can do the same for your child.

SCIENCE CONNECTIONS

You can make simple connections with science themes, too. A fun one shows how carbon dioxide works. Create the base of a rocket ship with seltzer water and Alka-Seltzer in a sealed film canister: ten seconds till blastoff! If your child is studying magnets, carve a couple hours out of a busy weekend to visit the science museum. Your local library often has free passes. Getting an annual pass is another way to visit different sections of the museum for short periods of time. If that's not realistic, show your kids how positive and negative electrons work at home. After you comb your hair, hold the comb next to a light trickle of water and watch the water bend. Another great way to bring science to life is to encourage your child to participate in the school's science fair, which is usually held in the spring. If he is hesitant, partnering with a friend might help. If you need ideas or don't have a science fair in your district, see the resources section at www.theparentbackpack.com for more information. Jump online and check out videos, games, and experiments related to science. A quality toy store will also carry interesting games and experiments. Since science is best taught by *doing* rather than reading, the more hands-on and experiential you can make the connections, the better for your child.

MATH CONNECTIONS

Beginning in the early years, count objects (like cereal Os and goldfish) by ones with your child. As they move up in grades, kids can count these same objects by twos, fives, and tens. Add and take away to demonstrate addition and subtraction. Fractions are a hard concept for many kids (math-challenged adults, too), but they're important because they form the basis for soon-to-be-learned percents and decimals. When your child is introduced to fractions (in second grade now), connect to this idea at home by making or ordering an uncut pizza. Cut the pizza (or a cake or a pan of brownies) and call out simple fractions with your kids. Have some fun with who's eating what fraction or percent of the pizza. This is a great way to reinforce work on fractions. Cutting up a play-money one-dollar bill into quarters is another way to help your child visualize fractions and teach money at the same time—a way your child is sure to remember.

As your kids move into double-digit addition and subtraction in second grade, dig out the Monopoly game (and your patience!) and let your child be the banker. It gives kids great practice in adding and subtracting whole numbers—what's known as "mental math." There are many board games that help build math skills, along with the skills of sharing and taking turns. Show your kids how to read and follow an athlete's stats in the newspaper. Puzzles are also a great way to improve spatial skills, and they spur good conversations, too. Invite your children to help you bake by measuring ingredients. How many one-quarter cups do we need to make a cup? Let them manage a lemonade stand on their own, money and all. It will take more time, but they will make valuable connections to math, money, and managing a business.

Math is everywhere. The more you can connect it to your children's learning at school, the better their understanding will be. If you're going on a road trip, turn that dreaded question, "Are we there yet?" into fun, family math. Help your kids figure out when you will get there based on how fast you're going. Throwing out wrong answers often encourages reluctant players. If you can make just one or two connections around math a week, your child will reap the benefits.

YOU'RE NOT MY TEACHER, MOM!

If, in your attempt to connect to your kids' learning, you hear comments like "Mom, I don't need another lesson" or "Dad, I already went to school today," it probably means you're trying too hard. Keep it fun and simple. Quick conversations and casual comments in the car are great opportunities to make links to what they're doing. These quick connections also keep your kids aware that you know what they're doing in school and, in turn, keeps them motivated to do well. As you make these connections around home, you will occasionally experience some magical "aha," "wow," or "oh, I get it" moments that will keep your child's curiosity alive. Children are naturally curious up until age nine or ten, so this is an ideal time to make links to learning. It only takes a few minutes each day. Be sure to praise their effort and progress rather than the outcome. For more on why this matters, see chapter 8.

Making meaningful links to your kids' learning is an important way to build bridges with school, but it's not the only way. The more you can connect with your child's teacher and classroom, the stronger your bridge will be.

Bridge Builder #2: Connecting to Your Child's Teacher and Classroom

Kristin stood at the bus stop, anxious to get her kids off to school so she could head to a busy day at work. While waiting, she overheard another mom and dad talking about volunteering in the classroom. She sometimes envied parents who worked part-time or from home. They could jump into the classroom or chaperone a field trip whenever they wanted. The mom seemed angry as she spoke about how different this year was for her daughter and herself. "Her teacher has very limited time for parents in the classroom. All she wants is more supplies and help in the copy room. No, thanks. How am I supposed to be involved in my kid's education if I can't even get into the classroom to volunteer?"

While classroom volunteering is one way to build a bridge with your child's classroom and teacher—and get a peek at what's going inside the classroom—it's only one of many ways you can get involved. Let's look at them all.

SHARE INFORMATION

A good place to begin building bridges with teachers is filling out the student information form that many schools hand out with teacher assignments or within the first week of school. It asks for information about your child—past school experiences, family makeup and siblings, personality and temperament, favorite activities, willingness to try new things, favorite type of books, strengths and weaknesses. Some teachers look at these immediately to get to know their students sooner. Other teachers choose to wait so they can form an opinion about your child on their own at first, then go back and read them for additional perspective. If your school doesn't offer student information forms, write a note to the teacher with a few key points about your child, using the topics above to guide you. It is important that teachers have the parents' perspective on their students, in addition to the file passed on from the previous year's teacher.

PARTICIPATE IN WELCOME DAY AND BACK-TO-SCHOOL NIGHTS

Most schools offer a welcome day, orientation, or a meet-the-teacher day before the school year begins for kindergarten through second graders and their parents. Plan to attend this important event or find a relative to take your child. My best advice for this day is to shake hands with the teacher and let your child get comfortable with her new teacher and surroundings. Let this time be about exploring the classroom with your child. Take in the different centers, details on the walls, and your child's cubby or seat.

Back-to-school nights are usually held within the first month of the school year to introduce parents to curriculum, classroom expectations, and how to best communicate with the teacher. Attending this event sends your child a message that you care about her education and that you know what's going on in his classroom. Teachers get annoyed with parents who come to these events and try to monopolize their limited time with questions or details about their individual child. But I see it happen all the time. Be gracious about a teacher's time, especially in the first couple weeks of a new year. It takes at least a few weeks to get to know each child and the class as a whole. If you feel it's important to meet, send a brief email with your concerns and request a future meeting.

READ THE COMMUNICATION COMPACT

Many schools and teachers now provide a communication "compact" between parents and teachers. This is usually a one-page document that lays out expectations for shared responsibilities between parent and teacher for the year. It is sent home in the first days of school or is handed out at open house. It outlines language and communication preferences—email, note, phone, or face to face. Some compacts also include classroom expectations and pledges between parents and teachers. You might be asked to agree to read the material the school sends home via student or via email, read with your child every day, support your child's homework, and play games that reinforce numbers with your children. If your school has not yet introduced the communication compact, you can find examples of it in the resources section at www.theparentbackpack.com.

VOLUNTEER IN THE CLASSROOM

Many, but not all, elementary teachers offer parents the opportunity to volunteer in the classroom. This can be a great way to see your own child interact in the classroom, get a sense of the teacher's style, and watch the learning unfold. It is both eye opening and interesting. But it's not for everyone. It takes patience to sit through multiplication tables, supervise art projects, or edit the "student newspaper." Some teachers are more comfortable including parent volunteers and will fold them into their daily routine; others will ask parent volunteers to cut out a project for an upcoming unit. Whatever the experience is, it's interesting to be in your child's classroom, to share a piece of his day, and help out the teacher. While it might seem logical that a school-wide policy be set rather than each teacher deciding about volunteers, union contracts don't require parent volunteers. That means it's up to the individual teacher to decide. This is yet another reason why it's important to build a healthy, positive bridge with your child's teacher. Before you can volunteer in any classroom, you must also fill out a CORI form (see page 55).

Be a Classroom Parent

If you have the time, volunteering to be a "classroom parent" or "room mother" is another way to build a strong bridge with your child's teacher. In most elementary schools, a classroom parent becomes a partner with the teacher in organizing (and sometimes planning) family-school events.

My experiences as a classroom mom varied significantly. In some situations, I organized classroom volunteers for the entire year, read with students regularly, and planned every party; in others, I organized a party or two. It all depends on the teacher and how she chooses to use classroom parents. Building a positive relationship with the teacher, no matter what your volunteer job involves, will go a long way in building a strong bridge for the future. This means following through on what you agree to do, respecting the teacher's requests, and lending a helpful hand—no matter how menial the task may be.

TOUCH BASE WITH THE TEACHER

At any point in the year, if you have questions or concerns about your child or your child's learning—whether it's about math homework, your child not being challenged enough in reading, or your child not getting along with a classmate on the bus—it's important to share this information with the teacher sooner rather than later. The teacher may be aware of it already, but it's helpful to hear the parent's perspective too. If you ask yourself, "Do I just wait until the parent-teacher conference to bring this up?" the answer is no—don't wait. Consider your child's teacher's communication preference and send a short message with your concern. If necessary, request a meeting to discuss the situation, but don't use email to discuss issues.

Anytime your child faces a difficult event—the death of a pet, a death in the family, a tough time with Dad or Mom being away, a bad phase with a sibling or a friend, or an obsession over something—give the teacher a "heads-up." Worry or hyperfocus on a situation often blocks children's learning. Teachers appreciate a quick note or email and can often connect with your child around it to help improve the situation. This is a great way to keep building your school-family bridge. If you're not sure how to ask or share, see chapter 5 for examples of how to effectively communicate this information.

ATTEND YOUR CHILD'S PARENT-TEACHER CONFERENCE

Make your parent-teacher meetings a priority. This sends a clear message to your children that you are invested in their education. If you cannot make the scheduled time, email the teacher and schedule another time that works for both of you. Most school districts are obligated to offer conference times in the evening so they don't conflict with parents' work schedules. Conferences are often sandwiched into ten- to fifteen-minute intervals, leaving little time for discussing issues of concern. If there is a problem or a specific area you want to review in more detail, let the teacher know and schedule a separate meeting. You're likely to receive better quality one-on-one time to discuss issues when conference week is over. Further details and examples of questions to ask at a parent-teacher conference are found in chapter 5.

PROVIDE CLASSROOM SUPPORT

Ever notice how kids often get sick within two weeks of a new school year if germ control isn't a priority in the classroom? Items like tissue boxes, hand sanitizer, and desk wipes typically fall outside of shrinking school budgets, so teachers often supply them with their own money if they want to maintain a clean classroom. That translates to fewer colds and sick days for your child, which in the end makes your life easier. Any help you can give is much appreciated. Many teachers put out requests, while some schools now require that every child bring in one box of tissues and hand sanitizer for the year. I think of this as a small price to pay for healthier kids—yours and the other two dozen in the classroom. It also helps the teacher stay healthy, which means your child will have fewer substitutes.

Teachers, especially elementary teachers, spend a lot of time in front of a copier or cutting things out for projects. They appreciate any help they can get from parents willing to do these types of jobs. The hours are usually flexible (some can be done at home), and it's also a good way to see what's coming up in the class. And there's an added bonus: meeting other teachers and volunteers in the copy room. You may pick up some helpful information and get to know other teachers at the same time.

ATTEND CLASS EVENTS

Teachers and principals will often plan special classroom or school-wide events where parents are invited to watch or participate. These can be centered on a play, a readers' theatre (where students act out a story), a party, a grade-level field trip, or a whole-school event. The dates and times of these occasions are often published in the teacher or school newsletters. If you or another family member can attend these events, your child will be thrilled. If you can't make it, let your child know in advance so she won't expect you. As a room mother for many classrooms, I've seen many disappointed kids watch and wait for an adult who doesn't show up. A simple heads-up email in advance to say you cannot be there (your child may not feel comfortable bringing this news to the teacher himself) lets a teacher know to pair your child up with another visitor.

HONOR CONFIDENTIALITY

Many schools require parent volunteers to fill out a confidentiality agreement. This informal contract states that you will honor the privacy of the children you work with. Working with students and teachers carries a big responsibility, whether it's in the classroom, in the gym, on the playground, or in the office. You will see and hear things about other students that need to remain private, rather than be shared at a parent pickup line or the bus stop. You wouldn't want parents sharing observations about your child with others, so don't share your observations of children (or teachers) with others. If you're confronted by a parent who wants to share information or gossip about a student, a simple, "It sounds like you learned a lot" or "This falls under 'too much information' for me," will usually end the conversation.

CORI FORMS

Before you can volunteer in a public school today, you are required by most schools to fill out a Criminal Offender Record of Information (CORI) form. Many private schools also require this information. This state form tracks your social security number and ensures that convicted criminals or sexual offenders are not permitted on school property. All school staff, from principals to cafeteria workers, custodians to teachers, is also required to a file a CORI. It often takes a number of weeks to be processed, so do it early if you want to volunteer. To ensure the safety of all children, schools cannot legally let you volunteer unless you have completed this form and are officially approved to volunteer. In some schools, you can visit a classroom as a "guest" for a conference or a welcome-back day. But since the tragic Sandy Hook Elementary School shootings, many schools have tightened their security. Your school's principal, its website, or your child's teacher will supply you with the latest safety and security procedures (see sidebar).

SCHOOL VISITATION AND SAFETY

Since 9/11 and the Sandy Hook shootings, most school districts have strengthened security procedures to keep our children as safe as possible. In addition to instituting the use of CORI forms for all staff and visitors, many schools installed a locked-door system (if they didn't already have one) that requires visitors and volunteers to ring a bell and be identified before being buzzed in. From there, visitors sign in at the office and are usually required to wear a visitor badge, or in some cases, photo identification. Schools also require that lock-down drills be conducted every year (like fire drills), and that personnel can see the entrance of the building from the office in all newly constructed buildings.

While a buzz-in system with identification may seem cold and uninviting, it's used for good reason. Honor this system and use common sense when entering and exiting your child's school. Don't let anyone slip through the open door unless you know them well. If you see someone lurking near a door, alert the office. Once you're in the building, don't open doors for anyone knocking. Let the office handle it. Finally, respect the sign-out system if you are picking up your child. School staff needs to ensure that the correct adult is picking up each child. This takes extra time and often frustrates parents but it's a necessary part of the school's procedure. Restraining orders, custody battles, and other adult behaviors require that these procedures be in place. School personnel are doing their best to keep our children safe.

Lastly, lock-down drills can seem scary to children and new kindergarten parents. But they are necessary to prepare for unforeseen emergency situations, including tornados, hurricanes, or an unwelcomed perpetrator. Like fire drills, lock-down drills are typically held once a year. Teachers explain to students why it's necessary, where to go, and what to do, while reassuring them that everything is okay and it's just a drill. Most schools will alert parents when they conduct a drill so you are able to talk to your child about it if necessary.

Bridge Builder #3: School-Wide Volunteering

When I was a PTA president, I received a hand written note one year from a mom who included a check. The note read:

> Dear ML,
>
> Enclosed is a check for $20. This is my donation to PTA/PTO to cover both my children for the coming year. I do this every year. As a single mom, working full-time, I have only minutes left in my day to connect with my kids. Please don't ask me to help with fund-raisers, I can't. Please don't ask me to be a room parent, I cannot. Please take me off the list for baking or helping or joining whatever committee. I hope you understand that aside from my time at home with them, this is all I can give. Thank you.

I loved everything about this note: how dedicated this mom was about connecting with her children and how she took the time and funds she could find to make some kind of contribution. Her "all I can give" was so much already. It reminded me as a parent leader that every family has limits and circumstances that affect the ways in which they can—or cannot—be involved with their children's school. Parent involvement looks different for every family. Bridge builders #1 and #2 are most important to your child's success in school: support your child's learning at home and connect with your child's teacher. If you can find the time or resources to contribute to bridge builder #3, school-wide volunteering, you'll benefit not only your own child, but also other kids in the school, the school at large, and your community.

Most elementary schools are affiliated with some type of parent-teacher or parent organization. This group is typically run by a group of parents—sometimes formal, sometimes informal—who work with school administrators. This group may appear to be an intimidating clique at first. Keep in mind, most members of that group started out knowing nothing more than where the school office was located. Even they got lost trying to find their child's first classroom. Hopefully, the group is welcoming and inclusive to new and incoming parents. If not, that's a good reason to join and help turn it into a more inclusive group.

The most well known parent teacher organizations are the PTA (Parent Teacher Association) and the PTO (Parent Teacher Organization).

These groups and others like them offer many different ways for you to get to know parents, teachers, and administrators, and influence the quality of your child's education. They also offer great leadership opportunities for parents. More fathers are getting involved with their kids' schools for good reason. The research shows that when dads come to school, kids care even more about their learning. Whether you are a stay-at-home mom or dad or a working mom or dad, there's a role for you. Find out when the meetings are, check one out, and raise your hand to volunteer for positions, events, or programs if you can. Before you know it, you'll gain an amazing understanding of how the system works, what it takes to improve your school, and how to give your child a better education.

PARENT TEACHER ASSOCIATIONS (PTAs)

Parent Teacher Associations are local affiliations of the National PTA, the largest volunteer child advocacy association. These groups pay dues to their state affiliate and the National PTA in return for member benefits, opportunities for parent leadership training, and a voice in advocating for national issues. Their local bylaws typically follow the national bylaws. National PTA leaders often speak before government bodies in Washington, DC, on child advocacy issues like homework and class size, and they encourage parent involvement in public schools. Locally, PTAs address school policy issues, advocacy, and fund-raising needs of the school. The PTA website (www.pta.org) provides a wealth of information for parents and parent leaders who want to get involved with and influence your children's education.

Kim Hunt is a mom of three who sits on the National PTA Board. A former PTA president, Kim works full-time and stays active in her kids' education. She finds many parents are already more involved than they realize. "Being involved in your kid's education means anything from helping your children with homework to feeding them a healthy breakfast," commented Kim. "Most schools offer lots of different parent volunteer options with different levels of commitment. It doesn't mean you have to attend a PTA meeting every month."

PARENT TEACHER ORGANIZATIONS (PTOs)

A Parent Teacher Organization, or PTO, refers to parent school groups that are not part of the PTA. Some schools use the term PTO, while others use PAC (Parent Advisory Council), PTG (Parent Teacher Group), or HSA (Home-School Association). Because these groups are *not* national organizations, they typically operate independently under an individual school or district with their own bylaws. A PTO organization does not pay dues to a state or nationally affiliated group, nor does it lobby Washington. Like PTAs, these groups encourage strong parent involvement, welcoming schools, and programs where teachers, parents, and communities work together. The magazine *PTO Today* and the website www.schoolfamily.com are also great resources for families and parent leaders on schools and education.

Tim Sullivan is founder of *PTO Today* and schoolfamily.com, a father of three, and president of his children's parent school organization. Tim believes that it takes students, teachers, and parents working together to make education the best it can be. "An involved parent doesn't have to run the PTO but does need to be an active part of the school equation," says Tim. "That means communicating with teachers (and not just at conference time), setting up habits at home that help learning, attending school events when possible, and making sure homework is done ahead."

POLICY AND DECISION-MAKING ORGANIZATIONS

Two other types of organizations exist within public schools that govern the practices and policies of a school and a school district. In both cases, parents serve a term, which is two to three years, depending on the policy of the school district. In both situations, monthly meetings are open to the public and a public comment section allows any parent or member of the community to speak to or address an issue.

School Councils or Advisory Committees
These are advisory boards often mandated by a state through No Child Left Behind. They are typically made up of two to five parents elected by the parents (unless the race is uncontested), teachers elected by teachers from the school, and a community member appointed by the principal. Together they serve as an advisory group to the principal on school

communication, budgets, practices, and some policies. There are usually equal numbers of parents and teachers on this council. The goals of the group revolve around school improvement. There are also many district-wide committees that school superintendents sanction for specific goals. These groups typically have a balanced mix of parents, teachers, and community members and make decisions on anything from hiring administrators to policies. Being a part of these committees provides great insight into the strengths and weaknesses of a school or school district and offers opportunities to improve your school in many ways.

School Board or School Committee

The primary governing body of a school district is the school board or school committee, made up of elected citizens at the town level. School boards will typically have from five to nine members, usually more for regional school districts. Responsibilities vary by state but typically include hiring and firing of the school superintendent, approving the local school

HOW TO ADVOCATE FOR YOUR CHILD OR A CAUSE

When you have a concern that involves your child, the first place to turn to discuss and resolve the issue is your child's teacher. Chapter 5 provides numerous examples on how to do this in a productive way using the technique I call the Power of P3. If you have a concern about your child or his teacher, and you have previously spoken to the teacher about your concerns, the next step is to go to the principal, not a governing board or a parent-teacher organization. It is wise to first inform the teacher that you're taking your concerns to another level because the principal will contact the teacher anyway. It's also important to understand that individual teacher complaints or comments cannot be discussed at any PTA, PTO, PAC, school council, or public school board meetings due to contractual regulations. If you hear a principal shut down a conversation about an individual teacher, it is for this reason.

If your concern goes beyond an individual child, specific classroom, or teacher level, most schools provide a chain of command to be followed. The first place to raise a general concern is at a local school PTA, PTO, or school council meeting, ideally when the principal or an administrator is present.

budget, and voting on changes in school policy. In some larger communities, getting elected to a school board can be costly, emotionally and financially, due to special interest groups or single-issue contested elections around controversial subjects. If budget and policy-driven issues interest you, and politics don't scare you, this role may be for you.

The Elephant at School

When the terms "school-parent partnerships" or "family-school relationships" are used, some parents and teachers question the authenticity behind "partnership." This is because there is a natural conflict that exists between parents and teachers when it comes to educating our children. It stems from the different perspectives that each expert brings to the table. While parents are interested in getting the best education possible for their child, teachers are charged with moving two dozen children from point A to Z within nine months. Likewise, administrators have a lot on their

Parents advocate for a range of school-wide issues from class size and healthier food in the cafeteria, to more recess time, tighter security procedures, saving a specific part of curriculum, and homework policies. Pulling together a few like-minded parents and finding a levelheaded spokesperson for the group often helps to create change effectively. Some advocacy groups exist nationally to help parents advocate for specific causes; many are listed in the resources section at www.theparentbackpack.com. Chapter 5 also provides tips on communicating with teachers and students.

From there, depending on your goals and the discussion, next steps will be decided. Addressing the district school board, at some point, may be in order if the issue cannot be resolved at the local school level. Either way, it's also a good idea to inform your child's teacher that you will be advocating for a particular cause. Bigger issues to advocate for, such as renovating or building a new school and raising town taxes to do so, often germinate from a small group that values education in your community and may include former school board members or teachers. The most effective way for change to happen in a district is for parents and teachers to work together toward a solution.

plates with schedules, budgets, and staff and often just don't have time to get behind a legitimate initiative. They also bear the shared responsibility of moving hundreds of students to proficiency or above on standardized tests every year. This is a tall order in today's school climate where testing dominates, new Common Core standards need to be learned and processed, and each child starts at different points. Teachers look at the whole of the class and how they will connect with each child. Parents look at one child individually and want what is best for their child. Meanwhile, the primal need to protect and fight for your baby is instinctual to parents, while teachers want to take care of all their "kids." This inherent conflict can lead to healthy tension that brings about positive change. Other times, it can lead to unhealthy tension in schools that ultimately infects our kids' education.

WHAT TO EXPECT FROM SCHOOLS

A school district's family-school culture is usually established at the top, with the superintendent. This climate is like a curtain between families and schools. In some distracts, that curtain is sheer and flowing, barely visible to parents. Schools are welcoming; partnerships are encouraged. In other districts, the curtain is heavy or iron clad, making parents feel like unwelcome intruders in their own school system. Here, schools are unfriendly aliens that intimidate parents.

Much has been written about what school districts can and need to do to "engage" parents versus "involve" them. "Engagement" suggests a commitment from the school to ensure that the culture is welcoming and friendly to families on a consistent basis versus just involving families in a few events throughout the school year by way of a newsletter invitation; it's a different relationship entirely to engage parents to be participants in the decisions that impact our children. Most educators know that family involvement leads to better schools and higher student achievement. But putting that into action consistently and making it happen is another issue. Encouraging meaningful, sustained parent engagement is a goal for most school districts today. While there is typically not a budget for family engagement, the good news is that accomplishing this goal often begins with a shift in attitude from superintendents, administrators, and educators rather than more dollars spent.

As a parent, you can expect your child's school to provide the highest expectations around family engagement and expect the same from principals, teachers, specialists, and office staff. Many schools now have a family engagement plan; some are hiring family engagement administrators. Expectations will typically include (1) a safe, welcoming, and friendly environment for your child to learn; (2) ongoing, accessible two-way communication about school events and what your child will be learning in class; (3) access to teachers and ongoing dialogue about your child's individual progress with any language assistance that is needed; and (4) opportunities for parents to be involved partners in the schools and contribute where they can. If these expectations are not what you see in your child's school, I encourage you to find a few C+ parents (see page 64), read chapter 5, and begin conversations with your principal and parent-school organization. A small group of parents can make a significant change in a school system—and a community—if they go about their goals in a productive way.

If this is not what you see or experience with your child's teacher, request a meeting with that teacher and use the tools in chapter 5. The more families can see the bigger picture and how their children's needs fit into the classroom culture, the better for the child. Likewise, the more a teacher can see and hear the parents' perspectives, understand the individual needs of each child, and strive to meet those needs, the better for the child. Parents know their child better as an individual; a teacher knows the child better from a grade-level standpoint. When the strengths of both experts are respected, tapped, and communicated, the child thrives and everyone wins. As I've stated before, how you support and advocate for your child makes a difference in getting what your child needs. Chapter 5 provides many examples on words that work so teachers can hear your concerns instead of react to your emotions.

Now that we understand why it's important to be involved, the many ways to do that, and what to expect from schools, let's take a look at the different types of parent behavior when it comes to advocating for your child's education.

Wanted: C+ Parents

When it comes to parent involvement, I've found that families generally fall into one of three groups. Parents may shift from one group to another as their children move through the system, and in two-parent homes, each parent may have a different style. A family's approach to involvement sometimes looks different from the first child to the last. And some parents start off in one category and never budge, while others move around depending on their individual child's needs or the situation.

The first two groups of parents fall into what I call "the A+ categories." In this case, A+ is *not* the grade to strive for. The first group is made up of parents who have the best intentions, but advocate for their children or cause in aggressive, annoying, or adversarial ways. These families are often trying to be assertive but are unaware of how their approach is perceived by teachers, administrators, or office personnel. The second A+ parent group is typically absent due to adversity, apprehension, or apathy. Many parents in this group feel anxious around schools and educators. They are often afraid to get involved.

The third group is what I call "the C+ category." These parents are calm, connected, and communicative around their kid's education. They are conscientious and collaborative and work to partner with teachers, specialists, and the office assistants that make up schools. C+ parents build strong bridges and are usually more successful in getting their children what they need. In the situation and examples below, see if you can identify the different types of parents.

It's mid-October and Mrs. Dennison cannot believe the homework hurricane swirling around the parents of her third grade class. Three parents have expressed strong and differing opinions about the homework being assigned. Sara's mom is angry that there isn't enough. Joe's father feels there is too much and it gets in the way. Alex's mother is frustrated that the homework doesn't appear to be corrected. Three different parents. Three different opinions. Three different approaches. Let's start with the A+ parents. Sara's mother feels third grade is the right time to enforce good study habits, so she emailed the teacher her thoughts about her daughter's homework.

Dear Mrs. Dennison:

I'm finding the homework that Sara is coming home with to be, frankly, mindless. As a third grader, I expect her to have at least thirty minutes of homework per night. She is finished in ten minutes and bored by the work. Clearly, she needs more of a challenge. I'd like to see higher levels of expectation for her homework and harder work by the end of this week—a plan that does not require Sara to ask for the extra work.
Thank you.

Next, Joe's parents feel the same homework assignments are getting in the way of sports activities and family time. Joe's mother thought she'd write a note to Mrs. Dennison but was quickly shot down by her husband. "It's our decision what we do with Joe at home. This amount of homework is ridiculous. Every night he's spending too much time after he comes home from football. He's eight years old." Joe's father scribbles across the top of his homework: "I told Joe he doesn't need to do any homework until football practice is over in November."

Finally, Alex's mother writes a handwritten note to Mrs. Dennison (she recalls that was the teacher's preference) about what she's heard from her son, who says that the homework isn't corrected anyway, so it doesn't matter if he does it.

Dear Mrs. Dennison,

I've been hearing from Alex for the past two weeks that his homework is not corrected. Because of this, he is not motivated to do it. I'm not sure how much of this information is accurate, so I'm hoping you can clarify for me what your homework policy is and how students get feedback on the work they've done. We want to reiterate the correct information to Alex and show our support for his homework. Feel free to email me back or give me a call to discuss further. Thanks so much for your time.

THE AGGRESSIVE, ADVERSARIAL ADVOCATE

Sara's mother's approach to asking for more homework falls into this A+ category. Her email alienates the teacher rather than raises a concern or requests a discussion. Parents who act in aggressive or adversarial ways are often not aware of how their actions or attitudes come across. Their attempt to advocate in an assertive way unintentionally becomes antagonistic or alienating. These A+ parents sometimes make accusations or assumptions before they acquire the facts. They may be angry about another situation that was never resolved and continue to play that anger out. They may appear to be absorbed in their child's needs with little attention on the effect it has on other children or the class. These A+ parents are more likely to be against, rather than for, a cause. Left unchecked, this behavior annoys administrators and agitates teachers.

Some parents in this category aim for A+ achievement from their kids. Others argue and demand answers ASAP. In extreme cases, A+ parents verbally abuse or physically assault an educator or school staff. While this group usually represents a small percentage of parents, they take up the most time. If you recognize some of this style in yourself, the fact that you are aware of it is the first step in becoming more of a C+ parent. Sara's mom will build a stronger bridge and have greater success if she moves over to the C+ camp where she will find a teacher more able to hear her concerns and respond to her needs. Let's look at the other A+ group, then we'll look at the C+ parent.

THE ABSENT OR APPREHENSIVE ADULT

Joe's father clearly falls into the other A+ group. He believes it's a teacher's job to teach and that academics stay at school. His priority for Joe at home is sports. He doesn't worry that the message he sends to his son—that school and learning are not a priority in this family—may be harmful to his success in school. It also sends the teacher a message that his family doesn't value education.

There are two subtypes of parents within this A+ group. The first abdicates their responsibility for anything academic. These parents are often not aware of the adverse effect this has on their children—or they're simply apathetic about education and educators. Sometimes adversity (family illness or unemployment) may keep them away. Sometimes the aftermath of a school-related situation leaves them so angry that they avoid schools or education altogether. The other A+ subtype is parents who are afraid around educated adults with authority. They feel awkward around teachers and anxious among administrators. Some in this group aspire to be more involved, but anxiety holds them back. They, too, may be afflicted with ailments or adversity that makes them less available. Some parents in this subgroup pay attention to their children's academics at home. They appreciate and value education, but don't access schools or get acquainted with teachers. While Joe's mother may feel differently, she is apprehensive about getting more involved herself, afraid of acting alone and alienating her husband.

Unfortunately, too many parents fall into one of the A+ groups— the Absent or Apprehensive group, as Joe's parents do, or the Aggressive, Adversarial group, as Sara's mother does. Often they overlap. The group that is most effective in their involvement is the calm, connected communicator.

THE CALM, CONNECTED COMMUNICATOR

Alex's mother is a C+ parent who will build the strongest bridges with teachers and schools for her child. She sends a note that shows she cares and wants to connect to her son's education. She approaches Mrs. Dennison with an open mind, not assuming she has the full story. She asks for clarification, shows support for her son's work, and respect for the teacher's approach. She also sends a message to Alex that homework and education are important.

C+ parents communicate clearly and collaboratively with teachers, especially when they're confused. They lead busy lives but understand the importance of connecting to their kids' education without pushing. They may question and confront but do so in a candid and calm manner. They use the power of being positive, professional, and persistent to communicate. (I call this the Power of P3, which I'll discuss in detail in chapter 5.) They want their children to compete and have compassion for other children, too. They consider all sides, compliment their child's efforts, and are conscious about what they say and do around their kids. They thank teachers and are careful not to talk critically about educators in front of children. This C+ parent is capable and confident, not antagonistic or entitled. When they get cranky, they own up to their conduct and correct it. They contribute to the classroom and the school in whatever way they can. For some, this is a casual contribution once in a while; for others, it's a continuous commitment for years. C+ parents are wanted by children, educators, and communities everywhere.

....

Now that you know why it's important to be involved, the different ways to get there, and what that looks like as you advocate for your child, you can build a strong bridge between your family and your child's school. The next ten chapters cover more specific topics and issues, beginning with kindergarten in chapter 4 and how to talk to teachers in chapter 5.

TOP TEN TAKEAWAYS

TO CONSIDER

- Research clearly links family involvement in a child's education to better grades, higher test scores, and fewer behavioral issues.

- Involvement at home that's connected to your child's learning has the greatest influence on your child; parent involvement looks different for every family.

- An inbred, natural disharmony exits between parents and educators in most communities, but it can lead to healthy tension; building positive bridges and relationships helps to bridge this gap.

- The approach you use to advocate for your child with teachers or in the school office makes a significant difference in how effective you are.

TO AVOID

- Don't overwhelm your child's teacher during back-to-school night or welcome day with specific details or questions about your child.

- Don't become an A+ parent: an absent, adversarial, or aggressive approach is not an effective way to advocate for your child or a cause.

TO DO

- Build bridges to your child's education by supporting your child's teacher and classroom, and attending or volunteering for school-wide events and programs when possible.

- Consider all the options for getting involved in your child's school and pick the right ones for you and your family.

- Extend your children's learning by making fun and casual connections at home to what they are doing in class.

- Become a C+ parent: a calm, connected communicator. C+ parents are needed to support their children's education in productive and meaningful ways.

CHAPTER 4

Kindergarten Matters

Play is to a child what gas is to a car. —KATHY HIRSH-PASEK, PhD, author of *Einstein Never Used Flashcards*

Bill and Suzanne sit on the edges of the chairs outside the principal's office, anxious for their meeting to start. Their oldest son, Sam, turned five in June and is scheduled to start kindergarten next month. Although Sam is excited to go to "the big school," Bill and Suzanne have watched his development this summer and worry that he's not ready. Suzanne reviews her notes, tapping her foot nervously on the chair leg. Bill glances at the clock. Finally, the office secretary leads them to the principal.

"Sam didn't talk until he was three. . . . He can't sit through a book and he still struggles to hold a pencil," Bill explains to the principal. "We've thought about asking for a waiver and waiting until he's six, but he's also the biggest kid in his preschool, pretty athletic, and he's already adding and subtracting. So, we're not sure that's the answer either."

Suzanne chimes in, "For now, we're trying to work on his vocabulary. We've read that is important for kindergarten, so we bought a children's dictionary and read it to him every night. We even started a game that he loves—for each definition he remembers, the next day he gets a piece of candy. But we're still not sure this is enough. How do we really know if he's ready?"

Kindergarten triggers parents' instincts to protect and preserve their children like no other year. Up there with walking, driving, and graduating from high school, it's a major milestone in childhood. Some parents are ready to let go. Some are not. For many first-time kindergarten parents, the experience is fraught with anxiety and stress. And it's understandable. Kindergarten marks the year parents begin to share their child with the outside world. How do I know if she's ready? Will his teacher be nice? Is half day or full day best for her? Will he make friends? Will she be able to sit still through all that work? Am *I* ready?

In the end, kindergarten is a leap of faith. And whatever option you choose for your child, the question really ought to be, is the school ready for your child? This chapter will clarify expectations for kindergarten and calm your fears about your child's readiness. It shows you how to keep his curiosity strong and how to support her learning. The best way to wrap your head around kindergarten is to read this chapter along with chapter 6 on reading, because these two chapters go hand in hand. I'll also explore the controversial issue of redshirting and the pros and cons of half-day and full-day options. Finally, I'll provide a few tips on transitioning your child to start that big first day so it goes as smoothly as possible, for both of you.

The New First Grade

Aside from accountability and testing, nothing has changed more in education in the past decade than kindergarten. When my five-year-old daughter hoisted herself onto that school bus step for the first time more than a decade ago, kindergarten was about playtime, letter friends, quiet time, and developing social skills. Today children learn how to read, write, add, and subtract in kindergarten, skills that were not taught until first grade less than five years ago. Two factors drive this trend. First, state standardized testing that begins in grade three. Second, brain research over the past two decades that suggests children are capable of much more than we ever realized. By the end of kindergarten, some kids will be reading one-syllable four-letter words. Some will be reading fluently and writing full sentences. Most will finish their kindergarten year somewhere in between. It's an exciting time for everyone. But no matter how high the expectations are, it's also a year best experienced in a developmentally appropriate environment—one that taps a child's natural curiosity and need for play.

Curiosity: A Child's Natural Motivation to Learn

A chapter about kindergarten would be incomplete without a discussion on curiosity, a child's natural motivation to learn. Curiosity is the root of all the questions your children ask, the source of their unyielding inquisitiveness. It is an innate human trait, very alive in five-year-olds. Human beings are born curious creatures, and most children are naturally wired to learn about the world around them throughout the early childhood years (preschool through grade two).

Curiosity cannot be taught, but it can be nourished, tapped, and channeled by teachers and parents. It's important that curiosity not be crushed in the process of teaching and learning skills. Of course, kids need skills in order to succeed in the world today, so it's a delicate balance. It's the job of parents and teachers to keep our kids' curiosity alive, to encourage their questions and support their learning, to guide and inspire them in a way that nurtures their spark for learning so it blossoms into a love of learning.

The Importance of Play

Wherever your children attend kindergarten, the most important factor is that they begin and end the year excited about learning and reading. This comes naturally for most five-year-olds, as their curiosity about the world is contagious. But it can only be sustained if learning and reading happen in a relaxed, inspiring environment. Play needs to be an integral part of every kindergarten day because children learn best through play in their early childhood years, preschool through grade two. Through trial and error, children use their senses, tap their imaginations, and discover their creativity and problem-solving abilities without even realizing it. Just as parents need to provide children with opportunities for unstructured play, schools and teachers also need to integrate hands-on, experiential play-based activities into their kindergarten curriculum. Unstructured play also helps to build attention spans and encourages social development. It's a child's work. In chapter 1, I talk about why play is vital to a child's early learning. These pages will help you understand the critical role of play in a five-year-old's development.

If you are exploring kindergarten options for your child, a key factor to consider is how play, or experiential learning, is integrated into instruction. Feeding five-year-olds daily worksheets, weekly tests, and daily homework will squash a child's natural excitement for learning. Most five-year-olds, especially boys, are not yet developmentally ready or able to sit at a desk and read or write for long periods of time. While some worksheets and pen-to-paper exercises are necessary to practice and reinforce skills, it's critical that teaching methods engage children and pique their curiosity. A combination of lessons, learning centers, and hands-on exploration throughout the classroom is considered a best practice for kindergarten today.

Choosing a Kindergarten

Jim is overwhelmed with a new job, three kids under six, and his loving and determined wife, Karen, who insists on only the best for their kids. While Jim agrees with most of Karen's decisions, he feels all she does lately is write checks—for the kids. So when Karen tells him she feels strongly that their oldest son needs full-day kindergarten—he loses it. "Karen . . . it's kindergarten. The public half-day program is free and you work part-time. Why would he need to be in school another three hours? He'll be fine!"

The irony behind kindergarten is that while it's become a critical first year in your child's journey, attending is still not a legal requirement in many states. While strained budgets keep this antiquated law on the books, it also means that kindergarten is not as well regulated as other grades. So the range of experiences, instruction, and facilities varies significantly. If you have a choice of kindergarten options, do your homework so you can make the best choice for your child. After you check out a school's website, set up a meeting with the principal or director, and visit the school. The next few paragraphs will give you ideas of what to look for.

When you arrive at the front door, take in the school culture. Does it seem friendly and kid oriented? Is student work highlighted, or is wall space dedicated to school rules? Were you greeted in a welcoming way in the office? Did you get a positive "gut feel" from the principal? Ask if you can arrange a visit to a classroom. Is the room filled with books of all different levels—from picture books to early readers? Are they displayed in an inviting way? Is there a comfortable place where kids can sit down and "read"? Are there tables that encourage group work? Is there a carpet for story time, reading groups, and calendar time? Reading to children and getting them excited about books, words, and phonics is an important part of kindergarten. Ask about their approach to reading instruction. Is it a balanced mix of rich literature and phonics? (Chapter 6 will explain this in detail.) Do they use small or close reading groups (a reading group lead by a teacher or a parent who reviews specific strategies)?

Do you see "manipulatives" for math—blocks, shapes, and forms that can be physically touched, combined, and played with? Worksheets play a role but should not dominate the day. Ask if there is a social skills philosophy or program used in kindergarten. Plants, animals, and science experiments make ideal hands-on learning experiences. Recess is important and a great way for kids to get outside, exercise, and build their social skills. Is there a place where kids can play store with a cash register, or use their imaginations and act out a story? Can you picture your child in the classroom? Is this an environment that you feel your child will thrive in? What feels right for one child may not be right for another.

Finally, ask about the class size of kindergarten. In private schools, it typically ranges from ten to fifteen students, with one or two teachers. In public schools, it's anywhere from eighteen to twenty-five, or more. A class of eighteen or more calls for two teachers, or a teacher and an assistant, as practiced in many public schools today. Many parents think of kindergarten as an easy, fun grade to teach. In fact, kindergarten teachers have a tough job because of the wide range of children's abilities: academically, emotionally, and socially. Are kindergarten teachers in the school you're considering trained in early childhood education or child development? This is not always required in private kindergartens. A few children come to kindergarten already reading, many come excited to read and write, while others are still learning how to hold a pencil. It's as challenging a year for teachers as it is for kids and parents. But what makes this year thrilling is that five-year-olds are typically high-energy, curious kids who like to be around other kids and want to please adults. They're excited to begin reading and eager to learn about the world around them.

Half-Day vs. Full-Day Kindergarten

Sheila has two kids and works part-time at home. She reads parenting books, gets the importance of play and reading, and feels her "mom" instincts are pretty good. Sheila also believes kids are at their best playing in their own environment, having fun, and working out social spats with neighborhood friends. "Just let them play" is her creed. So when it came to making a decision about the half- or full-day kindergarten (two and a half hours versus six hours) for her oldest daughter, Chloe, the decision was easy. It would be half day, no lottery application needed. Why would she do a full day so Chloe could play and learn to read in a structured way at school when she could get all that at home? But deep down, Sheila worries . . . will Chloe fall behind the other kids who go to the full-day program?

As kindergarten morphs into the new first grade, the debate over half-day or full-day programs magnifies. In 1995, less than half of U.S. schools offered full-day kindergarten. Today over 70 percent of all public school districts offer some variation of full-day kindergarten, and that number continues to grow. In some communities, it is built into the public school budget. In others, full-day kindergarten is offered as a tuition-based program, while the half-day program is free. In others, a lottery system is used to accommodate space limitations that full-day kindergarten creates. These options are common in states where kindergarten is still not a legal requirement and local budgets aren't obligated to fund it. But it does not make it easy on parents juggling busy lives, jobs, family values, and budgets.

My feelings about half-day versus full-day kindergarten have evolved over the past five years. The Common Core standards for kindergarten are exponentially higher than what most state curriculums expected even two to three years ago. And they don't take into account full- or half-day. Most kindergarten teachers I've spoken to feel two and a half hours a day is not nearly enough time to cover the new expectations and teach kids in an engaging way. Squeezing six hours of teaching and learning into two and a half hours a day seems unfair to teachers, parents, and most importantly, children, who often feel rushed from one activity to the next in two and a half hours.

Full-day kindergarten gives teachers and students time—time for hands-on, project-based experiential learning and more time for kids to create, explore, integrate play, and think about what they're doing. Kids have more opportunities to work on social and emotional skills in the classroom, an important area often cut in half-day programs that must focus primarily on math and literacy. Teachers need the extra time to get to know each student's strengths and needs, provide one-to-one instruction after group lessons, and to help those students who need either more support or more challenge. A full day also affords more time for social studies, science, and art, at-risk subjects in elementary schools. I'm convinced that our five-year-olds need the extra time to learn the new Common Core standards in a relaxed, hands-on environment. A full-day program is ideal to transition children into school without overwhelming them with two much curriculum, in too little time. But it's not for every child.

If you do have a choice of half day or full day for your child's kindergarten, in the end, visit the schools, observe your child exploring the classroom, and talk to the teachers.

Candy Weiler, a teacher, founder of an early childhood center, and retired principal of an elementary school in Massachusetts believes that every school needs to be ready for each five-year-old that enters its doors. "Rather than ask, 'Is my child ready for kindergarten,' the real question needs to be, 'Is this school ready for my five year old?'"

In the end, which kindergarten you send your child to is an individual decision based on what feels best for your child—and what works for your family. And if you have a child born close to your district's cut-off date for grade-level placement, there is also another consideration: redshirting.

Redshirting and Kindergarten Cut-Off Dates

My oldest daughter was due on September 7 but arrived five weeks early, at the end of July. The kindergarten cut-off date in our school district was September 1. So if I sent her to school at age five, she would be one of the youngest in the class. For years, every other mom on the playground asked me what I was planning to do. Would I send her or keep her out a year? Then it happened again—lucky me. My second daughter was also due the first week in September and arrived two weeks early in August. She, too, just made the September cut-off date and would be among the youngest in the class. For both situations, I did my due diligence. I read the latest research and consulted with my children's preschool teachers, pediatrician, and the principal at the elementary school. I spoke with family members and friends who faced a similar decision.

....

Redshirting, holding back a young five-year-old from kindergarten so he ends up one of the oldest in the class versus the youngest, sparks much controversy among parents and schools. Once used to give a child an athletic advantage, with the bar now raised for kindergarten, parents worry that their younger five-year-old might be at a disadvantage. Will he learn to read with his peers? Is she ready to sit in a classroom and transition all day? Is he mature enough? Redshirting can result in an eighteen- to twenty-four-month age spread in the classroom, making it even more challenging for teachers to teach and reach each individual child. Because of this, many schools hold a hard line on kindergarten birthday cut-off dates and don't allow exceptions, except in extreme situations such as illness. Redshirting is more common in suburban districts and is used approximately 10 percent of the time, more often with boys.

The two pieces of research that help decision making on whether to send a young five-year-old to kindergarten are gender development and social-emotional maturity. To my knowledge, no state or district has looked at standardized tests results by birthdate to determine if there is a long-term trend academically among those "redshirted." Though general research on the benefits of redshirting is inconclusive, studies have confirmed that five-year-old boys can be developmentally behind girls, by three to six months, particularly in fine motor skills. Redshirting a child in this situation may provide a short-term academic advantage—up until third grade when development evens out. Some argue it's better for a child to struggle early on when support systems are more available; others argue that "redshirted" kids who end up taller and bigger than their classmates feel alienated. The other area of research is social-emotional maturity. Children who aren't showing signs of independence or who are not yet able to interact or communicate with their peers or other adults in authority may not be ready for kindergarten.

If your child's birthdate falls near your district's cut-off date and you believe your child falls into one of these areas, initiate discussions with teachers and doctors who know your child. Listen to these experts who have seen hundreds if not thousands of five-year-olds in their lifetime, especially your pediatrician. Research the topic. I have listed some resources at www.theparentbackpack.com. It's important to take into account that a child who is bored in a grade year after year can become disengaged from school and learning just as easily as a child who struggles to keep up socially or academically. Some research suggests that kids who are redshirted often try risky behaviors in adolescence sooner than those who aren't. But a recent study tracked boys who were redshirted versus those who weren't through their teen years and found that the boys who waited a year appeared to be more confident and happier. The research is inconclusive and it's a very individual decision. Is your goal to give your child a competitive advantage academically? Could such a decision send an underlying message to your child that suggests "you need an edge, you're not smart enough?" Is your goal to ensure your child can keep up with his peers socially and emotionally, particularly for boys with late summer birthdays? In some of these cases, redshirting is more likely to be warranted.

Parents and school administrators struggle with these decisions because they are indeed difficult and individual choices. Be sure to include educators and pediatricians in your decision-making process because they have perspective on and experience with five-year-olds that you don't. Likewise, you have perspective on your individual child that they don't.

We ended up sending both of our summer birthday girls to kindergarten at age five. We concluded that they were both socially, emotionally, and academically in line with their peers, despite their late birthdays. But they were also girls. If they had been boys, the decision might have been different. When unique situations call for an extra year so a child can be socially successful within his grade level—and not just to gain an "edge" over others—redshirting may be warranted. Trust your own gut—not what other parents are saying or doing—and make a decision based on what's best for your child and your family.

Four Skill Areas for Kindergarten

No matter what school you choose, children need to know or understand some basic skills to experience a successful year in kindergarten. Your children will not need to master or be proficient in these skills when kindergarten starts. They will continue to be honed and sharpened throughout their kindergarten year, both at home and at school. But it is important that the foundation, the root of the skill, is understood so kids get off to a solid start.

The four skill areas are social-emotional awareness, reading and writing readiness, numbers knowledge, and physical abilities. Keep in mind your children's capabilities today look very different from what they will look like in three months from now or even three weeks. Visualize your child's journey: the first ride on the bus, the first day in the cafeteria may be a leap of faith for both of you. But it's a leap your child will take and succeed at when you support, encourage, and guide him. Remember, it's totally natural to feel some fear as a parent, especially if this is your first child heading off to school. Kids are often more ready for kindergarten than parents are.

SOCIAL-EMOTIONAL AWARENESS

Our children learn core social-emotional skills at home and in kindergarten that will serve them for the rest of their lives. This is especially true today as children enter a world more culturally diverse than any in history. Skills that answer the infamous question, "but can he play in the sand box?" In other words, can he get along with other kids? Four areas make up the skill of social-emotional awareness: respect for authority and ability to follow two-step directions, ability to function independently, communication of emotions, and ability to share and take turns. Let's take a closer look at each of these areas now.

First, does your child respect authority and follow two-step directions, such as "Go back to your chairs now and take out your writing journals"? Five-year-olds succeed in their first year of school if they have had some discipline and rules to follow in their toddler through preschool years. In order for children to listen to instructions and interact with others, they first need to know and understand that someone else is in charge and, once in school, it's no longer Mom or Dad. They need to accept authority and recognize when they're following directions and when they're not. This skill will be developed as the kindergarten year progresses, but the basic foundation of respect for an authority figure other than Mom or Dad needs to exist so simple directions can be followed.

Next, can your child separate and function independently without continuous adult guidance? An independent five-year-old can dress himself, put on a jacket, tie shoes (maybe not yet in in our Velcro world), and use the bathroom independently. Of course kids need help with zippers, ties, or putting on boots sometimes, but they can usually handle these skills on their own. A child coming to kindergarten also needs to feel comfortable separating from a parent, once the short-term transition is complete, and enjoy playing next to others, *without* an adult alongside at all times. A child who hides in a corner or behind an adult's leg for extensive periods of time may not be socially ready for kindergarten. Likewise, a child who needs constant one-on-one supervision for safety reasons or who puts other children at harm may not be prepared for a kindergarten class environment.

Third, a child needs a basic understanding that emotions are communicated with words rather than by hitting, biting, or throwing. This does not mean that five-year-olds have emotional control at all times. There will be many times when they get angry and yell or throw something at school. But this needs to be the exception rather than the norm. With this skill comes the knowledge that others have feelings too, and with time they will learn to better understand those feelings and communicate their own. The ability to communicate feelings in a polite, productive way is the basis for a child's future emotional intelligence and a foundational skill for their social-emotional readiness in kindergarten.

Finally, does your child understand the idea of sharing and taking turns? Kids will not always succeed in doing this as five-year-olds, but they do need to have a root understanding of what sharing means and what it looks like. As they sharpen this skill throughout their kindergarten years and beyond, children come to understand the give-and-take of sharing and playing cooperatively with others as well as communicating their feelings in productive ways. The more you can reinforce this idea at home with siblings and friends, the more successful your kindergartner will be.

If your child shows signs of developing these four areas of social-emotional awareness, she is most likely ready for kindergarten. If she lacks more than one of these skills and it's determined she needs another year for the roots of the skills to take hold, what you do with your child that year will make a critical difference to her readiness the following year. Some schools make recommendations that children attend kindergarten for two years to accommodate social issues. Talk honestly about your child's strengths and weaknesses with preschool teachers, school principals, and pediatricians. Together, you can make an informed decision.

READING AND WRITING READINESS

The best way to prepare your children to read and write is to shower them with words from the time they are born. I introduced this concept in chapter 1 and expand on it further in chapter 6. The more books, conversations, and words you've shared with your children during their first five years, the more likely they will be reading by the end of kindergarten.

Your children's appreciation for language comes from three sources. First, it comes from your reading *with* your kids, not just to them. This means being excited and asking questions about the plot and the characters, and making connections between the book and experiences in your child's life. Picture books are a great resource for initiating lively discussions. Point to the words as you read so they know you're reading left to right; this will also help your children begin to associate the word with the image. The more books your children experience, the better. Second, make a habit of talking about what you're seeing and doing with your children. Having daily conversations with your children may sound obvious, but we often speak *to* our kids rather than engaging them in conversations or considering their thoughts. In the midst of our busy lives, we quickly tell them what to do when, and by doing so, we quickly dismiss their inquiring minds. Finally, model reading in front of your children. Let them catch you reading and writing every day—books, newspapers, magazines, e-readers. What you read doesn't matter. Kids are masters of imitation. The more they see you reading, the more likely they are to sit down and "read." Pretend reading is a natural step in the reading process.

If you wish you had read more or had more time to do it now, it's never too late to dial up the reading. Even reading just fifteen minutes a day with your child will help. The more consistent your reading is, the better. Which books you read doesn't matter as long as your child is interested in them. Through this daily exposure to words, language, and books from their parents and family, children will be able to sit and listen to a story in the classroom or at the library. Ask them to identify rhyming words and the beginning sounds of words. Encourage them to sing and recite the alphabet, and understand that l-m-n-o-p is not one letter. By kindergarten, most children are beginning to write their name and identify the letters in it. Some kids can identify and write letters of the alphabet, and are beginning to learn some "sight" words (common words, like *the* or *when*, that must be memorized because they are difficult to sound out). Less than 5 percent of children come to kindergarten already reading.

Let's revisit Suzanne and Bill, whom we met at the beginning of this chapter. Their son, Sam, cannot sit through a book, so his parents read a children's dictionary to him every night and reward him for each word he remembers. There are two problems with this approach. First, kids need context to understand and retain what they read. The more connections children make to the words and ideas, the more interested they are and the more they get out of it. Reading a dictionary may give an immediate boost to a child's short-term memory of vocabulary, but it will not translate to long-term memory or prepare a child to read. Second, rewarding a child with candy for learning undermines a child's internal and natural curiosity about the world around him. What could they do instead? If Bill and Suzanne find books on sports that interest Sam, read with him every night and increase the time by one minute each day, they will be well on their way to developing Sam's ability to read for himself. Every child has an interest in something. We just need to listen closely enough to discover what that is, and then head to our local library and let our child take home some books related to that subject.

NUMBER KNOWLEDGE

Kids used to learn to count to ten in kindergarten. Today children will count to one hundred by the end of the year, so kids who have a basic sense of numbers will be off to a strong start in kindergarten. This includes knowing their age, phone number and address, counting to twenty, and being able to identify numbers one through ten. Recognizing that numbers are also words and knowing one through ten as sight words will happen as they progress through the year. As I mentioned above, by the end of the year, your kindergartners will be able to count to one hundred. They will also be able to identify numbers out of order and learn how to add and subtract single-digit numbers. They'll learn how to count by tens, fives, and twos, or what's known as *skip counting*. And the good news is all these skills are easily reinforced at home though board games, play, and computer apps. Chutes and Ladders, any games with dice that involve movement, and blocks will teach your child basic number sense while having fun. Driving in the car and food shopping also provide great opportunities to reinforce numbers and practice counting so your children come to kindergarten prepared to learn to add and subtract.

Kindergartners also need to understand the basics of money and, by the end of the year, be able to identify a penny, nickel, dime, quarter, and dollar. This is a hard concept for many kids. When a child discovers that five pennies make a nickel, two nickels equal a dime, and there are many ways to create twenty-five cents, it's an "aha" moment, which usually happens by second grade. Giving your child the chance to pay or find the right change while you're at a store is the ideal situation to teach these skills, as long as you have a patient cashier. Buying a toy cash register, filling it with a few real coins, and encouraging your kids to play store also goes a long way in building this skill.

Telling time is a skill that takes most children years to grasp. This is not something mastered by many five- or six-year-olds. Kindergartners can understand that the big hand tells the minutes and the small hand tells the hours. They should be able to associate parts of the day—breakfast, lunch, and dinner—with 7:00 a.m., 12:00 noon, and 6:00 p.m. Time is an abstract concept and children's brains at this age absorb literal ideas. This is also why the concept of "today, tomorrow, and yesterday" is often difficult for kids to grasp at this age. The same holds true for days of the week and calendar dates. While some recognition is needed of time and dates, these skills are practiced from kindergarten through second grade and are mastered by third grade. Using an analog clock (one with a face) instead of just digital clocks in your home will also help the process along.

PHYSICAL (KINESTHETIC) SKILLS

Just as there are social-emotional skills a child needs to acquire, five-year-olds who have mastered certain aspects of the world around them and their physical self will experience a positive kindergarten year. Beyond colors, the parts of the body, and five senses, kindergartners need to be able to identify basic shapes—circle, square, rectangle, and triangle—and sort objects by color, size, and shape. There are many games and computer apps that reinforce these skills. While some five-year-olds learn their right from left hands early on, many children mix up their right and left sides through third grade or even later. This is a developmentally common trait and nothing to worry about. A weekly game of Twister (with the L or R written on hands and feet) will usually do the trick. But, as is the case with all five-year-old teaching and learning, keep it fun and interactive.

Kindergartners also need to know how to be able to hold a pencil correctly, trace a line, and use scissors, crayons, and glue. The best way to practice these skills at home is to have your children cut, trace, write, draw, and glue. Let them explore and experiment. These are skills that boys often need more time to master. Be sure to get left-handed scissors for lefties and fatter age-appropriate pencils with grips for kindergartners. Coaching your kids to cut accurately by turning the paper instead of the hand or scissors often helps the cutting process. Kindergartners who know how to climb stairs, jump, skip, hop, and swing independently will also be well on their way to a successful first school year. All these skills are motor-based activities that moms, dads, grandparents, older siblings, family, and friends can encourage in fun, enjoyable ways.

Transitioning to Kindergarten

Now that you have a sense of kindergarten expectations, how to choose a kindergarten, and the four skill areas children need to begin kindergarten, let's turn to transitioning to that big first day. Once you officially register your child for kindergarten and fill out necessary forms, you will receive information about school bus schedules, student pickup policy, dress codes, cafeteria accounts, and a school supply list. If your child will attend a public school, you will schedule a hearing and vision test. You will be notified of your child's teacher, sometimes two or three weeks before school begins or earlier in some districts. You'll also be informed of dates when you and your child can finally meet the teacher and visit the classroom. And there are also medical requirements for immunizations and annual physicals that verify your child's health. Your pediatrician can supply you with the appropriate forms.

No matter how excited your child appears to be about kindergarten—or how ready you yourself are—this is an emotional milestone for both of you. Beneath the surface of details and stuff-to-do lurk emotions that range from "I can't wait!" to "I'm scared of the big kids on the bus." Parental emotions can range from, "What if he doesn't make any friends?" to "It can't come too soon!" Oftentimes, kids don't recognize their feelings; they simply act them out in other ways. Even adults may find themselves harboring feelings they weren't aware of.

As your child begins to imagine himself in his new school, I offer a few transition tips below that will help you both get ready for kindergarten.

CLIMBING THE V-TREE

I use an acronym called the "V-Tree" to highlight the steps you can take:

- Visit
- Talk about transitions
- Read
- Empathize
- Establish a routine

Be sure to visit the new school with your child more than once.

It's important to visit the school, the playground, and the cafeteria so your child feels comfortable in each place, especially if you have a more reserved child. If you go for a vision or hearing test, take the time to walk your child around the school. Check out the gym and the bathrooms. The more times you visit, and the more your child sees and experiences the school environment, the smaller and less scary the school will feel to your child—and you. When you visit for the second time, bring a cousin or a grandmother with you so your child can play tour guide and show off what she knows about her new school. Walk the school route or take the bus route. Many schools have a "ride the bus" day. Some schools offer Countdown to Kindergarten, a transition program run by parents or educators in the community to provide a place for kids to meet and get to know their new surroundings before kindergarten begins. If there isn't a program like this in your district, consider starting one. More information can be found at www.countdownto kindergarten.com.

Discuss transitions with your child and how they work at school. Just like going from the drug store to soccer practice to the grocery store, your child will transition from literacy to math in the classroom, to recess on the playground, to lunch in the cafeteria, back to the classroom for more literacy, and then to art, which may be in a different location, and back to the classroom. That's a lot of transitions in six hours, even more for a half day, for a five-year-old. Talk about using the bathroom, using a tray in the cafeteria, and walking quietly down the hallways. Talking about this new territory will bring up feelings that need to come out, and it will help prepare them for their days ahead.

Read with your children every day for at least fifteen to thirty minutes. Read whatever they want. Let them read picture books and "pretend" to read before they can. Let them see you reading and writing. Shower your children with a waterfall of words—books, descriptions of what you're doing, and stories—every day. Reading aloud with your children is the most important step you can take to prepare for kindergarten. Talk about what you're reading, the characters, and ways this story might connect to your child's life. Most importantly, keep reading to your children even after they read themselves.

Empathize with your child's emotions because they will change every day—and so will yours. Let your child know how excited you are about kindergarten and that it's okay if they feel a little scared. Most five-year-olds fear mean teachers, going to the bathroom, the big kids at recess, and eating lunch in the cafeteria. They also often fear not knowing how to read when the other kids do. Let them talk out their concerns and assure them there will be adults all around to help them. If you're nervous about the school you've chosen for your child but this can't be changed, be careful your feelings don't taint your child's natural enthusiasm for school and learning. Find another adult with whom to talk out your concerns. If your child senses your stress or anxiety, he will not feel comfortable or confident heading off to kindergarten.

Finally, establish a different schedule in your house on school nights. Going to bed earlier for a week before school begins is one way to gradually move into the ten to eleven hours of sleep elementary kids need for their brain to function at its best. Show your children how to get their backpack ready to go and lay out their clothes the night before so you have fewer headaches the next morning. Establishing simple habits and routines at the beginning of your child's school journey will save you lots of time, conflicts, and missed buses—more than you could ever anticipate.

....

I hope this chapter makes the leap to kindergarten a little easier for you and your child. We looked at the changing expectations of kindergarten, the importance of play and curiosity in your child's development, half-day versus full-day options, redshirting, the four skills it takes to be successful in kindergarten, and how to transition smoothly to the big day.

The next section of the book discusses specific areas where you can connect with your child's education. Chapter 5 provides strategies and tactics for communicating effectively with teachers; chapter 6 will discuss the stages of reading and what it takes to get your child reading well. From there, you'll find other helpful hints in the remaining chapters on everything from dealing with bullying to homework and organization.

TOP TEN TAKEAWAYS

TO CONSIDER

- Expectations for kindergarten are much higher today than even a few years ago, but the curriculum should still include play-based, hands-on, and experiential learning.

- Full-day kindergarten gives a child time to process, to play, and to think, both socially and academically, versus a half-day program that must cover the same curriculum in half the time.

- The research on redshirting five-year-olds is inconclusive; each decision is individual, based on the unique needs of the child and family.

TO AVOID

- Beware of academic "readiness" tests for kindergarten. Your child's social and emotional skills must also be taken into account. Ask this question: is the school ready for my child?

- Don't push your child into reading books that are too difficult; she will move into the next level of early readers when she is ready.

- Don't let your own anxieties about kindergarten cloud your child's perception.

TO DO

- Read to your kindergartner every day for at least fifteen to thirty minutes and play with words in an engaging, fun way.

- Transition your child into kindergarten by visiting the school, talking about transitions, reading every day, empathizing with his feelings, and establishing a new routine.

- Nurture your child's curiosity and answer his questions; connect to what he is learning, especially when he is excited about it.

- Play board games and car games with your kids that reinforce numbers and letters.

PART TWO

Connecting to Your Child's Learning

CHAPTER 5

Words That Work with Teachers

Bad things happen when teachers are made to feel like "the hired help" by powerful and influential parents. And raw feelings result when teachers flaunt their status, withhold information, and infantilize parents. —SARA LAWRENCE-LIGHTFOOT, author and professor of education, Harvard University

Sarah, Jill, and Alicia claim to be BFFs (Best Friends Forever). But recently their fourth grade teacher, Ms. Sweeney, sensed some tension between the girls and made a mental note that it might be time for a seat change. She was not entirely aware of what had happened among the girls the previous week—that is, until she opened her computer Monday morning to find two parent emails: one from Sarah's mom and another from Jill's.

What Not to Write

Ms. Sweeney:

I'm sure you know by now that Alicia is bullying many of the girls in your class. Alicia is a mean girl who's been harassing our Jill for two weeks now. She steals her cell phone, decides where girls will

sit on the bus, and even kicked Jill at recess today. We've had it! Jill is clearly the victim here and it's obvious you are not properly supervising the girls. I've heard from Sarah's mother that Alicia is also bullying Sarah.

Starting immediately, we want Alicia kept away from our daughter at ALL times—in the classroom, at lunch, and at recess. I'd like you to inform the bus driver of this situation so he can stop Alicia from bullying our daughter on the bus. This problem must stop immediately. We want to know ASAP what you plan to do about Alicia so I can assure Jill that this problem will be taken care of. We expect to hear from you today and will contact the principal tomorrow morning if we do not.

Susan Richards

While this email may appear to be an honest, assertive way to advocate for your child, it's problematic. First, Susan's email is focused on the behavior of another child rather than the feelings or needs of her own daughter, Jill. Susan pounced on her daughter's attacker—a natural, emotional reaction from parents who see or feel the hurt their child is experiencing. Second, it assumes that Jill's story conveys what actually happened rather than her version of the story. Third, it tells the teacher what to do, which is never a good idea. Rather than motivate action, this email is likely to put Ms. Sweeney on the defensive. Finally, it uses the word *bullying* in a misleading way. (We'll look at bullying in detail in chapter 10.)

Now compare this to the email from Sarah's mother.

What to Write

Good morning, Ms. Sweeney:

It seems that the social rivalry in the triangle of Sarah, Jill, and Alicia is escalating. I'm hearing about hurt feelings, seat exclusion, nasty texts, and "bullies" at the lunch table. While I'm not exactly sure what is going on, I do know that Sarah is feeling afraid and she can't focus on her work. I know you agree that Sarah needs to feel safe in and around her classroom. I'm wondering what you are seeing and hoping we can resolve this situation soon. The best way to reach me today is by cell phone.

Thank you,

Clare Lewis (Sarah's mother)

Clare relays to the teacher what she is hearing from her daughter, Sarah, with an open mind rather than blame. She channels her emotions and focuses most of the message on how either she or her child is feeling (scared, angry) and what Sarah needs (to feel safe, not threatened). Most importantly, she conveys this information in a positive, professional way.

When children are distracted by social or emotional issues and don't feel safe or comfortable, their learning stops. Most teachers know this and appreciate a heads-up when social issues become a pattern, meaning three or more incidents. It's helpful to flag these issues before they become a bigger problem. But how you go about doing that, and the words you choose to use with the teacher, make a big difference in getting the issue resolved and your child's needs met.

Remember, the majority of your relationship with this important person in your child's life is built through indirect communication—notes, emails, or phone calls. Anything you write, email, or say to your child's teacher either strengthens or weakens the bridge you're trying to build.

Reread the two emails above as if you were the teacher receiving them. Which one makes you want to help the child? Teachers, just like students and parents, are people too, with emotions and opinions. If you keep that simple idea in mind when you communicate, your bridge will get stronger and your child's needs are more likely to be met.

The Power of P3: Be Positive, Professional, and Persistent

Regardless of how you are treated by your child's teacher, the office assistant, or even your child's bus driver, never lose sight of the power of your own behavior. The success of your involvement with your child's education at school hinges on how effectively you communicate with teachers and other school staff. When blame and accusations seep into our words, educators feel the need to defend themselves rather than hear and respond to our concerns. When this happens, very little gets accomplished.

I developed a communication strategy I call the Power of P3 that keeps communications professional and focused on a child's needs instead of the emotions surrounding the situation. You can single-handedly affect your child's education by following the Power of P3. If you can be Positive, Professional, and Persistent (the three *p*'s in the Power of P3) on an ongoing basis—and I recognize it's not an easy feat in some school settings—you will have a greater influence on your child's educational experience.

BE POSITIVE

Begin with an optimistic, collaborative attitude. Once the issue is identified and discussion begins, think about the outcome you want and make affirmative statements that move the situation forward. Agree on some action steps. "I'm confident we can solve this problem; what can I do at home to help?" "I know you agree that Sam needs to feel comfortable on the playground and at recess. How do we get him there? Would it help for Sam to speak to a counselor?" "What's most important to us is that Rachel enjoys reading. What can we do to help her get there?"

If you go into a discussion believing the outcome will be positive, it's more likely to turn out that way. Asking teachers what you can do to help at home will often motivate them to develop a plan or a strategy that will help the child beyond what they had considered before. Teachers like it when parents get involved at home to support the child in ways the teachers suggested. Sharing information about your child and his interaction with the teacher also helps. "Jack loves when you talk about baseball. It's a real connection for him."

BE PROFESSIONAL

A simple way to remember how to be professional is to use PROF as an acronym: be Polite and Respectful in your Observations and Feelings. First, remember to respect the chain of command at your child's school. That means going to the teacher first with your concerns. Focus on how you or your child feels about the situation rather than accuse or judge the teacher.

"I" and "my" language are more likely to be polite and respectful than using "you" or "your" language. *I'm wondering. I'm concerned. I'm worried.* Be specific. Ask questions. Using "I" or "my child" language keeps you focused on your own feelings and observations or your child's needs rather than blaming or attacking an educator. *You haven't . . . You need to . . . You are not . . .* are judgmental and will usually put an educator on the defense. When delivered with a positive perspective or in an inquisitive way, focusing on your observations keeps things moving forward. It centers the conversation on the child, where it belongs. This does not mean you think only about yourself or your child, but it does draw out feelings and promote conversation rather than accusations and blame. These words build trust. Stay away from "you" language that is demanding, entitled, or alienating.

BE PERSISTENT

If you're not happy with the outcome of your discussions, the action taken, or the progress made with your child or your child's teacher, then it's time to restate your concerns. This is where the persistence phase of P3 kicks in. Keep in mind that being positive and professional is imbedded in being persistent.

Follow up in a positive, professional way and use a slightly different approach than the first time. Remember that teachers and administrators are very busy people. Give them a reasonable amount of time to get back to you. If they don't, put the Power of P3 to work again. You'll find if you do this with a positive and professional attitude, persistence will pay off.

In your discussions, be sure to restate next steps or the agreed-upon action. If you decide to go above the teacher, always tell the teacher your intention and that you're unsatisfied with the outcome of the situation. Principals will loop back to the teacher before they respond to you 99 percent of the time so it only hurts your relationship if you go blindly around the teacher. Use words that are professional and positive as suggested later in this chapter.

Of course, P3 is easier to do when things are going well; the real test comes when there is conflict with a teacher or other school staff member. You will not be able to be positive and professional all the time. There will be moments when you can't help feeling like being rude back to the crabby administrative assistant in the front office who hasn't smiled in fourteen years. Using the Power of P3 doesn't mean that you keep things superficial or avoid bringing up the real issues or concerns. And it doesn't mean you let people take advantage of you, or treat you or your child in disrespectful ways. P3 is a tool that helps you respond to issues and address your concerns by communicating in effective ways—ways that keep the communication meaningful and respectful.

Reflect back for a moment to the perfect storm I laid out in chapter 2. What does this have to do with being positive, professional, and persistent? If you can empathize with the craziness and complexity behind a typical school day, you are further ahead than most parents who want action right now and cannot see beyond their own child's needs. Let's go back to another situation with our moms Susan and Clare.

Susan is at work while her babysitter waits at the bus stop for her daughter, Jill, so she can drive her to soccer. It's week three of school. Susan learns through the babysitter that the neighborhood bus is already fifteen minutes late dropping Jill off. She hangs up and calls the school, outraged.

What Not to Say

"This is Susan Richards. My daughter's bus hasn't shown up yet, and I need to know what is going on immediately! Jill has a soccer game in fifteen minutes and if she doesn't make it there on time, her coach will not let her play. I need to know where that bus will be in five minutes so that my sitter can go and meet it. This is the third time this month it's been late and I've had it. I don't have time for this nonsense."

Marcy, the secretary, has three lines going at the moment and is agitated by Susan's tone and attitude. She looks up the bus number for Richards but takes her time to volunteer the "just in" information about the bus. Marcy puts her on hold, radios back to figure out the "exact location" of the bus, and eventually gets back to the phone. By this time, though, the bus drops off Jill and Mrs. Richards hangs up. Sarah's mother, Clare, takes a different, more effective approach.

What to Say

"Hello Marcy, this is Clare Lewis calling. I was wondering if you had any information about bus number sixteen and when it will arrive?" Relieved by her pleasant attitude, Marcy responds, "Well, yes, Mrs. Lewis, we just got word from the dispatcher that bus sixteen is running about twelve minutes late today. He's a new driver and still having some trouble with the route, but it should be there in about three minutes."

Clare starts off positive. She is polite and efficient. Problem solved. She gets right to the point, doesn't labor in negativity or blame, and gets what she needs in less than thirty seconds. Note that Clare also addresses the office assistant by name (a good idea) and knows the bus number, saving a step for the busy office assistant. Susan drones on about her issues with the bus timing and alienates the assistant with her demanding and condescending demeanor. It's noted that Susan Richards is not pleasant to deal with, while Clare is a likable and respected parent.

If you take the time to remember P3, you will stand apart from alienating, antagonistic, or aggressive parents who often treat school personnel like second-class citizens. Sometimes this is because parents feel *they* are treated this way and they give it back. Wear a smile, no matter what you come across. Be enthusiastic and ask for what you need in the most professional and positive way you can. It can be hard work and sometimes takes biting your tongue. But P3—being positive, professional, and persistent—can be contagious. It will help you build a stronger bridge between you and your child's school.

The Power of P3 in Practice

When anger, frustration, or mama and papa bear emotions run deep, finding the neutrality to be positive and professional can be hard. But it's important to do so that teachers hear and respond to your concerns rather than your emotions. When parents make demands in unprofessional ways, educators hear entitlement rather than concerns about the child. In response, teachers defend their actions and the schools, and a downward spiral of disrespect results. This negatively affects your child's learning and weakens the bridge you are trying to build. In many cases, parents have legitimate, reasonable concerns. But the tone and the approach they use to express their concerns make a significant difference to the administrators on whether an issue is successfully resolved or not—and how quickly. One approach makes an educator want to help and strengthens your parent-school communication bridge; the other puts educators on the defensive and weakens your bridge. Take the time to step back and think before sending an email that attacks a teacher. Parents who are respected in a school are more likely to get what their child needs.

RECOGNIZE THE SOURCE OF YOUR EMOTIONS

Before "words that work" can work, it's important to understand and acknowledge what lies beneath the bridge you're building with the teacher. Much of the time, parent waters look relatively calm. But at some point during your child's thirteen years in school, you will likely experience some frustration, anger, or resentment. It's inevitable, given the pressures on our overburdened school systems and your diligence to ensure your child gets the best education possible. Your emotions are natural and understandable. It's what you do with your emotions, however, that makes all the difference.

Anger and resentment usually stem from a hurt or a fear, perhaps the result of a prior situation or experience with the school where you felt your child was treated unfairly or put at a disadvantage by the system. It could have happened last week or last year. It may feel like it happens repeatedly: mediocre or "bad" teachers two years in a row, a teacher being replaced by a disastrous long-term substitute midyear, a bullying situation with your child that no one did anything about. Often anger or resentment result from a decision that parents didn't agree with or, more often, a conflict left unresolved. Sometimes the anger comes from shame or resentment from your own school experiences, feelings you buried decades ago.

If, as you read these words, certain situations or memories come to mind, it means you are aware of some feelings hiding below. Your resentment is bound to seep into communication between parent and teacher—in an email, an innocent note, or in parent teacher conferences.

Deborah is a senior copywriter at a New York advertising firm and the mother of twins, Lisa and Molly. With two third graders in different classrooms, she gets a day-by-day comparison of her children's teachers. While Deborah understands that a child won't always get ace teachers every year, she's angry. When teachers were assigned in August, she met with the principal and requested that Lisa be switched to Molly's class. In Deborah's mind, Molly's teacher was "stronger and more seasoned with a good reputation in writing." Deborah values writing and she wanted both her daughters to benefit from this teacher. Her request was denied and no legitimate reason was given.

For the past month, Deborah has noticed that Lisa's teacher makes careless spelling errors on her worksheets. On one paper, a word was misspelled twice, which aggravated Deborah to no end. Then she caught another spelling error two weeks later. She thought to herself: "How can this teacher teach my daughter to read and write if she can't even spell herself?" Frustrated, she made copies of the worksheets, circled the misspelled words, and scribbled out a note to the teacher that read: "Perhaps your students would become better spellers and writers if the words on your worksheets were spelled correctly." She put the paper in a sealed envelope and sent it to school with her daughter.

Deborah's anger about not getting the teacher she wanted for her daughter seeped into her message about the worksheet. Unfortunately, Deborah wasn't aware that this was happening and damage was done. What could Deborah have done here to communicate her concerns? If this happened once or twice, nothing; it falls under the category of "pick your battles." Remember that teachers are only human and make mistakes, too. If it becomes a pattern, pull together three to five solid examples and write a brief, handwritten note to the teacher stating that you've noticed that this is becoming a pattern but, more importantly, so has your daughter. Keep copies of what you send. An effective teacher will acknowledge and correct the issue. If the teacher gets defensive and the problem persists, then send your evidence to the principal with a quick note and let the teacher know you are doing so. A good principal will handle the situation carefully because it reflects poorly on the school, too.

Can Deborah fix the bridge she weakened? She can repair it by being honest and offering an apology to the teacher in person. In most cases, simply stating "I handled this situation poorly" is enough. Then have a productive, honest discussion about your wish for Lisa to become a stronger writer. Anger is not productive for your child, the teacher, you, or your family. When negative emotions affect your ability to effectively communicate on a regular basis, the bridge you've built between parent and teacher weakens. Establishing strong communication and building on that throughout the years helps you deal with issues when they happen. Be aware of how your anger or fears affect your communication so you can maintain and build a strong bridge.

BUT MY CHILD DESERVES BETTER!

Often parents feel that an action by a teacher or a school is blatantly wrong. What makes managing emotions so difficult is that parents are sometimes right in their convictions that their child was mistreated. Parents often feel violated and taken advantage of for valid reasons. Blaming the schools or attacking a teacher (or an administrator) in an unprofessional manner feels justified. After all, your child's education is at stake.

But a reasonable parent will ask these questions: What does this accomplish? How does it affect my future relationship with the school my child will continue to attend? Blaming will usually get you into deeper, more turbulent waters that can be even more difficult to navigate. When agreements cannot be reached as you move up the administrative ladder, mediation or a lawsuit may be considered. But whatever route you take, an angry, "you owe me" attitude of entitlement will not get you closer to the education your child needs. What will help is channeling your emotions and energy into focusing on your child's learning and what productive steps can be taken to move forward.

Ryan is a smart boy whose parents are greatly concerned he is "not being challenged" in the classroom. He consistently scores the highest grades on all tests and barely needs to study. His mother sends an email to his teacher.

What Not to Say

Dear Mr. Messing:

Ryan has become very bored with school. His homework is done in fifteen minutes, or finished on the bus, and he says he hates school. You may be concerned about his social skills, but we are not worried about his life on the playground. He is in school to learn and we feel he is an exceptional child who is slipping through the cracks. We want and need you to challenge him, especially in math and science. We expect this to happen as soon as possible, or we will need to request that he be moved to a teacher who is willing to challenge him. Thank you.

While honest and open, the words used in this note weaken the communication bridge between parent and teacher rather than strengthen it. Teachers pride themselves on recognizing, understanding, and meeting the needs of each individual student. This speaks to a best practice in teaching called *differentiating instruction*, or individualizing instruction so each student is reached and challenged. Some teachers are better at differentiating instruction than others, and it's a difficult goal to attain with a 24:1 ratio, but most teachers are sensitive to phrases like "my child is bored" or "my child is slipping through the cracks." They are more likely to defend what they've done rather than hear your concerns when this kind of language is used.

Here's the message with specific words that a teacher will be able to hear and act on.

What to Say

Dear Mr. Messing:

For the past month, Ryan is moving through his work quickly. He feels he could be doing more, beyond the extra credit you've been diligent about giving him. He finds he is repeating past work. We've noticed he completes his homework within fifteen minutes instead of the forty minutes expected for fourth grade. We wonder if you are seeing this in class and what can be done to address his needs. I know we both want to keep Ryan challenged and ensure that he reaches his potential. What can we do to support him at home? Any thoughts you have are appreciated. Would it make sense for us to come in, with Ryan, for a conference? I look forward to hearing from you.

Thank you for your time.

This response uses the Power of P3. It's positive and professional. Ryan's mom focuses on what her son is doing or not doing rather than on the teacher's performance. It is not accusatory or judgmental. "We wonder if . . ." suggests that the teacher consider possibilities; it doesn't tell the teacher what to do. Asking questions is often an effective way to communicate with teachers. Remember you are your child's first teacher. Your job is to work *with* the professionals who help educate your child, not against them.

Using Words that Work

How well you advocate for your child depends on how effectively you communicate and phrase requests. Do your words create a stronger or weaker bridge? The following "I" (or "we") and "my child" language is helpful to remember when raising issues and concerns about your child. If you can get comfortable using these phrases consistently when you communicate with teachers and schools—in person, via note, or by email—your requests are more likely to be respected and you are more likely to get what your child needs. Try them out and practice using them, or they will come off as disingenuous:

- I've noticed Jane seems to be more anxious than before.
- I am thrilled that Carlin has passed [her state standardized test], but we're still concerned.
- I've noticed that Avery is moving quickly through her work. Are you seeing this, too?
- I'm wondering if you have suggestions for Kevin when he can't focus on his work?

- I'm concerned that Chris is consistently forgetting to bring home his homework.

- I am seeing . . . at home. I'm wondering if you are seeing this in the classroom?

- I'm worried that just moving Charlie away from distractions won't be enough.

- I'm confused about what I read in your newsletter and what my son is telling me.

- What can I do to help my child be more successful in school?

EMAIL ETIQUETTE

Similar to a work environment, email messages between parents and teachers should be simple information exchanges. The rule of thumb in many schools is that teachers try to return emails within twenty-four to forty-eight hours, but this is not always adhered to. If you use P3 with language that works and keep the length of your email to no more than four to five average-length sentences, you will be more successful both in getting a response and in getting what your child needs. Lengthy or excessive emails often indicate that an issue exists that might be better handled face to face. Give a heads-up about your concern, followed by a request for a phone call or a meeting. Any email longer than five sentences usually means anger is stirring.

When you feel the burning need to blast a note or email to the teacher about something that's happened to your child, go ahead and write that email. Get it all out on the screen, emotions and all. But don't hit Send. Instead, send it to yourself, a trusted friend, or your spouse. Then reread it the next morning and get some feedback. Channeling your anger first, and then choosing words that work will make a big difference. It will help you engage in meaningful dialogue with your children's teachers and get the outcome you're looking for. Once you've let go of your anger, draft a simple email, using P3 and words that work to state your concern, ask questions, or request a meeting with the teacher.

Likewise, using the following "my child" language will help you channel strong emotions and keep focused on your child's needs. Remember to keep the language detailed:

- Alex expresses frustration about math on a regular basis.
- Jamie is not feeling safe on the playground because of a clique of kids.
- Susie feels she is consistently being singled out in the classroom.
- Ryan doesn't understand the writing instruction.
- We find that Karen is more successful when instructions are repeated.
- Olivia is experiencing anxiety over math every day. I'm wondering if she needs extra support? What would that look like?
- Dylan has many strengths. What do you see as his challenges?
- Allison has her challenges. How can we tap her strengths?
- We've noticed that William has difficulty reading aloud. Are you seeing this in the classroom? What can we do to help?

When conflict arises, it's important to avoid accusations and judgment that puts people on the defense. Generally, the more defensive an educator becomes, the more entitled a parent becomes, and the conversation spirals down from there. Likewise, the more entitled the parent becomes, the more defensive an educator becomes. Reflect back what you hear from the teacher. Then use "I" and "my child" language to help the conversation stay focused. Be aware of mama and papa bear instincts and focus on your own feelings or your child's needs. In difficult situations, both parties are often stressed, so words that defuse and disarm are helpful. Examples include:

- I'm feeling frustrated that this situation is not improving. Do you have another idea?
- While I was hopeful last month, I am now concerned that time is slipping away.
- I'm not following what you're saying. Could you rephrase so I can better understand?
- It sounds like you are disappointed, too. Is there another strategy we can try?

- I'm hearing a difference of opinion here. Where do we go from here?

- We're feeling worried about Tommy's reading. What else can be done?

- I'm not feeling comfortable with that approach for my child. Is there another option?

- It sounds like we are in different places. How do we resolve our different opinions?

- Are we in agreement that Joey needs more math support at school and at home?

- We respect where you're coming from but disagree with your final decision. We will need to take this to another level.

As you think through how you might phrase a request or a question, it's also important to keep in mind that there are a few phrases frequently used by parents that immediately throw up roadblocks. Oftentimes these come from parents who feel they are smarter than the people who teach their children. Sometimes they come from parents because they don't realize how they are being perceived. In either case, try to avoid using them and be mindful of your tone of voice. The tone you use has a significant impact on your message.

What not to say to an educator:

- I need you to . . .

- You need to fix this . . .

- This school needs to . . .

- I don't care about the other kids in the classroom. . . .

- I know many other parents who feel this way. . . .

- Everybody else feels this way, too. . . .

All of these commands or assumptions sound as if they are being directed to a subordinate or a second-class citizen. This is not language that builds bridges or follows P3. These words will weaken your communication and make your next conversation more difficult. Commands and accusations do nothing but put an educator on the defensive and make it difficult for your child's needs to be heard, let alone met.

The comments "I know many other parents who feel this way" and "Everybody else feels this way, too" are made frequently by parents when speaking to teachers or administrators because they often *do* know other parents who feel the same way. But even if you do know other parents feel the same way, saying so is a big mistake. While it's logical to think that making this point will help your case, in fact, the opposite is often true. These words can cause the teacher to feel ganged up on or that you're jumping on the bandwagon of complainers that someone else is driving. The teacher only wants to focus on your child at the moment and isn't interested in hearing about "everybody else." If administrators feel you are simply following the crowd, it can discredit your individual concerns. It's best to focus on your own child unless you are advocating for a greater cause.

Now that you have some perspective on language that puts the Power of P3 into action, you're ready to communicate with your children's teachers in writing and at parent-teacher conferences. But before we dive into parent-teacher conferences, here's one more reminder: If there is a serious issue or concern that you have about your child, the regularly scheduled conference is not the time to bring this issue up for the first time. Give the teacher a heads-up as early as possible that you have some concerns and set up a separate time to discuss these apart from the very busy, overscheduled week of parent-teacher conferences. It is not necessary to wait for the biannual parent-teacher conference time. In fact, your meeting may be more productive outside of this scheduled time.

Parent-Teacher Conferences

Since many schools now sandwich conferences into a revolving door of ten- to fifteen-minute blocks, every minute counts. The most important part of the parent-teacher conference is to commit to going. Carve out the time, sign up for an early slot, and prepare. Going to the conference sends a critical message to your kids and their teachers that you care about your children's education. And if both parents can possibly be there, it's even better. If you can't make the proposed times, email the teacher and request another option. By most union contracts, parents must have access to a teacher to discuss academic progress at a time that mutually works and in a parent's preferred language.

Once you make the decision to go, there are two ways to handle parent-teacher conferences. One is to allow them to play out as they sometimes do with unproductive, superficial dialogue. This is where the teacher and parent exchange pleasantries about the child for a few minutes, while emotions churn below the surface, and the next parent waits not so patiently outside the classroom door to get in. The other is to take the time to prepare to get the most out of this short meeting.

PREPARE: TALK WITH YOUR CHILD

Begin by listening to your child. If you don't already know, ask your child what he likes most and least about school. Ask about math, English, and social studies. Something your child dreads or says isn't explained well offers a clue about what's not connecting for him. If you're not sure what questions to ask, take a look at your child's schoolwork. Identify patterns: Where does she struggle? Where does the teacher write the same comments? Is the work sloppy? Does your child churn through homework too quickly? Socially, does she have at least one good friend in school? Make notes for a couple of weeks before the conference and write down questions before you go.

LISTEN WELL AND RESPECT BOTH EXPERTS— YOU AND THE TEACHER

As the parent, your in-depth knowledge of your child gives you insight that a teacher can't possibly acquire in a few months. Remember, you are your child's first teacher and the expert on your child's quirks and what makes him tick. On the flip side, the classroom teacher is trained in what is socially, emotionally, and academically appropriate at this developmental stage and knows your child best in a group setting. Respect both positions—yours and the teacher's—and listen carefully. Take notes. Listen to what is said and what is not said. The more sharing that goes on between you two experts and the more candid and respectful the dialogue between teacher and parent, the more successful your child's experience will be. Try to paint a picture of your child by sharing two or three details about your child's style and passions at home that the teacher can take away: She loves everything animals these days. He reads better when he keeps a bookmark under each line.

USE P3 IN THE CONFERENCE

If you follow the Power of P3—that is, if you're positive, professional, and persistent—you're more likely to get your questions answered and your child's needs met. No matter what the situation, keep that P3 turning. Again, this doesn't mean you are superficial or avoid the real issues. On the contrary, decide ahead of time what you want to discuss. Any behavior or language that is less than positive, professional, and persistent can lead to a battle for control that takes the focus off your child.

Here are some questions to keep things positive and focused on solutions for your child. Remember to always think in specifics. I've organized the questions into three groups depending on whether your child is (1) doing well, (2) struggling, or (3) needing more of a challenge. Your child may exhibit a mix of these characteristics—for example, she may do well in one area but need more support in another. Not all kids fall cleanly into one group. If you have a specific concern you know you want to talk about for the majority of the conference, send a short email to your child's teacher in advance. He will appreciate a focused discussion as much as you will. If there are things going on at home, tell the teacher. Those things affect your child's learning more than you know.

For the child doing well:

- Everything seems to be going well for Jake academically. How is he doing socially?

- Do Eric's classmates see him as a leader or a follower? Does he get along with his peers?

- I'm wondering if Hannah is performing up to her ability. How we can be sure of that?

- Do you see any area that Jessie can improve upon? What makes her spark?

- What can you tell me about Alex's work ethic? How's his attitude toward learning?

- What are Annie's strengths? Weaknesses? What's her primary learning style?

- Have you noticed any other interests that could be encouraged?
- If Bobby was your child, what would you ask his teacher that I haven't yet asked?

For the child struggling:

- Does Jamie stay on task, or does she need frequent reminders?
- I'd like to understand the grade level that Stephen is performing at in reading (math) and how this compares to last year.
- How often are fluency tests given? May I receive results of the past year's testing?
- What do you see as the problems or factors contributing to this situation?
- What support can the school offer since Jill is not on a special plan? Do you use RTI?
- Specifically, what kind of small group reading instruction support does William need? Will this be the support group he receives?
- At what point should Ryan be tested? What is involved in the testing?
- What can we do at home to support these efforts? How often should we do this?
- I'm wondering what else we can do to make sure Caitlin doesn't fall behind?
- What strengths does Tyrone have that we can tap to offset his weaknesses?
- How does Chris work in small groups? Does she participate in class?
- When can we meet again to monitor and follow up on Sophie's progress?

For the child who needs more challenge:

- We've noticed Debbi finishes her homework very quickly. Are you seeing this in class?
- We're feeling that Emily may need some additional challenge in her work. What are your thoughts on that?
- What subjects does Don excel in and in what areas can he improve?

- What can I do as a parent at home to support Lisa's learning?

- How is Sam socially? Does he participate in class? How do his friends see him?

- Is Jackie a candidate for the school's gifted program? Should she be tested?

- Do you see children Arie might be grouped with so he is more challenged?

- If there is disagreement: May I offer my point of view on why I disagree with this assessment of April? Could you help me better understand your point of view?

If your discussion has focused on your child's struggles or need for more of a challenge, then a follow-up meeting is in order. It may make sense to set up monthly touch points until you're feeling more comfortable that your child is indeed thriving. Or you might keep each other updated briefly by email. Do what feels right in your gut and what works for you and the teacher.

....

This chapter showed you how to communicate effectively with teachers. It explained why managing strong emotions and finding the neutrality to be positive, professional, and persistent is often difficult, though necessary, for teachers to hear and respond to concerns. When parents present issues in a demanding or entitled manner, educators often respond defensively. This may result in a downward spiral of disrespect. Being an effective communicator in email, in person, or at parent-teacher conferences pays off and gets you much closer to ensuring your child receives the best education possible. The Power of P3, a technique used throughout the remaining chapters, ensures parents communicate effectively so their children's needs are met. The next chapter discusses reading and why this is the foundation for your child's journey.

TOP TEN TAKEAWAYS

TO CONSIDER

- Children thrive when parents and teachers connect.
- Reading classroom newsletters and respecting teacher's preferred communication style—email, note, or phone—keeps you connected to your child's education in productive ways.
- Everything you write, email, or say to your child's teacher either strengthens or weakens the bridge you're building.
- When teachers feel accused or blamed, they are more likely to defend their actions rather than focus their energy on helping your child.

TO AVOID

- If you find yourself writing a lengthy, accusatory email to your child's teacher, don't send it.
- Don't accuse or blame a teacher or administrator. Recognize your emotions and find an adult who will listen to you and help you identify what you want in the situation.

TO DO

- Use the Power of P3 to communicate effectively. Acting in a positive, professional, and persistent way builds strong bridges and is more likely to get your child's needs met.
- Use "I" language that focuses on your child's feelings and behaviors, or your own observations. Use email for basic communication or to set up meetings.
- If you have questions or concerns about your child, request a phone call or a meeting with the teacher to discuss this further; it's not necessary or wise to wait for the regularly scheduled conference.
- Prepare for and attend parent-teacher conferences; ask candid questions to use the limited time wisely.

CHAPTER 6

Why Jack *Likes* to Read—and Write

The more that you read, the more things you will know.
The more that you learn, the more places you'll go. —DR. SEUSS

Panic grips Melanie as the school bus door closes behind her six-year-old daughter, Kara. As the bus speeds off, she catches sight of Kara's smile and her small hand waving in the window. Melanie waves back, swallowing tears. Her mind races with what she just learned from another mother standing beside her at the bus stop— that all the other girls are reading chapter books. Melanie thinks, "How can Kara's friends be reading chapter books already? They've only been in first grade for two months. Where did we go wrong?!" Melanie cries throughout her long drive to work. Within an hour, she cancels Kara's art class, adds a tutoring session, and emails Kara's teacher demanding a reading plan immediately. Melanie knows she's losing perspective, but she feels compelled to give her daughter whatever edge she needs so she doesn't fall behind.

Reading is the most important—and most misunderstood—part of a child's elementary journey. It's the catalyst for everything else. One of the greatest gifts you can give your child from kindergarten through grade five is a love of reading. And it all begins with your waterfall of words discussed in chapter 1—the language, books, and experiences that you shower your child with from birth throughout his elementary years.

Regardless of socioeconomics, race, or nationality, students who are read to more are better readers, achieve the most, and stay in school the longest. It's hard to believe that only one-half of U.S. students who start college actually finish, but it's true. And the percentage of students who graduate from college compared to those who don't graduate is directly correlated to how strong of a reader they are. Standardized tests also show that if children are not reading proficiently by the end of third grade, they are less likely to graduate from high school.

By the end of this chapter, you'll understand what it takes to get a child ready to read, the stages of reading, and why reading aloud to your child is crucial. It will ease your mind about "fresh" books like *Junie B. Jones* and *Diary of a Wimpy Kid*, and show you how words, curiosity, and a love of reading lead to lifelong learning.

Learning to Read: The Crucial Waterfall of Words

Learning how to read is like learning how to walk. Your child didn't suddenly get up and walk one day. Though it may seem like that, it takes months of preparing the body and brain, coaxing, and practicing before that first step happens. Just as your child learned to sit up, then crawl, stand, discover how two legs work, and finally take that first step, reading also happens in stages. But unlike walking, it takes years rather than months for the reading synapses to gel in the brain. Every child learns at a different pace: 2 to 3 percent of children learn to read by age four. On the other end, 2 to 3 percent learn to read at age eight. The other 95 percent will learn to read somewhere between the ages of five and seven. Becoming a fluent reader happens after that. Reading to your children every day and exposing them to language, books, and experiences makes a significant difference in your children's future reading and writing skills. This waterfall of words creates the source from which your child identifies sounds, connects sounds to words, and then links words to meaning.

The Debate over How Children Learn to Read

Controversy over how children learn to read has raged for years. Is it more effective taught as a "whole"—reading words and sentences in literature—or in parts with a greater focus on the mechanics of sounds and syllables (phonics)? Educators once believed that children learned to read by absorbing words, stories, and meaning. The theory went that when children were surrounded with language, literature, and rhymes, sounds would turn into symbols that would translate to words and meaning. Comprehension was caught, not taught.

For the past three decades, brain research has revealed that reading is a far more complex process than previously thought. Some of that research links explicit instruction in phonics to significant increases in reading ability. In most schools today, a best practice in reading instruction is a combination of these two worlds, your child's exposure to language and literature combined with interactive instruction that builds skills in phonological awareness and phonics. Most educators believe that this dual approach yields the greatest vocabulary, fluency, and comprehension in children.

It's important to acknowledge that there are many learning, reading, and textbook companies today that claim they can teach your child—or even your toddler—how to read in just a few months, often before the age of three. Some believe reading can be taught through showing vocabulary cards to babies and toddlers as young as nine months old. The reading industry is a huge, multibillion-dollar business that often feeds on parents' anxiety about their children's performance in reading. It's only natural to worry about your child's reading ability. But it's important to remember that reading is a skill that takes years to acquire. It doesn't happen overnight and if it appears to, it's likely that a child either has memorized sounds and their association with an object or falls in that 2 percent of children who do learn to read before the age of four. Memorizing words doesn't translate into comprehension or a love of reading. So beware of reading-industry claims and let your child learn to read in the way he was meant to learn.

There are five basic stages of reading or literacy: understanding sound, sounding out words, developing vocabulary, acquiring fluency, and mastering comprehension. Some educators refer to these stages of reading as *emergent literacy*. Let's take a closer look at these five important stages.

STAGE 1: UNDERSTANDING SOUND—
PHONOLOGICAL AND PHONEME AWARENESS

The first stage of prereading is your child's ability to notice words, syllables, and sounds. This is referred to as *phonological awareness*. It's the ability to distinguish sounds and symbols that work together to make words. This is the basis for reading and writing. In the beginning, children may not be able to say the sound or word themselves, but they begin to unlock the code. An abundance of research suggests that the more words your children hear, the more language they are exposed to, and the more images they connect with by kindergarten, the better their foundation for reading. That's why reading aloud to your children is the single most important activity you can do for your child's education. *Phonemes* are the smallest form of sound—such as the *ch*, *sh*, *th*, *ee*, *a*, *b*, and so on—that work together to create a word. There are forty-four phonemes in the English language and twenty-six letters, or symbols.

Remember when your child could not stop saying "What dat?" fifty-nine times a day? She was building up and stockpiling her sounds, syllables, and phonemes. Children discover that some sounds rhyme, and some don't. "Cat" sounds like "hat." "Clock" rhymes with "dock." "Dock" starts with the same sound as "dog," but "dog" rhymes with "log." Rhymes and rhyming books are important to a child's development through kindergarten because they help strengthen a child's phonological awareness. The poetic rhythm they hear in nursery rhymes, the notes you hit in the ABC song, the cadence in your voice when you read a funny story all contribute to your child's understanding of sound and words. After rhyming, children then begin to identify and count syllables. They hear and see endings of words and begin to blend different segments of words together. They can identify which word doesn't belong in a list: sad, mad, kid, had. Magnetic letters on a refrigerator are a great, inexpensive way to play with, blend, and rhyme words. Your children's skill level in phonological and phoneme awareness usually predicts their future success in reading.

Not long ago, I was in a store looking at cards. Two moms stood next to me, one on each side. Both had toddlers. One little girl sat in a stroller while the other girl squirmed in a store cart. I noticed this scene because, while both girls were awake and alert, they behaved quite differently. The girl in the stroller was quiet. Her mother silently read the cards while they exchanged glances and smiles. Meanwhile, the girl in the cart pointed to and labeled everything she saw. It was an interesting comparison. The chatterbox's mom described the objects she pointed to and answered her every question. A natural dialogue flowed between them. I was stunned when this little girl pointed to a display and said, "Mama . . . man. . . .kin?" As her mother tried to understand her words, the little girl repeated, "No-ize, mama, no-ize." She was trying out the word *mannequin* and associating it with no eyes. Eventually, her mom picked up on it. As she rounded the corner, I heard her mother say, "Now where did you learn that word, Lucy?"

Lucy knew the word *mannequin* because her mother showers her with words every day. Her phonological and phoneme awareness is high. When you see parents or adults engaging in conversations with their toddlers or preschoolers and verbalizing much of what they are doing or seeing, they understand the value of words, language, and talking with their children. The sounds children hear as images, objects, and feelings are strengthening their phonological and phonemic awareness.

Let's go back to Melanie and Kara at the beginning of this chapter. Melanie panicked because Kara was not on the same "timetable" as the other girls for moving onto chapter books. Remember, your child's river ebbs and flows. Reading earlier does not mean better. If children are pushed into reading books too quickly, they will no longer associate reading with pleasure, and they will not feel as secure or confident moving forward. Because most parents misunderstand the process of reading, there's natural anxiety around whether or not your child has begun to read and whether he'll keep up with his classmates.

Reading every day with your children and engaging in conversations about books and stories will strengthen their phonological awareness and make them stronger readers. The key is to keep reading fun. There are also many reading apps and computer games that will help reinforce phonological skills (see the resources section at www.theparentbackpack.com). But remember, your children will read when their brains are ready to read, just like they walked when they were ready to walk.

STAGE 2: SOUNDING OUT WORDS—PHONICS

Phonics refers to the letter-sound relationship in processing words. It's about decoding and the mechanics used to break down sounds and syllables so a word can be sounded out, associated with an image, and understood. The letter *n* represents the sound /*n*/, for example, which is the first sound in "nest." The sound /*ch*/ represents the beginning sound in "cheese." Phonics allows children to read new words and expand their vocabulary. There are over one hundred phonics rules and three thousand words that children can learn through phonics.

Phonics is a critical prereading skill for most children, but on its own will not teach children how to read. Some children absorb phonics naturally and effortlessly through being read to. Others need small-group instruction or one-on-one practice to break down the blended sounds, prefixes, and endings before they can actually read and comprehend syllables and words. Phonics instruction is part of the curriculum in many preschools today and continues through kindergarten and first grade. Jim Trelease, author of the best-selling book *The Read Aloud Handbook* says, "Giving phonics drills to children with no access to books is like giving oars to people who don't own a boat."

Most educators agree that, in conjunction with that waterfall of words that we give our children through talking, stories, and books, most children benefit from explicit phonics instruction that's systematic and interactive—meaning a consistent back-and-forth exchange between teacher and student. While worksheets and memorizing have a place in phonics instruction, the world of literacy instruction has evolved significantly in the past several years. An involved parent will ask what approach is used in a school and look for a combined approach—lots of books, reading aloud in small groups, and an interactive approach to building phonological awareness and teaching phonics.

STAGE 3: DEVELOPING VOCABULARY

The next stage in reading is *vocabulary*—that is, learning and associating more challenging words with images, experiences, and feelings. This is the heart of reading and writing. Children's vocabularies are best developed through reading aloud to them, telling stories, and having conversations on a daily basis—that waterfall of words again. Every time you read to your child, tell him a story, or talk with him, you're helping him to soak up more vocabulary and experiences that will enable him to become a stronger reader. By age two, a child understands anywhere from three hundred to one thousand words, usually driven by socioeconomics. From there, that number expands exponentially. The more books children are exposed to, the more stories, words, and conversations they hear, the greater their vocabularies, as we saw with Lucy. By the time children enter kindergarten, they have heard millions of words. The greater their exposure to words, stories, experiences, and conversations, the more inclined they will be to like reading. One of a child's most primal instincts is imitation. Children pick up words and sounds by imitating those around them. Research shows that children with the largest vocabulary when they enter kindergarten generally have the easiest time understanding the teacher's instructions, and tend to have greater success in school.

Most schools supply a list of "sight words" and "high-frequency words" that need to be memorized by sight in kindergarten and first grade. Sight words are "rule breakers"—words that typically don't follow phonetic rules or patterns and can't be sounded out, like *by*, *over*, *all*, *that*, *some*, and so on. I've included some sources that offer these lists in the resources section at www.theparentbackpack.com. Your school or teacher will usually supply a list of sight words, too, as they will vary slightly from school to school. If you do make flashcards for them, it helps to include a visual of the word where appropriate or to use it in a sentence. *High-frequency words,* as the term implies, appear frequently. They include words such as *the*, *is*, *it*, *on*, *my*, and *you* and can be phonetic or irregular. The ability to identify and understand sight and high-frequency words helps build fluency. Sometimes these words are used interchangeably by schools.

STAGE 4: ACQUIRING FLUENCY

Fluency refers to the ability to decode individual words and sentences with appropriate diction, emphasis, pronunciation, inflection, and attention to commas and exclamation points. The more your children read or are read to, the more fluent they become, unless there is an issue beneath the surface, such as a reading disability. Fluency is the precursor to comprehension and can be taught in whole-group (meaning the whole class) instruction, small-group instruction, and one on one. Just as your kids master computer games by playing them again and again, reading improves with practice. Most teachers use some form of small, close, or shared reading groups to work on fluency and comprehension strategies. Modeling reading for your child at home also helps with fluency. Shared reading—"You read to me; I read to you"—is another great way to improve this skill. When you pronounce and emphasize the words correctly, your child will follow. Again, the more repetition, the more fluent your child will become.

STAGE 5: MASTERING COMPREHENSION

When children can make a mental movie in their mind of what is going on in a story, they are on their way to comprehending or understanding the meaning behind the text. There are three levels of understanding in

MEASURING READING PROGRESS

Fluency is typically used as an oral measurement tool (meaning kids read aloud) in schools to test whether kids are reading at grade level or not, from grades one through five. Common testing tools used are DIBELS (Dynamic Indicators of Basic Early Literary Skills), CBM (Curriculum Based Measurement) Maze, ORF (Oral Reading Fluency), and DRA (Developmental Reading Assessment). A teacher or a reading specialist administers these tests, and students are given a passage to read silently or aloud for one minute. Students are typically tested at the beginning and end of the school year. The results are compared to grade-level benchmarks that are used to assess the level of reading instruction your children need. Children at or below grade level are usually retested throughout the year to make sure they continue to make progress.

If a child is identified as falling below grade level in reading, a best practice in schools today is using Response to Intervention (RTI). This approach has proven to be an effective teaching strategy used to target a child's specific need and keep her on track. Different tiers are used for different levels of support. Teachers break out kids into small groups based on their skill level in phonics, fluency, or comprehension. Different strategies are used depending on kids' needs. Coteachers, instructional assistants, and teacher's aides work with kids in the small groups. If one program does not improve a child's reading. The first level involves the ability to respond to basic questions about facts and themes. The second level moves on to exploring these facts and themes by comparing and contrasting parts of the story, the characters, or the themes themselves. This stage is typically fully developed by fourth grade. The third and deepest level of comprehension involves applying what you've learned to critical thinking, understanding what the author is trying to say and why, and using that in writing an essay or an opinion. These levels progress naturally throughout grades one through five.

You can help children with their comprehension in a number of ways. Reading aloud to your children allows you to ask questions that help their comprehension. Helping them predict what a book or passage is about also improves comprehension. By reading titles and headlines (especially in nonfiction books) and connecting them to what children may already

reading, another strategy may be tried. Continual assessment and review of the child's progress is necessary to keep RTI effective. Most importantly, if your child needs phonological or phonics instruction, it's critical that she be placed in a program that will benefit this particular skill. If you find your child receives extra support in reading, be sure to identify what skill is lacking and that the program is indeed reinforcing this skill. Once you know the skill your child needs help on, you can reiterate the strategies at home, using one of the many resources provided at www.theparentbackpack.com.

Some schools may be reluctant to give out student data to parents for fear it will be misinterpreted. If you have any concerns about your child's reading level, ask for a copy of your child's fluency scores and discuss them with the teacher. Keep in mind that the trend in these scores is more important than one individual score. Benchmark levels can be looked up online if your school uses one of the main tools, DIBELS, CBM Maze, or ORF. Students will often start off the new school year lower than where they left in the spring due to inconsistent reading during the summer months. If your child's fluency rate is lower than grade-level benchmarks, talk to the teacher about your concerns (see chapter 5, Words That Work with Teachers). There is much more that goes into reading beyond fluency. Phonics and comprehension are also areas that can be measured and addressed. More information about reading testing can be found in chapter 9.

know or an experience they have had helps the children look for clues in the book that will help with their comprehension. To help children predict and begin to create pictures in their minds, ask questions like these:

- What is this book about based on the title and pictures?
- What do you think will happen? How do you know that?
- Do you like this character?
- What's really going on here?

Another time to improve your child's comprehension is when you watch a TV show together. Ask your child about the main idea of the show and what the primary conflict or the problem was. Compare the characters. All this helps build a child's skill level in comprehension.

But what happens if your child still can't sound out basic words?

Kindergarten Skills

If, toward the end of kindergarten, your child has not mastered the skills named below, he may have a phonological weakness that will hinder his reading ability. It's important that you raise your concerns with the teacher, if the issue hasn't been discussed. By the last month of kindergarten, children can generally write their own name, recognize and create rhyming words, identify the beginning sound of a word and label other objects that begin with that sound, have fun with words such as counting syllables by clapping (Mon-day) or pulling words apart (up = u-p, cup = c-u-p). (Note: Segmenting phonemes /ch/ /a/ /t/ is a much more difficult task that often takes children more time. This is not the same as pulling words apart). If your child has not mastered these skills despite small reading groups or RTI and discussions with the teacher, request in writing that your child be screened or tested. Phonological deficits can be turned around with targeted small-group or one-on-one instruction. The key is identifying the weakness early and getting the right supports in place. Generally, the earlier these deficits are caught, the quicker they can be corrected.

Getting Past Reading Levels

Andy approached the bus stop with his second grader, Charlotte, and was surprised to hear the kids talking about what color reading group they're in. "I'm in the yellow group. My mom said that's the highest group," said his daughter's friend Ellie. "I don't want to be a yellow," said another friend. "I'm in the red group. I'm just glad I'm not a greenie. That's where the slow pokes are." Andy turned to find Charlotte walking away from the group with her head down. He walked over to Charlotte and didn't even need to ask what reading group she was in. "I'm in the green group, Dad," said his daughter with tears in her eyes. "I hate reading."

By second or third grade, kids begin to recognize what reading group they're in and where they fall in the pecking order. While many teachers mix up groups and focus on different strategies, it's only logical that distinctive reading levels will fall into similar groups. If your gut reaction is "my child belongs in a higher reading group" and you're feeling the urge to contact the teacher to get your child's group changed, remember that this is where she is this month. She could be in a very different place a few months from now.

Children in the lowest reading group often dislike reading, and that's typically why they are there. But the energy spent worrying about where your child is among peers on the reading group scale would be much better spent making a commitment to read to your child every night for thirty minutes. Read books your child likes—from picture books to chapter books. Picture books provide great opportunities to work on comprehension. Share the reading with your child without pressure and make it fun. And continue reading to your kids throughout elementary school and even into middle school if they don't mind. Most kids enjoy being read to by their parents, though they won't always admit it to their peers. Reading aloud with your kids and sharing the reading is the best way to boost reading ability and instill confidence. If it's done in a fun, enjoyable way on a consistent basis—and this is key—they'll usually grow to like reading.

While many books are "leveled," or rated, based on how difficult they are, it's critical to know that there is no universal rating system for books—be they picture books, primary readers, or chapter books. Different companies use different rating and coding systems, so it's impossible to compare them. One universal rule of thumb is that nonfiction is generally much harder than fiction. One way to gauge if a book—fiction or nonfiction—is the right level for your child is the "five-finger test." Have your child read the first page and count the number of words he does not understand. If there are more than five words he doesn't know on that page, the book is probably too hard for him. Forcing your child to read books that are too difficult hurts his confidence.

GETTING RELUCTANT READERS TO READ

Donna was growing more and more frustrated with her son Connor's lack of progress in reading. Connor's older brother was reading chapter books by the age of seven and it seemed like Connor should be too. Perhaps he would be if it weren't for those picture books taking up room on his bookshelves. They were always the books Connor wanted his parents to read to him. Convinced that Connor would be reading chapter books if those picture books were out of sight, Donna went into his room one night and removed all the "baby" books from the shelf. She told Connor that it was time for him to read "big boy books," and they'd be giving away the picture books to little kids who couldn't buy books.

Donna enacted the perfect play for what *not* to do, especially with children who are *reluctant readers*, meaning they are not inclined to pick up a book on their own. Creating a reader is no longer a mystery. Unless there are phonics deficits, a learning disability, or processing issues, the formula works: shower children with a waterfall of words from birth through their elementary years, provide basic phonics instruction in an engaged way, and encourage and nurture reading for fun. Children love to reread books because they can predict what will happen. They love to "master" the story. Once they are comfortable with a level of reading and feel good about the effort they've put in, they will typically move themselves up to another level of books. Be sure to praise the effort your children put into reading and the progress they make, no matter what level book they read. They will move up naturally to harder books when they feel they've mastered their current level.

Creating a R-E-A-D-E-R

Now you understand the stages of reading and the fact that it's a much more complex process than we ever thought. Next, I'd like to share what it takes to create a reader. I've spelled out what it takes by using the word *reader* as a mnemonic.

R = READ ALOUD TO YOUR CHILDREN

Read with your children, to your children, and in front of your children. This is the most important thing you can do to get your child reading more. If you're like most parents, you respond to this idea with "Yeah, we did that when they were little, now we're beyond that. They need to be reading on their own." Reading to kids of all ages, those who are becoming fluent readers and even those in middle school, benefits your children's reading in many ways. First and most important, your children have your undivided attention. They are sitting next to you cozy and comfortable, which makes reading an enjoyable experience. Most kids enjoy being read to until they are adolescents, and some even beyond that. Because they hear and see the story, they are more likely to remember it and comprehend the details. Point to the words. Read about the author. Look at the pictures and predict what might happen.

Your children hear the expression in your voice. They catch your rhythm. They hear you pronounce new words correctly. All of this helps their fluency. It also gives you a chance to ask questions about the book. And this time together "counts" as reading. If your child has reading homework for fifteen to thirty minutes a night, it can be you reading to her with your child following along. Use your finger to help your child follow the words, and she will often imitate this. Share the reading—you read to her and she reads to you—but don't push this on a child. Let reading be the reward.

Most of the time, just sitting with and being close to you is half the experience for your children. If you have any doubt of the importance of reading aloud to your children, read Jim Trelease's book *The Read Aloud Handbook*. You'll understand the mounds of research that support why it's so important to continue to read to your children. Finally, let your kids catch you reading for enjoyment. The more you model reading, the more your child will imitate you. Read the newspaper, books, or magazines. If you're reading on a tablet or the computer, let them know you're reading a book or an article, and talk about what you're reading so they associate computers with reading, too.

E = USE ENTHUSIASM AND EXCITEMENT AS YOU READ

Read to your children with energy and enthusiasm. Let your excitement for whatever you are reading come through in your inflection and tone. Read with different voices. Find a book you are really excited about reading to your child. Your enthusiasm will be contagious. This won't always be easy to do. We're all busy and tired from a hard day's work. It's okay to let others share the reading. When your "reading time" melts down to "we have to do it now" time, it might be better to just read quietly to yourself and let your child see you reading. Or give him a book to "read" to himself. Emergent readers can "read" the pictures and make sense of the story. It's also a good idea to mix up the readers. Moms, dads, grandparents, aunts, uncles, and siblings can all share this reading experience. It's natural for a child to associate one particular book with one parent or the other. Let your natural enthusiasm for a subject or an author come out in what you read to your child. Grandparents are often wonderful readers, full of excitement and enthusiasm because they love to be with their grandchildren. Siblings can be great readers, too, as long as this isn't forced.

A = ACCEPT ANY AND ALL READING MATERIAL

When my oldest daughter turned six, she received a Junie B. Jones book for her birthday from a friend. That night I heard my husband reading it to her. The fresh language I heard horrified me. I couldn't imagine how this kind of reading could be good for kids. I literally took the book away the next day and then asked the librarian, her teacher, and even the principal their opinions of these "awful" books. To my surprise, they all said the same thing: it doesn't matter what she reads as long as she is reading. It took me a while to understand that the key to getting a child reading—and reading fluently—is reading something she's interested in.

Cast a wide net for reading and let your children read whatever they want if it is age appropriate, meaning at their level or below. From picture books to magazines to a chapter book on funny sounds your body makes, kids will read more when they like what they are reading and they can relate to it. The funnier it is, the more interesting the material is to a child, and the more likely they are to read it and keep on reading. That is the goal. Have them read to themselves, aloud to you, along with the audio, or to the dog. Just read. *Diary of a Whimpy Kid* falls into the same humor category. As long as these books aren't the only books your kids read or you read to them, their reading will flourish. My daughter devoured every Junie B. Jones book written and then graduated to Harry Potter books. If you can get your children hooked on a book series they love, they are well on their way to becoming a fluent reader. And remember, your local children's librarian is happy to help you find books that are just right.

Many kids love Guinness World Records books—they love to read the gory, amazing stories. *Sports Illustrated for Kids* is a great way to get kids reading as is the old standby *Highlights* magazine. *Discovery for Kids* is another good one. Kids love getting a subscription in the mail. Balance out your child's reading with a classic children's story or a book that you remember as a child. In my family, we let our kids read anything they want to themselves, and we read a more classic book with richer vocabulary to them. But if they're tired and just want to read something fun that involves little effort, my kids love to pull out the book of poems that sits next to the bed, *Where the Sidewalk Ends* by Shel Silverstein.

D = DIGITAL NATIVES NEED DIRECTION

One of the toughest things about getting kids to read today is the huge number of digital distractions before them. There are literally hundreds of thousands of apps and games at their fingertips on computers, tablets, and cell phones (which are really just tiny computers in tiny hands). Computers and digital sensations vie for our children's attention at all times. Games that light up, buzz, and ding offer instant rewards, which are often much more interesting and immediate for kids than using their imaginations with a good book. Our children are digital natives, born into a different world than we were, and it's a world we must accept. But managing their intake of this endless digital world and balancing it with reading online and printed books will help you raise a reader—and increase a child's attention span. The good news is that playing games on a computer is far more interactive that watching television in a passive mode. Although some games and reading apps can help your child and reinforce skills, they cannot replace the need for the waterfall of words and reading instruction. Nothing can take the place of reading full-length books on screens or the old-fashioned way—on paper. Talking with children about their experiences and having conversations about books will round out their reading exposure.

E = EXPERIENCE EVENTS AROUND READING

At one of my most memorable mother-daughter book clubs, we decided to read a book from a local children's author. I called her and asked if she could visit the group and talk a little bit about her book. She was delighted to come. And her delight turned to tears of joy when she rang the doorbell and stepped into a room to find all the girls dressed up as the main character in the book—pigtails and all. To this day, her book is one of my daughter's favorites.

Creating events around reading is a good way to bring another dimension to reading. Take weekly trips to the library and bookstore. Give your children their own library card. Nothing puts a smile on children's faces faster than signing their own free library card and being able to borrow books. When kids associate fun with reading, they are likely to want to do it again. Take advantage of story times, activities, and just hanging out in your local bookstore or library. Surround yourselves with books: books in baskets in the bathroom, bookshelves in every room. Some families use the "number of library books per age" rule: when you're five, you can take out five books of your choice; if you are six, you take out six. Another great way to make reading fun is through a book club. Thanks to Oprah, book clubs have become a common occurrence at all ages, from age eight or nine and up. If you do establish a mother-daughter or father-son book club (or any mix, grandparents, too!), the key is to keep it fun. It should not be full of worksheets or essays like school. The more experiential it is, the better.

Children who become readers have parents who make reading a part of their everyday experience. Instilling reading as a routine, part of going to bed at night along with brushing teeth, is an easy way to create a habit of reading. Having a good light and a bookshelf or basket with plenty of books available will help. Adding some incentive into the ritual of night-time reading can also help. In our home, bedtime for many years was at 7:30 p.m., but if my girls wanted to read, then it was 8:00. If you find your child reading under the covers with a flashlight, congratulations! You've raised a reader. Praise his commitment to reading. Ask questions about what he's reading. Share books with him and continue to read to him. Other ways you can make reading and words fun and part of a routine is in the car: find words that start with each letter of the alphabet, read signs along the streets, read the letters on license plates. The grocery store is another great place to encourage readers: read cereal boxes, have your children search for certain items and check prices, teach them how to read nutrition labels. Keep it fun.

SSR/DEAR Time: Sustained Silent Reading and Drop Everything and Read

Barbara was outraged. Her third grader, Emily, came home from school and told her that the teacher had started a new program called SSR. For fifteen minutes every day, they would have Sustained Silent Reading. They could read any book they wanted while sitting at their desks. "No talking, just reading. And it's okay to lip the words if you want to," said her daughter, excited about the program. Barbara was convinced it was a waste of time to spend time reading in a classroom when they already did this at home. She called her sister in Texas and asked if she'd ever heard of this in her kids' classrooms. Barbara's sister told her they had a similar program called DEAR time: Drop Everything and Read. Like SSR, it runs for about fifteen minutes every day and the kids can read whatever book they want. Still convinced it was a waste of time and just an extra break for the teacher, Barbara wrote an email to the teacher demanding an explanation as to why such a program was necessary.

SSR and DEAR time have become a best practice in many schools over the last decade, and for good reason. Research shows that when kids read every day and make a routine out of that reading, they actually look forward to it and begin to ask for it. But it must be every day—and it must be free from judgment, grades, worksheets, or drills. The key in either program is that the teacher reads, as a role model for the kids. Equally important is that the kids read whatever book they want. The idea is to make reading fun and a pleasurable experience on a consistent basis. Even if you read at home daily with your children, it will only help your kids to read to themselves at another point in the day. If your child's school or teacher practices SSR or DEAR time, you're lucky. Many schools find they don't have the time to do it anymore. If your school doesn't offer SSR or DEAR time and if you're so inclined, check out www.readingrockets.org for some key reasons why this is a best practice. Use this information to make a case for the adoption of SSR or DEAR time in your child's school. (For tips on how to communicate this information effectively, see chapter 5.)

How Children Learn to Write

Talking about reading without talking about writing is like having a school without teachers. A child's writing ability typically parallels their reading readiness. Children also like to imitate adults writing, just as they do in reading. The most important factor in writing, as in reading, is to keep it positive and enjoyable. If there is too much pressure placed on children to write clearly before they are able, they learn to dislike writing and will turn away from trying to master it. Writing can be a frustrating experience for child, parent, and teacher alike if the steps aren't introduced as a child is ready for them. Remember that every child learns at a different pace. Many boys' fine motor skills are not as developed in kindergarten and first grade, making writing even harder for them.

With the additional focus on keyboards and touch-screen computers today, kids have fewer and fewer opportunities—other than in school—to write unless you create them at home. Simple things like asking your child to be the grocery list maker each week, writing a thank you note, or making a to-do list for the day will give her a feeling of competence, as long as you are forgiving of phonetic spelling and hard-to-read letters. These tasks are all age appropriate.

Just as there are five stages for learning to read, there are six different stages for learning to write: holding a pencil, prewriting, forming letters, writing words, learning sentence conventions, and mastering complete sentences and spelling. Children move through these stages from kindergarten through grade three. Let's look more closely now at each stage.

HOLDING A PENCIL

During the scribble and drawing preschool stage, children experiment and practice "writing." They imitate adults and begin to understand that symbols, letters, words, and numbers have meaning. In preschool and kindergarten, their "scribbles" will often tell a story that they love to tell you about. A child will begin to learn to hold a pencil at this stage. Depending on the child, this fine motor skill may come naturally or may take some time. Some come to kindergarten knowing how to hold a pencil; others do not. Given the higher expectation levels in kindergarten today, working with your child to get closer to this skill—in a way that does not put pressure on the child—will help. Some boys have an interest in holding a pencil; others run the other way. Use fatter pencils and pencil grips to make the process more comfortable for your child. A quality book or toy store will typically carry different pencil grips to try out.

PREWRITING, CIRCLES, AND LINES

Before children can form letters or numbers, they need to be able to draw lines (straight and diagonal) and circles that close. Keep this stage fun and practice on lined and unlined paper. Once they've mastered this stage, they are ready to write letters. Tracing paper works for some kids, but others will get frustrated tracing. Some want to copy them. Experiment and listen to your child's likes and dislikes.

FORMING LETTERS

Kids learn how to write letters by copying them and practicing till they get it right. There are no shortcuts. Your child's teacher will usually have them bring home the correct size of lined paper. Another way to help your child practice is to draw letters on grade-level lined paper with a yellow highlighter. Put a green dot where you start and a red dot where you end. And let your kids have fun tracing and following the lines. A great resource to use for this stage is www.handwritingwithouttears.com.

WRITING WORDS

Once a child understands that words make up sentences and there is spacing between the words and sentences, the real writing begins. The "one finger between each word" method is typically used. Many of your child's words will have phonetic or inventive spelling, and this is developmentally appropriate. Giving your kids a special journal that they can practice writing in inspires some kids to write. Keeping grade-level supplies—paper, pencils, erasers—on hand and ideas (known as *writing prompts*) to write about will also help inspire your budding writer.

LEARNING SENTENCE CONVENTIONS

By first grade, students are expected to get punctuation and capitalization down in their sentences. This is an important habit to form and one where, the more reading children do, the more naturally they grasp this idea. Remind your child to pause at each period when reading to reinforce this rule. As children move from grades two through four, they will learn more conventions like commas, semicolons, and quotation marks. Again, pointing out these things as children read will make it easier for them to master them in writing.

MASTERING COMPLETE SENTENCES AND SPELLING

In grades one through five your child will be tested on weekly spelling words and asked to use them in sentences. By the end of first grade, most children can write a complete thought in a sentence and expand that idea to full paragraphs. By third grade, they are writing multiparagraph reports, and by fifth grade, they are writing longer compositions, stories, and persuasive documents. At various points through the grades, your child may have an opportunity to create a published story. While this used to be a labor-intensive project involving many parent volunteers and a big commitment from teachers, technology and a variety of software options (listed at www.theparentbackpack.com) now make this process much simpler.

LEARNING HOW TO ORGANIZE WRITING: GRAPHIC ORGANIZERS AND RUBRICS

From second grade and up, most schools use graphic organizers to teach kids how to organize writing. A *graphic organizer* is a visual tool for categorizing thoughts. A common graphic organizer is the Venn diagram. Your child's teacher may list preferred graphic organizers on her website. You can find many others available by googling "graphic organizer." Depending on how your child learns, one organizer may be easier to follow than another. Another best practice that most schools use is a rubric for writing. *Rubric* is a fancy word for expectations—that is, what the teacher looks for in a writing project. The expectations and grade delineations for each writing assignment are clearly communicated so kids can measure their work against the rubric. They are usually helpful and easy to follow. Ask your child if he received a rubric before you review any writing or draft. This makes the evaluation process much less subjective and much easier on the parent.

Writing Expectations

The truth about writing in many school districts is that it hasn't received the attention it deserves—until recently. Writing is difficult. Teaching and correcting writing is even more difficult. But with lots of practice, consistent reading to support and reinforce the ideas behind the writing, and parents and teachers who are supportive and encouraging, your child can and will master writing. The Common Core standards put a greater emphasis on nonfiction, critical thinking, and writing. So you can expect to see more writing in the next few years, particularly persuasive writing that is supported by evidence rather than narrative reports that tell a story. This is all in an effort to create stronger communicators who are well prepared for the real world.

Some districts have instituted a Writing Across the Curriculum initiative, where kids write paragraphs and papers in every subject—not just during literacy. Some schools invest in writing curriculums, such as the 6 Traits Writing Program. No matter what program your school district uses, there are some basic principles in elementary writing that are helpful for parents to know. First, most kids are taught that there are five steps to writing. Prewriting, where the child thinks about what to write and then uses a graphic organizer to get ideas down, is the first step. Then drafting, revising, editing, and finally publishing—writing or printing the final paper. The most important part of this process is revising because good writers revise again and again. Once students get the content where they want it, the next step is to edit for punctuation and grammar. Many schools use a five-paragraph system for the first few years of writing. While this can get a bit rigid, it helps kids understand that a paper begins with an introduction, where the topic sentence, or thesis, is conveyed. This main idea is then supported with three detailed paragraphs, followed by a conclusion.

A model frequently used in elementary grades is the 6 Traits Writing program or a similar approach. Centered on six areas of instruction, this approach is also used as a rubric to evaluate writing:

1. **Ideas and content:** How creative and rich is the student's thinking?

2. **Organization:** Is it effectively organized based on a logical graphic organizer?

3. **Word choice:** Are verbs and adjectives strong? Do they tap the imagination?

4. **Voice:** Does the writer's personal voice or point of view come through?

5. **Sentence fluency:** Is there a variety of sentences for rhythm and flow?

6. **Conventions:** Call the COPS in for Capitals, Overall appearance, Punctuation, and Spelling.

By grade three, kids are introduced to metaphors, similes, and personification. By fourth and fifth grade, most students are learning how to write a persuasive document with research and supporting evidence.

Be sure to praise your child's effort—not the outcome—as much as possible during the process of writing. When you ask questions about what they're writing, they feel your interest. Display their work. Keep samples of your children's writing at each grade level with their report cards to show them their progress. Kids love to see how they've developed over the months and years, just like tracking their height. This is far more interesting to them than report cards. Finally, keep in mind that phonetic spelling and mixing up some key letters—like *b*, *d*, *p*, and *q* along with numbers 6 and 9—is a natural part of a child's learning process, as we saw in chapter 1 with Will and his dad. Letter reversals can occur up to third grade and do not necessarily suggest a problem.

....

Reading and writing are critical skills that lay the foundation for all other learning in the grades to come. Read aloud to your child, read for fun, and give your child opportunities to write. And remember to keep the focus positive and encouraging. A child who likes to read—and write—is a child who usually succeeds in school.

In the next chapter, I'll discuss teaching, how classroom placement is handled, and what you can do to influence your child's classroom assignment.

TOP TEN TAKEAWAYS

TO CONSIDER

- Reading is best learned through words, books, and experiences in combination with phonics instruction. Each child learns to read at his own pace.

- Reading aloud in an engaged way with your child is the single most important activity you can do to raise a reader because it associates reading with pleasure.

- Writing gets better with practice; the Common Core standards expect more writing from students.

TO AVOID

- Don't make your child read books that are too difficult; kids will naturally gravitate to harder books once they've mastered the level they are comfortable with.

- Don't force children to write before they are physically ready; keep the experience fun and full of scribbles.

continued

TOP TEN TAKEAWAYS, *continued*

TO DO

- Shower your children with a waterfall of words—conversations, books, and stories—from birth through elementary school to create stronger readers and writers.

- Make sure your children read every day and read books that are not too difficult for them

- Create a R-E-A-D-E-R: Read aloud, with Expression, Any book or magazine your child wants to read. Do it Daily. Experience books. Make reading a Ritual and a Routine.

- Strong readers make strong writers; providing writing opportunities for your kids makes them more successful writers.

- Reading ability is often measured through fluency tests at least twice a year. If you're concerned about your child's reading ability, ask to see the trend in his fluency scores.

CHAPTER 7

It's All About the Teaching

I cannot teach anyone anything. I can only make them think.
—SOCRATES

By the end of second grade, Rachel had declared she didn't like school. It wasn't fun, her teacher was mean, and recess wasn't worth that long, boring bus ride. She didn't like to read, wasn't interested in learning about new things—unless it was related to sports—and all the coaxing and encouragement from Mom and Dad couldn't change her mind. Certain she had a learning issue, Rachel's parents requested she be tested. The results surprised everyone: Rachel was an intelligent, confident, eight-year-old girl who just hadn't hit her stride in school.

When Mrs. Harrison stepped into Rachel's classroom, she was a different kind of teacher from day one. "Welcome to Team H," she said with her hands stretched out. "Each one of you was placed in my classroom because you work hard. You are not afraid to ask questions. And you have high expectations for yourself—just like I do for you. On Team H, we find fun and interesting ideas in everything we learn, and we share those ideas with our friends here and families. This morning we're going to get to know each other a little. Who would like to share one way that you worked hard this summer and tell us what you learned from that experience?" Excited to think and talk about how hard she worked at soccer camp, Rachel's hand shot up. "Maybe this year won't be so bad," she thought.

Next to a parent, teachers have more influence over a child's education than any other factor. Teachers shape young minds. They change lives. It doesn't take long to figure out that it's all about the teacher. This chapter shows you what capable and effective teaching looks like, how to support your child's teacher, and why the teacher-student match and class makeup are so important. It will also cover how schools place students, what role you can play in your child's classroom placement, what to do when your child ends up with a less than ideal teacher, and the changing rules in unions and teacher evaluations.

Teachers: The Trump Card

A school system can tout state-of-the-art buildings, terrific administrators, an award-winning superintendent, but if the teacher in front of your child's class is not an effective, skilled instructor who knows how to connect with kids, the rest doesn't matter. Teachers are the trump card. We don't need a lot of research on teaching to reinforce what intuition has already etched on our brains from our own school days. But I'll share some of it because the data is remarkable. From Stanford University to Johns Hopkins and many research institutions in between, studies reveal some remarkable findings:

- The quality of teaching has six to ten times more effect on student achievement than all other factors combined.

- Three years of effective teaching accounts for an improvement of 35 to 50 percentage points on average on students' standardized tests.

- The best teachers in a school have six times as much impact as the bottom third of teachers.

- Students with a teacher in the top 5 percent gained a year and a half's worth of learning while students with a teacher in the bottom 5 percent learned only half a year's worth of curriculum.

As in any profession, there are wide-ranging abilities and results in teaching and many factors that influence them. But until recently these factors had not been measured on a consistent basis. We'll talk more about union regulations and performance evaluations later in the chapter. First, let's spend some time reviewing what makes a teacher effective and look at a typical day in an elementary teacher's world.

What Effective Teaching Looks Like

Just like parents, teachers come to school with a wide range of experiences, styles, and approaches. Teaching is both an art and a science. It's a juggling act that looks different every day, in every classroom, making it that much harder to define and measure. Based on my experience with and exposure to hundreds of teachers, I conclude there are four critical skills that excellent teachers master. These include connecting with kids, setting high expectations for each child, using and communicating about student data, and managing their classrooms skillfully. Let's take a closer look at each of these.

EFFECTIVE TEACHERS CONNECT WITH KIDS

A great teacher genuinely cares about kids, looks for ways to connect with them, and has the patience to build a rapport with each child. While this may sound obvious, I have met teachers along the way who don't seem to like kids or connect with them. Despite each student starting at a different place, this teacher strives to connect. The connection may look different with each teacher, but it shows up in the classroom, every day. Some teachers do it through sharing their own life stories. Others tell funny jokes. Others create a team spirit that kids thrive on. A great teacher will connect individually with your child and take the time to get to know what makes him tick or what makes her spark. Effective teachers are accepting and respectful of children's opinions. They know kids don't always come to school excited to hit the books; that's why it is so important for teachers to establish relationships with their students and build community in their classrooms.

EFFECTIVE TEACHERS SET EXPECTATIONS
THAT INSPIRE EACH CHILD

There are many teachers who connect well with kids, but don't encourage them to reach the highest level they can. As the saying goes, "An average teacher tells, a good teacher shows, and a great teacher inspires." A skilled teacher sets high goals for each child, motivates students to take what they've learned and apply it on another level, establishes clear expectations from the beginning, and expects success from all students. She understands that each child starts in a different place. He builds community in the classroom. She conveys the knowledge that students need to know, shows why and how it's relevant, and engages students to think about what they've learned in new and different ways.

EFFECTIVE TEACHERS RESPECT STUDENT DATA
AND COMMUNICATE CLEARLY

Teachers are inundated with data on their students today, more than ever before. They know exactly where each student stands in reading and math and what skills each child needs to move to the next level. Effective teachers work with this information and praise progress. They meet each child individually where she is, differentiate their instruction to reach each and every child, and move each child nine months forward by the end of the year (or more). But skilled teachers also make sure they know and understand the whole student, not just data points on a chart. Effective teachers communicate clearly with students and parents, explain themselves well, and listen for feedback. They teach in different ways to reach different kids and adapt again when needed. And they have fun doing it. Great teachers learn from their students every day. It's a herculean job teaching in a data-driven, digital age.

EFFECTIVE TEACHERS MANAGE THEIR CLASSROOM SKILLFULLY

Teachers who have earned respect from their class maintain order and discipline. They can get the undivided attention of their students with the clap of their hands. I'll never forget the experience I had in my daughter's kindergarten class as a classroom parent. When I asked Mrs. T to step out for a moment so I could talk to the kids about the end-of-the-year class gift, within three minutes, the classroom was utter mayhem. When she walked back in the classroom and flicked the lights, a calm silence returned within three seconds. Because teachers compete with so many sources of information and distractions today, this expertise is critical. For most teachers, classroom management is a learned skill that comes with time, good mentorship, and training from the school district. Teachers need to be respectful of and respected by their students. When classroom management is weak, teaching and learning suffer.

Supporting Teachers' Hard Work

Teachers have a tremendous impact on our children, and it's important for parents to recognize that and show respect to teachers who are doing great work. And the majority of teachers are doing just that. Elementary teachers do far more than we know. They supervise squirmy kids for more than six hours a day, five days a week. They prep three to four lessons each day, teach a whole class lesson in literacy, reteach some kids and challenge others, manage small-group instruction, and know exactly what's going on in the back of the class. They organize a small reading group in one corner, an enrichment group in another, and redirect behavior all within five minutes. They answer questions, recalibrate the latest piece of technology, attend a meeting, fill out paperwork, review data metrics, check an IEP, and get ready for recess duty. They blow noses, give tests, connect with kids, teach a math lesson, zip jackets, and stay up late correcting papers and tests. They worry about the students they're not reaching. They care and connect with each of "their kids" every day of the school year. They teach a third lesson on science, handle a "bullying" issue, walk the kids to the gym, direct the parent volunteer, plan the field trip, update their website, input grades, and attend a staff meeting. It's an exhausting, challenging job.

Teachers also have days when their students don't focus, the math lesson doesn't go as planned, the fire drill ruins the day's rhythm, the projector dies, and a parent email feels like a stab in the heart. On days like these, teachers can't hide in the bathroom, close their office door, or take a long lunch. They still have to be there for all their kids until the bell rings.

SAYING THANK YOU AND DOING YOUR PART

Many teachers I know keep a special drawer of thank you notes from families of kids they taught in previous years and even the distant past, from students they still remember twelve years later, from families who took the time to acknowledge their hard work and say "thank you." It's at the end of those bad days when teachers open their special drawer and read those notes again. Often with tears in their eyes, they remember how much they love teaching, how much good they are doing, and how much they are appreciated.

So take a few minutes and write a note or an email of thanks to your children's teachers. This could be a short note acknowledging a hurdle overcome or a lesson that sparked your child, or a great year so far. Copy the principal on your email if you want. Or even better, have your child write a thank you note. The teacher will appreciate it more than you'll ever know. There's no better gift you can give a teacher than a personal note showing your appreciation. And, once again, it makes that bridge you're building even stronger.

Another important way to support your children's teachers is to do your part. Be involved in your child's education every day. Teachers know which parents are supporting their kids' learning and they appreciate this more than you know. Check your child's homework every day and make sure it's finished. It doesn't have to be correct. Teachers get frustrated when parents make excuses for why their kid's homework isn't done or wasn't even attempted. We'll talk more about homework in chapter 12. There are also many ways to connect to, extend, and enrich your child's learning discussed in chapter 3. Read to and with your child every night. Teachers know which families are doing this because it makes such a significant difference in a child's progress. And encourage your children to respect their teachers. These steps go a long way toward supporting a teacher's hard work and being involved in your child's education in productive ways.

Now that you have a sense of what makes effective teachers, what they do every day, and how to support them, let's look at how teachers and children are matched up in classroom placement. This is usually the source of much parental angst at the beginning and end of each school year. Will my child get a "good" teacher? How does placement work and how can I influence this decision?

Child-Teacher Placement

Marilyn thought about that hot day in August when her daughter, Hadley, ripped open that long awaited placement letter—the letter that would decide her daughter's fate for third grade.

"Ohhhhh. . . I hope I get Ms. Perkins," said Hadley, repeating the mantra of every other third grader in town. Karen recalled the names of the "best third grade teachers," from a friend whose children had just finished Baker Elementary. Ms. Perkins was on her list, too. When Hadley screamed, "Ms. Perkins! SWEET! Grace will be in my class!" Marilyn sighed with relief. They got lucky. It was sure to be a good year.

Never did Marilyn imagine she'd be sitting at her kitchen counter three months later with Hadley in tears, saying she hated school. Considered to be one of the "star" teachers in the school, Ms. Perkins wasn't working out for Hadley. Their styles and personalities didn't click. Hadley was more of a reserved child; Ms. Perkins seemed to connect more with outgoing kids. "She doesn't like me, Mom," cried Hadley. "She yells at me almost every day, and she's mean. I hate school, and I am not going."

As parents, we evaluate our kids' teachers from three perspectives: our children's, our own interactions, and through the observations of other parents and kids, i.e., the rumor mill. While this three-pronged assessment is natural, it's important to keep in mind that what everybody says does not always match up with what you observe or with your own child's experience. Every child, parent, and teacher relationship is different. Some will be better matched than others. Teachers, like everyone, have good and bad days. And the makeup of the class can play a significant part in the culture of the classroom. While a structured teacher with high expectations may work well for one family, it may be a mismatch for another, as was the case with Hadley's third grade assignment.

Parents worry more about which teacher their child is assigned to than any other factor, especially if the match the previous year wasn't the best. No parent wants to deal with a child in a mismatched situation or with a less-than-effective teacher two years in a row. The teacher matters too much. Most parents make a quick prediction once they hear who their child's teacher will be, based on their own experience or what they hear from others. But this prediction doesn't always pan out. Marilyn and Hadley's situation is not unique. While there are certainly "ace" teachers under whom many children thrive, those teachers are not always the best match for your student.

HOW CLASSES ARE FORMED

While the process of creating classes looks slightly different in each school, there are many common threads across districts. The days of elementary principals arbitrarily placing kids into classrooms are long gone, as is the practice of placing kids purely by their academic standing. While most public schools will not allow parents to select a teacher for their child, many will accept a note from the family indicating a preference for a "different experience," if an older sibling had a teacher that did not work out so well. Although each child is unique, this type of communication helps minimize placement conflicts. Some, but not all, schools will also allow—by letter or a face-to-face meeting—parent input on placement.

There are many layers involved in creating what most public schools today strive for: a heterogeneous class with a reasonable mix of students for each teacher. Class placement is a complicated job that most elementary principals take very seriously. Most administrators would rather put the time in up front than deal with mismatched students and teachers once the new school year is underway. I know many principals who spend months laboring over this process. Multiple factors go into classroom placement decisions including academic level of the student, time demands the student will place on the teacher, the student's interpersonal skills and peer relationships, whether the student requires special programs (IEP or 504 Plan—see chapter 9), how the student's learning style matches a teacher's teaching style, and feedback from the previous year's teacher.

The size of your child's school also makes a difference in how class placement is handled. In some schools, especially where there are five or fewer classes per grade, the teachers are more likely to know the strengths, weaknesses, and tolerance levels of teachers in the next grade. They also tend to know most of the kids at their grade level by the end of the year. In these schools, teachers may be given greater responsibility for student placement in the succeeding year. The principal then reviews and revises the class lists based on her broader knowledge of teachers, children, and parents. In schools that are larger, meaning six or more classes per grade, the current teachers may group their students on many variables including ability, how they work with other children, how much time they require, and what peers may accompany them to the next grade level. Once groupings are identified, the principal usually creates the final class lists. The larger your school is and the less likely your principal is to really know your child, the more important it is for you to advocate for a well-matched teacher and classroom for your child.

INFLUENCING CLASS PLACEMENT

The more the teacher or principal understands your child's strengths and weaknesses, what motivates him, how she learns, and your goals for him, the more likely your child is to be placed with a well-matched teacher next year. This is another reason why building a bridge with your child's teacher is so important. Let's take a look at a letter that a mother wrote to the principal after her son's not-so-great second grade year.

Dear Mrs. Glick,

After a wonderful first grade year with Mrs. Arpin, we feel obligated to tell you that Jack's placement in second grade with Mrs. Pendy did not work out as well. Jack was often confused by lessons, unclear about the expectations, and distracted by the classroom noise. Though we discussed this and met with Mrs. Pendy, there was little change. To her credit, however, we could see she made a concerted effort to focus on Jack.

Our hope is that for third grade, Jack can be placed with a teacher who, like Mrs. Arpin, is structured, with strong classroom management skills and high expectations for students. Jack wants to do well in school, is excited to learn, and we want to keep his flame of curiosity lit. Thank you for considering our thoughts.

The best letters related to placement are brief and to the point. Jack's mom kept her points focused on Jack's experiences, his needs, and her observations. There is no blame or accusation, just a clear reference to what they feel Jack needs in order to thrive in third grade. Some schools allow parents to name students with whom you don't want your child placed due to a prior experience. Be cautious about overdoing this. The more kids you list, the more you limit your child's placement options. Depending on how strongly you feel about the placement, set up a meeting with the principal. If you remain professional and positive in your approach, it will strengthen the home–school bridge you are building and enhance your child's chances of getting a well-matched teacher and classroom. But if your child does end up on the wrong end of teacher placement, there is a protocol to follow.

Managing a Bad Experience with a Teacher

I cringe at using the word *bad*. But let's face it, even the best schools harbor less than effective teachers. The most important thing to remember in this situation is this: how you handle the problem makes a big difference in the outcome. Putting the Power of P3 (see chapter 5) into action will help. Even if you're halfway through the school year, it's never too late to provide feedback. No matter what happens in the current situation, remember that you're also paving the way for the following year.

Here are my recommendations on what to do when your child has a bad experience with a teacher.

- **Keep your external attitude positive and professional.** Your child is with this teacher for six hours every day. Be sure to empathize with her feelings and reassure her that "we" will get through this. She needs to know that you are there to help and support her. Acknowledge what is working in the classroom. Just like parents and kids, every teacher has strengths. Try to help her see that. If the teacher is super demanding about organization, remind your child that this is an important life skill and the teacher is preparing her early. If the situation is handled well, this experience will make your child more resilient. It can also positively impact your child's placement for next year if handled effectively.

- **Keep notes.** This can be a hard, tedious, and frustrating job for parents. But if you want to remedy the problem, it's crucial. Get a small notebook and jot down what your child tells you without it being obvious to your child that you're doing this. Write down the date and anything that your child reports that the teacher says, does, or writes that you feel is inappropriate, unprofessional, or substandard. Keep in mind that I used the words *what your child reports*. While you may trust that what your child says is accurate, this must also be verified. Note the effect the actions or words are having on your child. It's never too late to start. Be specific—the more details the better. Keep in mind that every teacher has bad days, just like parents. Maybe even a bad week. If something occurs once or twice, it's not a cause for concern. If it becomes a pattern of three to five similar situations, then it's time to do something.

- **Meet with the teacher when you see a pattern.** If there are three or more similar comments or actions on different dates that negatively influence your child and her learning, it's time to meet with the teacher. The level of impact on your child is important. If these issues do not affect your child, don't create an issue that isn't there. If it's quite obvious these incidents are impacting your child and most likely your family life, use the Power of P3 (see chapter 5) for words that work. Be positive, professional, and persistent when you discuss your concerns. Convey your own and your child's observations and feelings without blame. Focus on how these actions upset or disturb your child and your family. Write down the key points of the discussion and what the teacher agrees to do. Set up regular meeting times to review progress. Be genuine about what is working and what's not.

- **Meet with the principal if things don't improve.** Send a short email expressing that you want to meet to discuss your child's situation and indicate that you have documented data and have met with the teacher previously. Let the teacher know you are doing this. Follow up with the principal's secretary. If you don't get a response within forty-eight hours, email again using the Power of P3 from chapter 5. Some principals will invite the teacher to join the meeting. This may be uncomfortable for you, but don't be intimidated. If you have documented your concerns and have previously met with the teacher, this should not be a problem. It may not be the first time the principal hears these concerns.

THE TOP FIVE MISTAKES PARENTS MAKE WITH TEACHERS

1. **Telling the teacher what to do.** This makes any teacher feel like hired help. No one likes to be told what to do, or how to do it, especially from someone other than their boss. This leaves most teachers demoralized and less willing to "partner" with you. Use the Power of P3 to communicate effectively.

2. **Undermining the teacher at home or gossiping.** It's not uncommon at the elementary level for things that are said or heard at home to leak back to the classroom. This happens more than you know. A teacher can often tell from a child's words or reactions when parents are not supporting her efforts or are speaking disrespectfully about her. Beware of "little big ears."

3. **Hyperfocusing on your own child.** Yes, you are your child's best advocate, but the teacher also has valid observations about your child and has to consider two dozen other students' needs, too. Showing no deference to their professional judgment frustrates teachers. It's difficult for them, too, if you don't respect their many responsibilities and, for example, try to hold a conference about your child during an open house, in the hallway, or when volunteering.

4. **Going over the teacher's head to the principal.** This aggravates teachers and weakens your communication bridge. Ninety-nine percent of the time, the principal will go to the teacher before holding a meeting or responding to the parent, so it's best to communicate up front and not hide the issue.

5. **Not showing up or doing your part.** Whether it's making sure homework is complete, attending parent-teacher conferences, reading the newsletter, or turning in forms on time, when parents don't make an effort to get involved with their child's schooling on a basic level, it lowers the teacher's expectations for your child. Teachers work hard and appreciate when parents do their part. They genuinely want parents to be involved because they know the child will be more successful.

A number of years ago, my daughter was placed with a teacher whose teaching style did not match my daughter's learning style in any way. This teacher seemed better suited for kids who were auditory learners, who could grasp a lesson when it was verbalized with minimal visuals or interaction. My daughter needed to visualize lessons in order to process them, and her frustration in the classroom was beginning to affect her health. I met with the teacher, explained my concerns, and documented the effect that some of her actions and language had on my daughter for three months. After many follow-up meetings with the teacher and the principal, and demonstrating how my daughter's learning style was not well matched with the teacher's singular style of instruction, my daughter was finally moved to another class.

The process was hard work, and I often felt frustrated. But I persevered following the Power of P3 because I knew what was best for my daughter. When she went to the new classroom, the dark cloud that hung over her and our house lifted overnight. The difference was remarkable. I felt like we had our daughter back.

Between the ages of five and ten, I'm convinced that a year or two of dealing effectively with a mediocre teacher will provide a child and parents with the coping skills they need to accept and make the best of a year. However, as the research shows, two years of ineffective teaching at the elementary level can hurt a child's curiosity and love of learning. It's our job as parents to advocate for the best teachers possible during these early years. But how you do that makes all the difference.

Once children move into their middle school years, my feelings about advocating for better teachers changes. When children are eleven or twelve, and the foundation for learning is in place, I believe they will become stronger students by dealing with all types of teachers. When they get into the real world, they will have demanding bosses, bothersome neighbors, and trying times. Learning how to manage themselves and work within these situations in school can be a positive learning experience for them, especially when parents are there to support and guide.

It's important to keep in mind that the majority of teachers enjoy kids and are very effective at what they do. While I wish I could assure you that having to deal with a bad teacher-child match is unlikely to happen to you, it could. For many years, dealing with less-than-effective teachers has been difficult for kids, parents, and administrators, but that is beginning to change. Let's look at why.

Ineffective Teachers: A Historic Problem

Elementary teachers have one of the most isolated jobs in the world, even when they coteach or plan lessons together. Some lack sufficient supervision, observation, and evaluation. Often, evaluation procedures are limited by teacher's union contract regulations, which were historically designed to support equal hiring practices, job security, and compensation. In many contracts, these regulations allow one preannounced supervisory evaluative visit per year. With some contracts, if a supervisor shows up unexpectedly in a teacher's classroom once too often, the teacher has the right to file a grievance. Within this system, 95 percent of teachers are rated excellent. This frustrates effective teachers as much as it does parents. And, once a teacher is "tenured," meaning he receives professional status after three years on the job, only the best of schools continue to monitor that teacher's progress. Under these collectively bargained contracts, many state and local school leaders find their hands to be tied in carrying out effective teacher evaluations.

Although effective instruction is proven to have the greatest impact on student achievement, the isolated nature of a teacher's job, teachers' union contract regulations, and historical evaluation processes have little to do with monitoring or rewarding great teaching. In a system that rewards teachers who have the greatest number of degrees, certifications, and longevity, the fact is that these qualifications don't necessarily translate into better teaching or learning in the classroom. Moreover, highly unionized contracts whose regulations apply equally to all teachers have, in some cases, protected the weaker teachers and failed to acknowledge and reward excellent teachers. Teacher-training programs in colleges and universities have also been faulted for not adequately preparing teachers for real-world classroom experiences. And, finally, in our financially pressed school systems, there is often insufficient time and money to train and mentor the promising teachers we do have in classrooms. Thankfully, all this is beginning to change in many districts.

Improved Teacher Evaluations and Unions

For the first time in the history of our school system, a movement is afoot in many states to improve teacher evaluations. Driven by Race to the Top incentives (a federally run program to improve accountability in teaching and learning), many states and school districts are beginning to agree to a multifaceted teacher evaluation process. This process links teacher performance to a new system of evaluation that includes SMART goals (specific, measurable, attainable, results oriented, and time bound) and student achievement on standardized tests. Rather than the annual preannounced evaluation date, teachers will be evaluated multiple times a year for brief, unannounced periods of time. Teachers are understandably nervous about this new system, no matter where they stand, because change is always hard. This process will take some time, given the three-year cycle of union contract negotiations, but progress toward improving the evaluation process and insuring that your child's teachers are as effective as they can be is underway in many districts. Check in with your school board. If this is not happening in your district and you'd like to advocate for more effective teacher evaluations, talk to your school superintendent or state representative.

Some districts are also starting to use Interest Based Bargaining (IBB), a more collaborative approach to collective bargaining that is less industrialized, uses fewer lawyers, and starts with goals from each side rather than muddy details. In a *Boston Globe* column about the need for IBB and why it will improve schools and ensure fairness for teachers, columnist Lawrence Harmon wrote, "Inflexible contracts steeped in minutiae about the rights of workers and managers don't lead to better classrooms. Teachers and school officials are embarrassed by the tricks they use to conceal their bottom lines. Parents, meanwhile, simply want a reliable education for their kids . . . Instead of issuing tough demands and counter-demands, the sides [in IBB] begin with a clear statement of their interests and objectives."

All this is good news for teachers, kids, and parents because it means that effective teachers are more likely to be recognized and rewarded for their work and that ineffective teachers will be held accountable to higher standards or removed. In some situations, parents fear that expressing concerns about a teacher will open up their child to class-room retribution.

Expressing Concerns and Retribution

The fear that your child's teacher will take out her frustration and anger on your child is understandable. I've met with many parents who share fears of retribution. What I have found in most cases is, if you handle the situation in a professional, positive manner—using the Power of P3 without yelling, threatening, or letting emotions take over—most teachers will make an effort to do a better job for your child. They may know they are not connecting well with your child and worry about it. They may welcome your insights on how to approach your child differently. If you are unable to communicate your observations and concerns effectively, some teachers may naturally harbor ill will toward your family. But if you can communicate your observations and concerns in a professional and positive way, rather than make accusations or judgments about the teaching, you'll be on your way to building a better bridge. It's all about how you deliver your message as discussed in detail in chapter 5.

If parents are to be partners in our children's education, we need to acknowledge the successes, address the challenges, and deal with the difficult situations in a professional way. Doing so will move our school systems closer to delivering the best education possible for our children. If feedback is given thoughtfully to both teachers and administrators, everyone wins because teachers receive the input they genuinely need and principals gain information they may not otherwise have. In situations where teachers might be abusing their power, this is critical. No one is perfect, parents and educators included. But we must work together and be respectful of one another so we can give our children the best educational experience the school has to offer.

....

In this chapter, we discussed what effective teaching looks like, how to support your child's teacher, what you can do to influence your child's classroom placement, and how to proceed when you get a less than effective teacher. In the next chapter, we'll look at connection and confidence and how to ensure these important characteristics are part of your child's educational journey.

TOP TEN TAKEAWAYS

TO CONSIDER

- Research confirms that the quality of teaching is the most important factor in a child's education—beyond curriculum, the principal, or the quality of the school buildings.

- An effective, skilled teacher connects with kids, sets high expectations that inspire, acts and communicates on student data, and shows strong classroom management skills.

- Many factors influence child placement including the student's academic ability, teacher-student match, class makeup, and teaching style; advocating appropriately for the right match is important through grade five.

TO AVOID

- Don't talk about teachers disrespectfully in front of your children because it confuses them and makes progress difficult in the classroom.

- Don't send a lengthy email to a teacher outlining all the issues you have with your child's situation or the teacher. Email to announce the concern and set up an appointment.

- Don't go over a teacher's head without communicating with the teacher first.

continued

TOP TEN TAKEAWAYS, *continued*

TO DO

- Support your child's teacher by sending a thank you note, making sure homework is completed, reading with your child every night, and teaching your child to respect teachers.

- Ask the teacher's opinion. You're an expert on your child, your child's teacher is the grade level-expert. Acknowledge that you know how difficult the teacher's job is given all the needs of the other students, and collaborate.

- Email the teacher a heads-up or ask for a meeting if you sense a growing problem. Most teachers want to know when parents are concerned and want to have an open dialogue.

- Use the Power of P3 to deal with ineffective teachers in a professional, positive, and persistent way. This will also help your child get a better teacher match next year.

CHAPTER 8

Balancing Academics with Connection and Confidence

If a child lives with criticism, he learns to condemn,
If a child lives with encouragement, he learns confidence.
—DOROTHY LAW NEITE

Mr. and Mrs. Parker perch themselves on the pint-sized chairs, ready to discuss their eight-year-old son, Shawn. As their legs and knees spill over the table's edges, the teacher praises Shawn's success in math and science. But when she begins talking about his lack of friends and playing at recess, Shawn's father abruptly cuts her off. "Look, I don't care what my son is doing—or not doing—on the playground," he says. "I give him a quarter for every answer he gets right in the high school science book. That's the kind of play he likes and it's obvious he's going to be an engineer like me. So let's keep this conversation focused where it needs to be—on academics. What is this school doing to prepare Shawn for the science and math he's going to need in high school and (knock on wood) to get into MIT? What are you doing to challenge him in these subjects? I'm not seeing anything but worksheets."

While it's natural for parents to focus on their child's grades and academics, it takes more than a good report card to raise a confident and connected child. And in today's competitive world, this doesn't happen by accident. With so much external pressure influencing our children—from parents, schools, coaches, social media, reality TV, colleges, and our culture at large pushing kids to do more, play harder, be smarter—it's no surprise that we have more children suffering from stress and anxiety disorders today than ever before.

This chapter discusses what it takes to keep our kids balanced—confident, connected, and resilient—so they get a well-rounded education and become happy adults. And what parent doesn't want their child to be happy? It's the number-one answer parents cite when asked what they want for their children in life. The problem is, we've lost perspective on what "happy" means. Many parents narrowly define happiness now as success—based on grades, achievement, or what level team or college accepts our children. This chapter will explore how we can instill confidence, connection, and resilience in our children without pushing, pulling, or labeling them. It will also reveal why praising effort versus smarts or outcome ultimately leads to a more competent and happy child.

Three Ways to Foster a Confident, Connected, and Resilient Child

Based on my twelve years of experience working with schools, teachers, parenting experts, and child psychologists, I've concluded that there are three ways to foster a confident, connected, and resilient child—and none of them have anything to do with grades or taking tests. Ironically, they begin with A, B, and C, so they are easy to remember.

First, it's important for every child to connect to an accepting adult (A), who encourages, empathizes with, and acknowledges the child for who he is, not what he does or who he'll be. This adult makes the child feel accepted. Next, every child needs to have a buddy (B), a similar-aged friend or relative with whom he plays and navigates the social and emotional waters of life from kindergarten on. Finally, every child needs a competence (C), a strength or interest (or more than one) that a child discovers and nurtures with help from others. This competence is best developed through praising hard work and effort. Let's take an in-depth look at each of these factors.

AN ACCEPTING ADULT

One of the speakers I've hosted through my nonprofit is Dr. Robert Brooks, author of many books, including *Raising Resilient Children*. Dr. Brooks maintains that children who grow up confident and resilient have at least one adult in their life (and perhaps more than one) from whom they draw strength. Dr. Brooks refers to that person as a "charismatic adult," a term coined by the late Dr. Julius Segal. This person may be a parent—or a relative, teacher, coach, or another adult who makes a child feel unconditionally loved and special.

Chapter 1 introduced the idea that our role as parents is to walk along the banks of our child's river to support, encourage, and guide (rather than push or pull) our child through his journey. In order to do this, we first need to accept the uniqueness and individuality of our children. From there, we love them and believe in them no matter where they are along their river. We may not always like their behavior or their grades but we still need to love them. Easier said than done, I know. Kids often turn out different from what we expect. And anyone who has more than one child knows that siblings often have completely different minds, bodies, and motivations. What works for one child doesn't work for another. It's what keeps family life so dynamic and interesting.

Woven within the idea of an accepting adult is an essential thread of empathy and respect. This doesn't mean there's a lack of discipline or accountability for behavior. It means that when conflict occurs—when kids misbehave, bring home a report card we're not happy with, or develop an interest in an area we don't care for—we still love them for who they are.

Dr. Brooks discussed this idea during a talk at The Parent Connection, explaining that "empathy is the golden rule in understanding your children. It's your attempt to appreciate and validate your children's viewpoints that makes them feel unconditionally loved. The true test of being empathic is when you're frustrated or disappointed. Think about individuals in your own childhood who were your 'charismatic adults' and try to model this type of behavior for your own children."

To become confident and resilient, a child needs to feel accepted for who she is—not who her parents want her to be. A child who is realistically praised or acknowledged for what she does well feels more accepted than a child who is constantly criticized for her wrongdoings. When our confidence in our kids' behavior wanes, it's especially important to stay focused on their strengths and what they're doing well. Dr. Brooks went on to say, "Even on the worst day there is something positive to say about your child. This is tough territory for most of us because we have hopes for our children. It can be difficult to accept that sometimes those hopes play out differently than we expected."

Recognizing and acknowledging how your child feels, without passing judgment on a given situation, is a skill every parent needs to develop to be able to accept who our children are. A child wants to feel understood. Listening, acknowledging, and validating the feelings you hear from your child helps to create acceptance. We may not like that our child kicked another kid in the shins at recess, but we can understand and acknowledge how he felt about doing it at the same time we dole out the consequence for the action. When we are empathetic toward our children, it also teaches them to be empathetic toward others. Empathy is a quality that can be nurtured at an early age.

My dad is at the top of my list of charismatic adults in my life. He is also a wonderful role model for teaching empathy. When I was nine years old, we moved from upstate New York to Michigan. My parents wanted to make sure we received a quality public school education, so they bought a house in a town that laid claim to one of the best school districts in the state—a town that also bordered a rundown city.

On a cold Sunday evening after Thanksgiving that year, my dad took my siblings and me for a ride. As we crossed the unmarked border to the city, I remember watching the perfect patchwork of lawns and neatly trimmed brick homes suddenly turn to broken slabs of concrete, washed-out brown fields divided by cyclone fencing, and boarded-up homes with gutters falling into overgrown bushes. We would occasionally see a person dressed in gray and black layers sauntering down the crumbled sidewalks. When we came to a large open field, my father stopped the car. We watched the scene in silence. I spoke first. "Dad, why are all those people standing around that garbage can watching the fire? Why aren't they trying to put it out? Is the fire department coming?"

My father's response left an indelible mark on my brain. "Those people, honey, are trying to stay warm. They started that fire because they don't have anywhere else to go." After a long silence, he added, "We have much to be thankful for."

That experience taught me empathy, acceptance, and compassion like no other. Adults who model acceptance and empathy teach kids to look at the world through a lens of compassion and empathy. Providing children with opportunities like this teach empathy and compassion at an early age. Children inherently want to help parents, coaches, teachers, other children, and those less fortunate. Involving kids in chores at home, joining the Best Buddies program at school (helping special needs children), and participating in charitable work—walks for hunger, food drives, soup kitchens—fosters empathy, compassion, and confidence. And children who are empathic and compassionate are more likely to find an easy time with the second strategy: making friends.

A BUDDY

The law of attraction dominates in elementary school friendships: like attracts like. Kids want to play with kids who have similar interests and activities. A six-year-old girl who likes to play dolls or house naturally gravitates to girls who want to do the same. An eight-year-old boy who likes video games or riding a scooter seeks boys who want to do the same. Temperament also comes into play. Two first-borns who are both on the bossy side or both on the shy side may not get along as well as an oldest and a youngest or two middle kids. Some kids want to be around many other children, others are more reserved and are content playing with one friend once in a while. These preferences are important to accept in our children and can sometimes be at odds when our kids are thrown into forced playgroups. Kids will begin to show marked preferences for whom they want to play with by age eight or nine; this occurs earlier for some girls. This is when many may have outgrown parent-arranged playdates, so it is best not to force the issue.

Most important is that your child have at least one buddy at some point during the elementary years with whom she can begin to build a friendship; a friend with whom she can start to understand what a two-way loyal, trustworthy relationship means. If this turns out to be just one special friend in your child's life, that's great. Some kids prefer to have one good friend that they request to play with regularly. This is completely within the normal range. Other kids may prefer to have three to five friends that they rotate between, and that is okay, too. What matters more is how your kids feel about their social situation.

If you hear your child constantly claim "no one likes me" or "I have no friends," or if you see a revolving door of a new friend every few months, it's important to acknowledge that something may be going on. This can be very difficult to deal with because no parents want to see their child hurt or excluded. Some kids are rejected because they come off too aggressively or because they are compensating for something else. This may play out as trying to be the class clown to win friends or picking on a smaller child to gain stature within a social group. Some kids struggle to pick up on social cues. The good news is that these are skills that can be learned. Whatever the case, your child is likely to benefit if you seek some guidance from a teacher or a counselor because the behavior is probably showing up at school, too. Teaching a child empathy and cooperative skills is easier and more effective during the elementary years than later on.

A note or email to your child's teacher will get the ball rolling: "I'm noticing some social issues that concern me. I'm wondering what you are seeing in the classroom and if we could discuss the situation." Nurturing the skills our children need to develop balanced and healthy relationships is important. Teach them how to be friendly: "Say hi and look them in the eye." Teach them to be empathic: "How would you feel if Becky dropped you for another friend when you already had a playdate scheduled with her?" Kids learn how to relate to others based on how you relate at home and what is discussed at home. Share your family values about friendships and why they are important. Talk about your own childhood friendships to help your children put things into perspective. I always tell my kids, "You don't have to be friends with every kid in the neighborhood, but you do have to be friendly." Many schools now have social skills groups set up at lunch—called "lunch bunch" or "banana splits"—that encourage kids to talk about their feelings and work cooperatively together. Including a model kid in the group is a plus, so if your child is invited, don't assume it's because she needs skill building.

Let's go back to Shawn at the beginning of the chapter, who has keen strengths in science and math but no desire to play with other kids his age. Shawn's mother came to me because she was concerned with her husband's refusal to acknowledge Shawn's lack of friendships. I explained to her that

Shawn may just be a slow-to-warm-up kid who hasn't found any like-minded kids in his class. As a first step, I recommended his parents seek out clubs or activities for him that are more likely to have other kids with an aptitude for math or science, like Destination Imagination, a LEGO Club, or any of the other resources at www.theparentbackpack.com. I encouraged her to speak to the teacher about helping to pair up Shawn with another child in class he could help. I also suggested she talk with the principal and request a strong math and science teacher and a peer with similar interests the following year so that both an adult and friend connection could be forged. While math and science may be a core interest for Shawn, it's also important his parents encourage Shawn to develop other interests and competencies.

A COMPETENCE

When it comes to a child's strengths in elementary school, I often hear parents say, "He isn't really showing a core strength yet" or "She's not really good at any one thing yet, she's trying a variety of activities." That's understandable because some children's strengths or competencies won't come out until later in their elementary years. Sometimes a child is doing many activities, but doesn't have time to practice and become good at any one thing. One of your child's aptitudes may be on the football field or the soccer field, in the pool or on the dance floor. Another may be math, reading, or science. Or he may like music, drawing, or working with his hands. Some may still be developing, but not yet discovered. When elementary kids experiment with different interests and activities—as they should be doing at this age—our role as parents is to encourage and praise the progress they make and the effort they put in rather than the outcome, the win, or the grade. Natural talent and hard work are only half the game. The other half is the child's mindset about what she is doing.

Psychologist Carol Dweck is an expert on the subject of a child's mindset. Her research shows that focusing on a child's effort or how hard she works—called a "mindset of growth"—rather than how smart the child is—called a "fixed mindset"—leads to developing competencies and better grades. I knew about this theory but never really understood the reasoning behind it until I read her research—and tried it out on my own kids—with great success.

In one of Dweck's studies, she gave four hundred kids a simple task to do. When they finished, they were randomly divided into two groups. One group was told, "Wow, you're really smart." The other was told, "Wow, you are working really hard." Dweck was testing whether these simple words could alter a student's mindset. Each group was then given a choice. They could take a hard test or an easy test. Ninety percent of the group that was told they were hardworking wanted to take the tougher test—they wanted to show how hard they could work. Two-thirds of the "smart" group chose the easier test; they did not want to risk losing their "smart" label. Then they repeated the first test. Though it was no harder, the scores of the "smart" group *dropped* 20 percent while the "hardworking" group *improved* by 30 percent. Dweck explained that emphasizing effort gives a child a variable that he can control. They come to see themselves as being in control of their success. Emphasizing natural intelligence takes it out of a child's control. Focusing on effort teaches children that they are in charge of their "smarts" and leads to self-confident kids who feel more competent.

Kids who think they are smart often feel that they don't need to make an effort. They can rely on their natural "gifts." When the smart label is continually reinforced, they are less likely to take on new or difficult challenges for fear of not looking smart. They can't control the outcome.

"STAC" YOUR PRAISE

Here's an acronym to help you move beyond "How'd you do on the test?" or "Did you win?" STAC your praise on your child's efforts and progress. This will help you keep your language focused on the hard work and effort your child puts in rather than the outcome or his smarts. If the theory holds, motivation, competencies, and grades will follow.

S: Be specific in what you praise.

T: Keep it timely.

A: Be authentic. (Don't praise effort when there was none.)

C: Praise only what your child can control.

Kids who believe they are hard workers are more motivated to try. They focus on the learning. They can control the results. This produces a more resilient kid who generally gets better grades, a kid who says, "I'm a hard worker; I can do it." The more a child is internally motivated to do something rather than externally motivated by an outside reward system, such as grades or treats for doing well, the more likely he will become a lifelong learner. (Internal motivation is often referred to as *intrinsic motivation* while external motivation is called *extrinsic motivation*. A balance between these two systems of motivation is key to success in school.)

Whenever I meet or speak with parents about their child and school, I find it helpful to get a sense of how their child is viewed in the family. When there is more than one child, the response inevitably moves to a comparison or labeling in some way. This is naturally how human beings process, so it's understandable that it happens. Here is a recent and typical response to the request "Tell me a little bit about Chris" from a mother who was frustrated about her third child's lack of success in school. "Well, I hate to say this, but Chris . . . is my lazy one. His older sister is my reader, my student. She flew through elementary school, no problem. And his older brother has done well—he's my athlete. No issues there, he finds a way around everything. But Chris is still trying to figure out who he is, other than a couch potato. We had him tested and he's got plenty of smarts. But he hates school, lives for TV, video games, and his friends, and occasional skateboarding—when he gets his lazy butt off the couch. He's also starting to play and hang around with some boys we're not too sure about. He only has one more year in elementary school. So we want to get him on the right track—before it's too late."

I cringe when I hear the "L" label from parents, partly because I've been guilty of using it myself. I hear it often from parents. Chris was probably labeled "lazy" in his family from an early age. As a result, he sees himself in this way. Children naturally define themselves based on how they are perceived by others. And the pronoun abuse—my athlete, my reader, my student—is common too, as if children are sheep that we own, shear, and shepherd along the path. Every child has strengths or gifts, waiting to come out. It just takes longer for some to unfold. The more labels or comparisons we slap on our kids, the longer it will take them (and us) to discover where their strengths are. They are crushed before they have a chance to bloom. The ideal age for children to nurture and explore different activities, interests, and hobbies is between the ages of seven and eleven. Kids don't always discover strengths on their own; they learn about and define themselves through others. They need an adult to foster and encourage their strengths by exposing them to different experiences and to accept where their interests are leaning so they can build competencies.

Mark's parents were tired of the school's negative perception of their third grade son. This had gone on year after year. In conferences, teachers continued to label him a distraction to other students, saying he played the class clown on a daily basis, probably as a way to mask his own deficits in attention and his ability to concentrate. Mark's dad believed he was labeled back in kindergarten and has suffered from a chronic carryover of this perception in each subsequent grade. This year Mark felt his teacher called him out for anything that happened in class and picked on him daily, no matter how hard he tried.

Meanwhile, his parents began to see some strength in his athletic and spatial ability. Coaches recognized his hand-eye coordination in baseball, and his parents noticed his amazing doodling and cartoon drawings on his notebooks. In a meeting with the school psychologist and the teacher, Mark's dad asked, "How can we tap Mark's strengths to shore up his weaknesses? We see some real strengths here, and I hope we can all work together to bring them out rather than hyperfocus on the bad things he does. Mark could use a little support around what he does well."

When I asked Dr. Brooks, the originator of the concept "islands of competence," about this idea of nurturing competencies, he told me: "Every child possesses islands of competence . . . or areas of strength. As parents, we must promote and praise these areas rather than focus on a child's weaknesses. Self-worth, hope, and resiliency come from experiencing success in areas of life that children and others deem important. Once children discover their strengths and believe in themselves, they are able to confront areas that are more problematic for them." So the more competent a child feels, the more motivated she is to try another activity or skill. Fostering islands of competence leads to a more confident child. The feeling of "I did it" breeds a desire to do it again and again and learn more each time.

Dr. Edward Hallowell is a best-selling author and clinical psychiatrist who writes and speaks frequently about childhood connection and competency. In his book *The Childhood Roots of Adult Happiness,* Dr. Hallowell shares the five steps that he believes lead to a confident, connected childhood: connection, play, practice, mastery, and recognition. The most important of these concepts is connection, which transcends the other steps.

1. **Connection:** The process begins with a child who needs to feel a close, satisfying relationship with an adult, a mother or father (or a single caregiver), and feel taken care of, understood, and loved unconditionally.

2. **Play:** Next, children need to play to learn to solve problems, discover their talents, and learn how to maneuver socially. Here Hallowell stresses the importance of human versus electronic connection.

3. **Practice:** In order to make progress—any amount—children must practice the same skill again and again. According to Dr. Hallowell, "The connection kids feel in making progress is more important than where the child ends up. Some gentle nudging may be necessary to ensure a child sticks to an activity, but keep the focus on progress."

4. **Mastery:** With practice and progress come mastery. "Mastery is a feeling, not an achievement," says Hallowell. "When a child achieves a new skill and feels good, he feels motivated to tackle new challenges. This leads to increased self-confidence, positive self-esteem, and a can-do, optimistic attitude."

5. **Recognition:** Finally, recognition is needed to link the bridge from mastery back to connection. "Kids need supportive, balanced acknowledgment and praise from parents, teachers, and peers for a job well done," reiterated Hallowell. "It instills personal pride and connectedness, which kids need to feel competent."

Multiple Intelligences

Woven within the ABCs of a confident, resilient kid—an adult, a buddy, and a competency—are different types of intelligences that go beyond the traditional IQ measurement.

Up until the late 1980s, people believed that intelligence was an inherited gene that could be assessed by a single measurement called IQ, or the intelligence quotient. Developed in the early 1900s, IQ measured a narrow slice of cognitive abilities. Ninety-five percent of people scored between 70 and 130, with the average score at around 100. It was used to label how "smart" a person was, and it is still used in some circles today. However, new research suggests that intelligence can be influenced through environmental factors that can effect an IQ score by ten to fifteen points. In the past few decades, different theories of intelligence have been developed, including Dr. Howard Gardner's theory of multiple intelligences, which has gained widespread support in educational circles. Gardner's book, *Multiple Intelligences*, suggests that seven spheres of intelligence exist in human beings, which include:

- **Linguistic intelligence:** the capacity to learn spoken and written language easily. Children who learn to read at age three or four usually have high linguistic intelligence.

- **Logical–mathematical intelligence:** the capacity to think logically, carry out mathematical operations, and reason deductively. Children with strong math skills at an early age are more likely to possess a high mathematical intelligence.

- **Musical intelligence:** the ability to recognize, compose, and appreciate musical patterns, tones, and rhythms. This intelligence often works in tandem with logical–mathematical intelligence.

- **Bodily–kinesthetic intelligence:** the ability to use one's body to solve problems and use mental abilities to coordinate bodily movements. Children who have strong eye-hand coordination at an early age are usually high in kinesthetic intelligence.

- **Spatial intelligence:** the capacity to recognize and use patterns of space and area. This may or may not correlate to logical mathematical intelligence. Children with strong art skills at an early age are usually strong in spatial intelligence.

- **Interpersonal intelligence:** the ability to understand the intentions, motivations, and desires of other people. Educators, salespeople, and counselors usually have a well-developed interpersonal intelligence.

Very young children with keen empathy skills often have strong interpersonal intelligence.

- **Intrapersonal intelligence:** the capacity to understand the self, one's feelings, fears, and motivations. This involves the ability to regulate one's emotions and impulses.

Dr. Gardner believes that every human being possesses a unique set of intelligences that reflect a mix of these traits. Some children may have an equal share of each; others have a particular strength or competency in one area. No matter what intelligences your child possesses, each and every child has competencies and strengths that can be nurtured well through the adolescent years. It's our job as parents and teachers, working together, to help recognize, nurture, and celebrate the efforts and progress our children make in these areas—whatever they may be—through their elementary years and beyond.

What children learn from the mistakes they make, a form of intrapersonal intelligence, helps them become more resilient. Self-regulating their own reactions to mistakes is key and often mirrors how parents react to their mistakes. To make a mistake is to learn a lesson. Let's take a closer look at how mistakes, which we tend to think of as "bad," can actually help build a child's resilience.

How Mistakes Build Resilience

Dr. Brooks contends that resilient children have learned how to view mistakes as learning opportunities. They can identify the problem, consider options, and judge what might be the best solution. "If you always have the answer for your child, they can't possibly learn to become resilient," Dr. Brooks stated in his talk. "Natural and logical consequences are what you strive for; hitting, humiliating, or using emotionally abusive words produces angry and resentful children." Dr. Brooks often uses the example of how parents react when a child spills milk. This example resonates with me because I didn't always handle this in the best way before I heard him speak.

Think about your reaction when your child knocks over a glass of milk. If it's along the lines of "How many times do I need to tell you . . . ? You need to be more careful . . . Why are you always so clumsy . . ." it's time to rethink. More appropriate reactions—such as saying nothing and getting a sponge to teach him how to clean it up, saying "It's okay, everybody spills milk," or getting the sponge to clean up together—will produce a more confident, resilient child.

As parents, we can help our children by not reacting to a child's mistakes with judgmental or derogatory comments. Rather, use mistakes as teachable, problem-solving moments. When children know they won't be condemned or criticized for their mistakes, they're more confident and motivated—and more willing to take realistic risks. Dr. Brooks suggests that parents ask themselves, "'Is my child a stronger person because of what I said today?' Monitoring and changing repetitive, negative scripts that often play out from our own issues may be necessary."

....

This chapter defined three ways to raise confident, connected, and resilient children. We discussed the importance of praising effort and progress over smarts, why labels are dangerous, how to reinforce competencies in our children, and why mistakes lead to greater confidence.

In the next chapter, we'll review what to do when you child needs extra support or special education services.

TOP TEN TAKEAWAYS

TO CONSIDER

- The three ways to foster a confident, connected, and resilient child from kindergarten through grade five include a connection to an accepting adult, a similar-age buddy, and a supported, nurtured competence.

- Recognizing and understanding your child's temperament will make you a more accepting and effective parent throughout the elementary years and beyond.

- Every child possesses islands of competence; it's our job as parents to recognize, nurture, and foster those interests or strengths that naturally unfold in our children.

- Research shows that the traditional method of measuring IQ is narrow and outdated; multiple types of human intelligence exist that can be influenced by environmental factors.

TO AVOID

- Don't label your children in negative ways; criticism blocks competencies in development.
- Don't criticize or react to your child's mistakes with judgmental or derogatory remarks.

TO DO

- Accept your children's uniqueness and who they are, even when you don't like what they do.
- Listen, acknowledge, and validate your children's feelings. Empathize with them so they feel accepted for who they are.
- Encourage your children to build healthy friendships through empathy and compassion.
- Praising your children's efforts and progress (rather than the outcome or their smarts) leads to a more confident, competent child.

CHAPTER 9

When Your Child Needs More Support

All children have gifts. They just choose to open them.
at different times. —UNKNOWN

Dan and Susan feel themselves going numb. As the teacher describes their son's situation, the words "failing to make progress" hang in midair. Dan takes the kick-in-the-gut staring straight ahead. Panic permeates Susan's body. Fragments of sentences echo around her: below grade level reading . . . not responding to RTI . . . intervention . . . expected to boost progress . . . not working . . . smart boy . . . struggling in phonemic awareness . . . his scores . . . not improving. Susan's hearing returns: ". . . so Michael needs to be evaluated to help us identify exactly where the problems are. It's likely he will need some extra support—either an Individualized Education Plan (an IEP) or some curriculum accommodations, what we call a 504 Plan. We'll follow up the evaluation with a team meeting as soon as possible. I'm sorry, Mr. and Mrs. Mallone, I know this is a lot of information for a fifteen-minute meeting. But I know this is the right step for your son."

"We were worried last year, we should have done something." Dan takes Susan's hand and breaks the silence. "We have no idea what all this edu-jargon means, Mrs. Mallone—other than Michael isn't reading at a second grade level. We'll do whatever we can to help him, but . . . we don't even know the questions to ask."

Learning that your child needs extra support, learns differently, or may benefit from special education services can be very distressing. Watching your child struggle to decode a word, add numbers that don't add up, or wrangle over how to spell a three-letter word while you sit helpless, wishing you could wave a wand and fix it all, is even more distressing. Perhaps your instincts said something seemed off, but you pushed them aside. Or maybe the teacher said she'll be fine, she'll catch up, kids move at different paces. But she didn't. You're still not sure. You knew something wasn't right, or you feel it now. But you have no idea what "it" is, what questions to ask, or how to begin the process of understanding the complex world of special education.

At some point in their six-year journey through elementary school, many kids will struggle on some level, in some area. It may be a short-term breakdown solved in a few months, or a longer-term disability that's diagnosed and solved through an IEP. Whatever the case, you are not alone—and your child is not alone. One in every ten kids lives with a diagnosed disability. Another 3 to 4 percent receive some kind of extra support or services for a deficiency. And many of them thrive. In fact, many of the world's great scientists, CEOs, and athletes, including Albert Einstein, JetBlue founder David Neeleman, and Olympic swimmer Michael Phelps all turned their learning challenges into greatness.

Entering the churning waters of extra help, special services, or special education for your child is one of the most overwhelming and scary experiences you'll encounter—and for good reason. This is complicated, emotional territory. Besides the legal terms, procedures, and acronyms that are foreign and intimidating, parents struggle with their own fears about the situation and their child's future. This chapter will give you an overview of special education and extra support—what it is and how it works. It will also give you a system for keeping your head focused on your child, where it needs to be. The most important thing as you begin this journey together is that your child gets the support she needs. This may mean Response to Intervention (RTI) for a few months, an accommodation plan (504 Plan), or an Individualized Education Plan (IEP) that will carry him throughout his elementary journey. But whatever form of support your child receives, your reaction to it, how you handle the situation, and the relationship you build with the school in the process will follow you for as long as your child is enrolled in school. You're building a new bridge, and an important one.

This chapter is not meant to be diagnostic or to help you analyze a complicated IEP. There are many clinicians and books that will help you do that, some of which are listed at www.theparentbackpack.com. This chapter will help you understand the signs of struggle and procedures schools use to evaluate and diagnose learning issues. You'll come away understanding how teachers know when kids are on or off track, how kids are evaluated, and what all those acronyms mean in the world of accommodations and services. Importantly, it will help you stay focused, support your child, and ensure she gets the services she needs.

Response to Intervention

Teachers today have more data on their students, more information on where they stand academically, than ever before. What's driving this trend is standardized testing and Response to Intervention, or RTI. *RTI* refers to short-term instruction strategies, or an approach to teaching, that provide students with different levels of support. As part of the regular classroom experience, RTI is now considered a best practice in elementary schools in literacy and math, and sometimes in behavioral areas. It is always data driven and evidence based, meaning the support levels are determined based on the results of your child's testing and assessments. Student progress is monitored very closely. If a program is working, that support is continued; if it is not working, a different program is tried.

RTI is typically tiered into three levels. Level one is general education that targets the whole class. After seeing the results of level one, students are separated into small groups of three to six kids based on their performance and instructional needs. These level two groups are given extra support in targeted areas, while level three groups are given even more targeted and often one-to-one instruction. For example, in a first grade class, a group of students may need extra support in phonemic awareness so they can master blending (putting prefixes with other letters, such as *push*, *pushed*, *pushing*, and *push-up*) or making compound words (like *backpack*, *backyard*, and *backward*). Another group of kids may require help with reading fluency strategies (such as recognizing commas, periods, and exclamation points). These two groups requiring extra support would both be considered level two interventions. A few of these kids may need even more support in phonics (sounding out basic words) and require one-to-one instruction. This is considered level three intervention. All levels are provided through the regular teacher and an in-class coteacher, special education teacher, instructional assistant, or teacher's aide. In school districts that use RTI, this targeted instruction may be done three times a week for eight weeks or twice a week for many months, depending on the needs. RTI benefits kids because they get a concentrated dose of specific instruction exactly where they need it. Once a child is tested, the results of the test are used to make decisions about next steps or additional support. This information can also help to diagnose learning disabilities early, or, in the case of behavioral problems, it can be used to redirect inappropriate behavior or target kids who need emotional or social support. While a few critics argue that RTI might keep kids off full special education plans longer than needed, most educators believe RTI is an effective instruction strategy for boosting kids' success and providing extra support where needed. If your school is not currently using RTI as a best practice, you may want to ask some questions about why not or what they offer in its place. If you don't like what you hear, find a teacher who's in favor of it, some like-minded parents, and consider forming a group to advocate for it.

Recognizing Signs of Struggle

Today many, but not all, learning issues that elementary children experience are caught between kindergarten and third grade. Some problems may appear later on. Generally, the earlier challenges are detected, the easier they are to remedy. Discovering your daughter has *dyslexia* (a language-based learning disability) by the end of first grade is far better than finding out in third grade. Diagnosing your son's *ADHD* (attention-deficit/hyperactivity disorder) in second grade is better than fourth grade. So follow your instincts and keep your antennae up. Many schools are responsive to children's needs and do a good job of recognizing, identifying, and screening children. Others are not. Sometimes the school is diligent, but your child's teacher isn't devoting the extra time your child needs. The reality is, when dollars are short, you don't want your child to be on the wrong side of the bottom line. When budgets are tight, as they often are in school districts today, schools wait for parents to request an evaluation, especially for kids who are borderline cases, rather than initiate it themselves. So don't be shy about asking.

ACADEMIC STRUGGLES

There are as many signs of academic struggle as there are learning disabilities. If your child refuses to go to school, fear probably lies behind his refusal to go. A fear that needs to be uncovered. It may be emotional; it may be academic. If it continually takes your child excessive amounts of time to do homework, alert your child's teacher. If he hates to read, refuses to read, or detests spelling and cannot get the words right despite studying them for hours, there is probably something else going on. If your child can read but doesn't understand what he just read, you need to talk to the teacher.

Your child's report card will also signal issues. This is where having a standards-based report card helps. Areas that should be developed or proficient by a certain time period are typically shaded. If you find your child's performance continually falls in "needs improvement" areas without showing any progress, speak to the teacher about it. If these issues have not been previously identified by or discussed with a teacher, ask questions. "Does my son need more support?" "What support systems are in place now?" "May I see the results of his reading fluency tests?" "Do you feel he needs to be evaluated?"

BEHAVIORAL STRUGGLES

It was easy to identify Jason in a classroom. He was always the one trying to be funny or distracting other kids. He would yell out when the teacher gave a lesson, tell a joke when it was time to read, or throw something when he was called on to answer a question. Jason was subconsciously deflecting a learning issue, but both his teachers and parents were continually focused on fixing his behavior.

Inappropriate behaviors sometimes mask learning difficulties. Kids don't want to look stupid so they act out to take the focus off the real problem. They'd rather look funny or be labeled a troublemaker than be thought of as "dumb." This is especially true closer to third grade when kids become more aware of the "smart" kids in the class. Raise a concern with the teacher if you think your child may fit this profile and it hasn't been explored before.

Identifying and Diagnosing the Problem

If your child's teacher has identified a challenging area for your child, as was the case with Michael, who was discussed at the beginning of this chapter, and you agree that further testing is needed, then a core evaluation of your student will be conducted. If the teacher doesn't believe further testing is warranted, but you do, a parent (or a guardian, pediatrician, psychologist, or day-care provider) can request that your child be evaluated by putting the request in writing to the teacher and sending a copy to the principal or special education director. An email is sufficient. By law, within five days of receiving your letter, the school must provide you with a consent form to test your child, or a referral letter from a teacher. Once signed, your child must be tested within thirty days (these are thirty school days, not weekend or holidays). A legal timeline kicks in once a consent-to-evaluate form is signed. At this point, a team is created for your student, consisting of the parents, teacher, school psychologist, special education teacher, and a team coordinator. Once the testing and report are complete, a team meeting is called. Each team member is expected to contribute to the meeting with insight and perspective on the child.

TESTING

A qualified psychologist administers tests and evaluates your child. This may be a school psychologist or, if you choose to do the evaluation independently with an outside organization and pay for it yourself, a credentialed child psychologist, psychiatrist, or neuropsychologist. Sometimes insurance plans will cover outside evaluations and sometimes they won't, so check with your health-care provider before making a final decision about how to handle the testing. Outside independent testing may provide a more comprehensive assessment than the public schools, but not always. Many public schools do a good job with evaluations; some don't. To better understand your school's reputation on testing and evaluations, ask other parents who have experienced it or ask a SEPAC board member (see page 185). It's important to note that the school doesn't automatically accept the diagnosis and recommendations from an outside psychologist, or even a neuropsychologist. Teachers and parents will also be asked to provide perspective in the form of questionnaires on progress, social, emotional, and educational history by the testers. This insight is very important to the evaluation process, so be sure to fill the forms out accurately.

Your child will take a battery of tests that assess the following areas: cognitive intelligence, language-based skills, visual-based skills, visual-motor integration, communication, memory, attention, executive functioning, social-emotional factors, and other assessments related to the suspected disability. This usually takes four to eight hours, over one or two days, depending on the number of tests given. The psychologist will then provide a written summary of the results, give their impressions, and define the student's needs in detail. For ESL (English as a Second Language) students, the law requires that parents receive this report in their first

SPECIAL EDUCATION AND ACCOMMODATION LAWS

There are two federal laws that protect children who receive extra services for their education. The first is called the Individuals with Disabilities Education Act (IDEA). Originally put into place in 1975, this law was reauthorized in 2004. Any state and school district that accepts federal funding for special education must comply with the minimum standards under IDEA. If your child's evaluation reveals a diagnosis or a disability that recommends "direct, specialized instruction," your child may be eligible for an Individualized Education Plan (IEP) under IDEA from the ages of three through twenty-one. If your child is transitioning from earlier support as a baby or toddler (known as early intervention) to preschool before age three, she may also be eligible for an IEP. The Free and Appropriate Education (FAPE) and Least Restrictive Environment (LRE) clauses are also embedded in this law. This basically means that your child will be educated, at no additional cost to you as a taxpayer, in the least restrictive environment possible. In other words, no child will be sent to another location to be educated unless it is necessary and agreed upon by the parents.

The second group of laws governing extra support in education is referred to as "Section 504." This is governed under Section 504 of the language. You have the right to receive a copy of this report two days prior to your team meeting, if you put this request in writing. At the same time, you may supply the team with any additional documents you want them to consider from your pediatrician, any prior testing, or schoolwork.

The Team Meeting

A team meeting will generally be scheduled two or more weeks in advance. Attendance by all members is critical. The purpose of the initial team meeting after an evaluation is to determine if your child is eligible for additional services and, if so, what those services look like to meet your child's needs—in short, what the IEP or the 504 Plan will include.

Rehabilitation Act of 1973 and the Americans with Disabilities Act (ADA) of 1990. Section 504 provides any child with a disability or deficiency "access" to the regular curriculum and after-school activities through "specialized accommodations"—any extra support that the child receives to help with a disability. In this simplest sense a pair of glasses is an accommodation for a child who has a vision problem. This law covers any disability that substantially limits hearing or vision, learning (reading and thinking), emotions, communication, health, or physical impairment. A child with a hearing loss may need a surround-sound FM system to learn in the classroom; a child diagnosed with ADHD may need to sit away from distractions to learn and concentrate; a child with a broken leg in a cast for twelve weeks may need a temporary medical 504 Plan to use the elevator or be excused from gym.

The distinction between an IEP and a 504 Plan is this: an IEP falls under special education. It requires "direct and individualized instruction" and possibly specialized services for the student. A 504 Plan provides a student with a disability "accommodations or access" to the general curriculum in the classroom, and may also provide some specialized services. In general, an IEP costs the school additional dollars; a 504 typically does not, but can, depending on the specialized services.

DETERMINING ELIGIBILITY FOR AN IEP

In the initial team meeting, determining eligibility is key. Subsequent team meetings, which happen at least once a year, involve setting new goals and adjusting the services as needed based on testing and progress made. There are three requirements for a child to be eligible for an IEP:

- The child is diagnosed with a disability based on the evaluation.
- The child is not currently making effective progress (this looks different for each child).
- Specially designed instruction to access the curriculum or related services are required for the child to progress. The recommendation from the evaluator must state "direct specialized instruction" and all team members must agree with this.

At times, members of the team may disagree with the evaluator's recommendations or diagnosis. When there is tension on these issues between parents and schools, or among team members in the school, meetings can get contentious. Parents are partners in this process and a critical part of the collaboration. It is generally in the best interest of parents to build a bridge with schools and use the Power of P3 in all communication related to special education and your child. This is not always easy, as emotions run high. Occasionally, a parent may choose to bring a special education advocate (a consultant or lawyer who is well versed in the laws and requirements of special education) to the meeting. If this is done, the school must be informed in advance or the meeting will be rescheduled. I'll discuss more about the relationship side of special education in the section titled "LISTEN and ACT" on page 181.

DETERMINING DISABILITY

A *learning disability* refers to your child's ability to store, process, or produce information. If your child is diagnosed with a learning disability or disorder, he learns differently than other children and usually needs to receive instruction in a way that matches how his brain neurologically processes information. Most learning disabilities are invisible because children with them seem to look and act within a normal range. Many of them, in fact, are very bright. But regardless of intelligence level, they will not be able to perform at the same level as their peers.

There are a number of specific learning disabilities:

- Attention-deficit disorder or attention-deficit/hyperactivity disorder (ADD/ADHD): problems with impulsivity, attention, or hyperactivity

- Auditory processing disorder: cannot distinguish between speech sounds

- Dyslexia: cannot process one or more areas of language or reading

- Dyscalculia: cannot comprehend math concepts

- Dysgraphia: severe trouble writing legibly with appropriate speed

- Dyspraxia: struggles with motor coordination

- Language learning disorder: trouble understanding spoken language and poor reading comprehension

- Nonverbal learning disorder (NLD): strong verbal skills but struggles with nonverbal cues such as body language, tone of voice, and social skills

- Visual perception disorder: struggles to notice or interpret visual information

Other, nonlearning-based disabilities include emotional disorders or disabilities, autism, speech impairments, severe mental and physical disabilities, and other health conditions. Emotional disorders often exacerbate or mask learning problems and learning disabilities can also hide emotional disorders.

Any of these conditions can be identified in the evaluation. Be sure you clearly understand your child's strengths and weaknesses once an evaluation is complete. An evaluator might indicate your child is strong verbally but weak in math and abstract reasoning, strong in rote memorization but shows slow processing speed. The testing—especially neuropsychological testing—covers a lot of cognitive and emotional ground. These are complicated tests and documents; it takes most parents, reading through the results multiple times and asking many questions, to grasp what the summaries mean. Teachers and counselors don't even understand all the data. Keep asking questions until you do.

Developing and Approving the Individualized Education Plan (IEP)

Once your child is eligible for an IEP, the team develops the plan. An IEP includes parent input or concerns, current progress, how the disability affects the student's progress, necessary accommodations and types of specialized instruction (content, methodology, and performance criteria), measurable annual goals, benchmarks to meet goals, a service grid of the specially designed instruction (the details of the service, frequency, type of personnel to deliver, and setting), extending school into summer and transportation (if applicable), and state standardized testing results. Sometimes, when the outcome is fairly predictable, a draft of an IEP is developed by the school in advance and presented to the team at the onset of a meeting. As a member of the team and your child's parent, be sure you understand and are comfortable with the recommendations.

When a parent agrees to the IEP and signs, it goes into effect. If there are some parts of the IEP the parent does not agree with, a parent can legally agree to the accepted parts that would begin immediately (this is considered partial agreement), while continuing to work out the remaining issues. When a parent outright rejects an IEP, it goes to the state for review and a stay-put clause goes into effect. This means your child's prior services remain in effect until a new IEP is signed. It's usually in the best interest of your child's progress to partially accept the services you are happy with and reject those that you want to discuss further. This way your child is at least getting some services to help her when she is struggling.

The 504 Plan

If your child is found ineligible for an IEP, it's usually because the majority of the team felt that "direct, specialized instruction or related services" are not necessary for your child to make effective progress—or there is not agreement on the diagnosis. At this point, you may agree to develop a 504 Plan. This is a less formal document, but a similar team approach (minus the special education personnel) is usually used to develop this plan. The coordinator for a 504 is often a school counselor. If you are in your first eligibility meeting and an IEP is ruled out, the special education folks may leave the meeting and it will become a 504 meeting. Or a separate meeting will be scheduled. A 504 Plan typically includes accommodations that will be made for a student's disability or disorder. A 504 does not require a full evaluation. An accommodation for a child who needs extra emotional support might be a hall pass to visit the school counselor at any point during the day; a student who has an auditory processing disorder may need to be placed in a classroom with a special sound system. Every accommodation agreed to in the team meeting is listed on the 504 Plan, and the school agrees to make these accommodations. If a child is diagnosed with ADHD, a few of the accommodations in a 504 may include being seated away from distractions, permission to chew gum in class, getting up to take breaks more often, or having extra time on tests. Because disabilities under 504 Plans now accommodate "concentration and learning," more children with ADHD are moving to 504 Plans rather than IEPs.

ADD/ADHD CONSIDERATIONS

Listening, sitting still, and concentrating are three skills required for success in school—and they are the three skills that children diagnosed with ADHD (attention-deficit/hyperactivity disorder) or ADD (attention-deficit disorder) struggle with the most. (For simplicity's sake, I will use the term *ADD* for the remainder of this chapter.) These are also skills that little girls are typically better at than boys. There's no question that the inherent structure of elementary education is biased toward girls, who are generally (but not always) more inclined to sit still, listen, and concentrate for longer periods of time. If you do have a child diagnosed with ADD, it's critical to build strong bridges so he ends up with teachers who understand—and accommodations that support—his needs and gifts, rather than fight his "deficits." The relationship you build with the teachers is far more important than a piece of paper with a list of required accommodations. Although children who are diagnosed with ADD have a neurological deficiency in their ability to concentrate and control their impulses—not necessarily an unwillingness—some teachers struggle with accepting this diagnosis. They misunderstand ADD, or lack the skills needed to reach and connect to kids with ADD. Getting your child placed with a teacher who understands and can relate to children with ADD is a good place to start.

Schools and teachers often recommend that kids diagnosed with ADD be medicated. When it comes to medication, ADD expert Dr. Ned Hallowell offered this advice when I interviewed him: "Schools are often too aggressive in pushing medication and parents are too quick to reject it. ADD medication has been around longer than most. It's safe and highly effective for many kids. Parents who do come around to it are usually amazed at the results." Hallowell also recommends that schools and parents take a strengths-based approach to ADD rather than harp on the deficit side. "Impulsive kids are often the most creative," says Hallowell. "Stubborn kids are also persistent, distractibility equals curiosity, and so on. Unwrapping the gifts of a child with ADD benefits kids, teachers, and parents." Helping a child with ADD feel positively connected to his strengths also boosts self-confidence. Aside from the accommodations a school provides for a child, parents can do a lot at home to support their children's ADD by making sure they get exercise every day and the right amount of sleep and nutrition, all of which play a big role in ADD. See chapter 13 for more information on fueling your child's body well and additional ADD resources at www.theparentbackpack.com.

AUTISM SPECTRUM CONSIDERATIONS

If your child is diagnosed with autism or is on the autism spectrum disorder (ASD) continuum, which includes Asperger's syndrome and PDD (Pervasive Developmental Disorders), other factors must be considered and specifically addressed by the IEP or 504 team. These include verbal and nonverbal communication needs; social-interaction skills development; needs resulting from unusual responses to sensory experiences; needs resulting from resistance to change in environment or routines; needs resulting from repetitive activities; needs for positive behavioral interventions, strategies, and support; and other needs that impact progress on the curriculum, including social-emotional development. Autism is one of the fastest-growing developmental disabilities in special education today, and many school districts are hiring specialists with autism expertise as a result. If your child has a diagnosis on the autism spectrum, and you have a choice in school systems, doing a thorough check on special education personnel and qualifications before deciding on a school would be in your child's best interest. Schools that have experts in applied behavioral analysis (ABA) are probably more able to service your child's needs than those without, even though you cannot specify personnel on an IEP. Visit the schools, meet the staff, and observe classrooms if you can. More resources on autism spectrum disorder are available on my website.

LISTEN and ACT: Managing Your Emotions

Now that we've reviewed the nuts and bolts around IEPs and 504 Plans, it's important to consider the emotional side of this world and all that it brings. Parenting today is difficult; add to that parenting a child with a learning disability or challenge, and you may find yourself over the edge. It's also easy to get too caught up in the process and procedures and lose sight of what's most important in all this: supporting your child and her needs, while maintaining balance in the rest of your family life.

Once you determine that your child learns in a different way or has a developmental disability, it's important to accept, embrace, and support the needs that grow out of the diagnosis. To help you manage the emotions and feelings involved in this process, I recommend a process called LISTEN and ACT. Anytime there is a new challenge with your child, and there will be many, this same cycle can be repeated. Here are the details for each step of the concept:

- **L**isten and empathize with your child.
- **I**dentify your own feelings about this situation.
- **S**hare your concerns and ideas with the teacher.
- **T**rust your gut and talk honestly about issues.
- **E**valuate the data or the evaluation.
- **N**avigate the options around your child's support and services.

- **A**dvocate for what your child needs.
- **C**onnect and communicate constantly with your child's teachers.
- **T**ake the time to do this.

If you can follow these steps using the Power of P3 (see chapter 5), you are more likely to get what your child needs in a reasonable time frame and to keep your child's self-esteem intact. It won't always be easy, but this will keep your focus where it needs to be. Let's take a closer look now at each aspect of LISTEN and ACT.

LISTEN TO YOUR CHILD

This is a key first step and one that is sometimes overlooked. Take the time to listen to how your child feels and how he learns. It may not be necessary to label the disorder to do this, but it is important to get your child to open up. Parents are often too quick to run to the teacher or jump to conclusions based on what they read. Or they want the discomfort to go away, so they grab onto simple solutions before they really know or understand the problem. Understanding the root of your child's situation is often as important as the solutions themselves. Listen to your child without labeling or judging. Empathize as you do this.

> "Michael, it must be really frustrating for you when you can't read the words. Tell me what that feels like. Tell me what your brain is thinking when the numbers don't add up. Tell me what you wish would happen. When the teacher says that, what does your brain think? How does it make you feel?"

Explain that many kids struggle in school. They just do it at different times. Take notes. Reinforce that you are here to help him and that you'll get through this together. If your child talks about feeling dumb, tell him that there are many different kinds of smarts and kids are smart in different ways. Remind him of something he did well this past weekend. If your child feels ashamed or is not comfortable talking with you about what he experiences, find someone else he can speak with. A child who feels understood is a happier child.

IDENTIFY YOUR OWN FEELINGS

When new information about your child comes at you quickly and you feel pressure to fix it, you may bury your own feelings about the situation. This is an overwhelming time. Try to take the time to quiet your mind and reflect on your own feelings. Finding another adult to support you in this journey is important. In many cases, disabilities are inherited, so this may bring up underlying issues about your own childhood and school years. It's important that you not let your own baggage cloud your vision and judgment on what is best for your child. Identifying how you feel and talking about those feelings will help you avoid that. In order for you to help and support your child, you need to accept and deal with the challenge yourself.

SHARE YOUR CONCERNS

While you are the expert on your child of five, seven, or nine years, your child's teacher is the expert on five-, seven-, or nine-year-olds. A special education teacher knows something about educating kids who learn differently. Respect this. Share your concerns and your ideas. Share what is working or not working at home. She may have other ideas for you; she may use your ideas in school. When the two experts on your child—you and your child's teacher—are exchanging information and hints about what works when, your child benefits in big ways. Remember, the relationship is more important than the piece of paper. Don't be afraid to share ideas or details. The more you share, the more she'll share.

TRUST YOUR GUT AND TALK HONESTLY

Trust is built through genuine and open communication, especially when issues or conflicts arise. Talk honestly about your concerns and your expectations. Relationships break down when trust is lost. If you are not feeling good about a service or a support your child is getting, trust that feeling and address it in an honest and open way with the teacher. Send a quick email or set up a meeting if it warrants discussion. Use the Power of P3 to communicate in an positive, professional, and persistent way. When issues build up, they only get worse. Don't wait for an annual team meeting to discuss a big concern. If your relationship is going well, there should be no surprises in your IEP or 504 meetings.

EVALUATE THE DATA OR THE EVALUATION

When the evaluation comes in, information overload will prevail for some time. Review it. Ask questions. Understand it. Use it. It's a tool to help get your child the support that is needed. Ask for results of benchmark tests in the classroom, reading fluency scores (MAZE, DIBELS, and others), and any other CBM (Curriculum Based Measurement) assessments. As long as you look at these results over the long haul and don't get hung up on one or two short-term results, they will help you get a clear picture of your child's needs. It's okay if you disagree with the school's perspective; just be professional in the way you approach your differences of opinion. Some people hire an advocate or a lawyer to help them out in IEP meetings. If you feel you need extra support in understanding testing and the special education world, this approach can be helpful. If you do hire an advocate, make sure you hire a reputable person who believes in building relationships with schools. Since advocates are not regulated by the state, you need to be sure to work with one who has experience and compassion. In most situations, you want to come to an IEP meeting ready to build a bridge, not fight the enemy. Keep in mind, the relationships you build with your child's special education teachers are just as important as the services written on a piece of paper.

NAVIGATE THE OPTIONS

Understanding all the possibilities around your child's support and services is important. Do your homework. An important part of understanding evaluations is to review the details and the subtest scores. There are lots of resources at www.theparentbackpack.com to help you. The more due diligence you do, the better your child's support will be. Parents who expect more from a school will generally get more, as long as their requests are within reason. Direct instructional support usually means hiring extra teachers or assistants to reach and teach your child. This is your child's right under FAPE (Free and Appropriate Education). If the school currently doesn't have the support in place that your child needs, then they may be obligated to get it, whether it's in the current budget or not.

ADVOCATE EFFECTIVELY AND ACT

Your school's director of special education or superintendent usually sets the culture for how special education is treated in the district. The best directors work with parents and keep open lines of communication. They also hire special education coordinators who recognize they are the face of special education in the district. Understand your school's reputation by talking to other parents and teachers. While you probably won't be able to change the culture in your child's short time there, knowing what you are dealing with will make you a more effective advocate for your child. You are building a long-term relationship when your child is on an IEP or a 504. The more professional you are in your approach with teachers and schools, the better the foundation your child will have in getting the support she needs. See chapter 3 to learn how to be a C+ parent, not adversarial or absent, as you advocate for your child.

Many public schools also have a Special Education Parent Advisory Committee (SEPAC), which can help you understand your rights in special education law. This group (formed and run by parents with the special education director as a liaison) meets regularly and will often provide parent workshops featuring specialists in learning and behavioral disabilities. If your school doesn't have a SEPAC chapter, and you feel there is a need for one, look into starting one by visiting a school near you that does. All it takes is some like-minded, dedicated parents on a mission and you'll find instant community. Check the resources section on my website for workshops, training, and advocacy.

CONNECT AND COMMUNICATE CONSTANTLY

The more regularly you communicate with your team, the better. Anytime there is new information, alert your child's teacher or the special education teacher. The better your connection to the teachers, school psychologist, and special education coordinator, the more likely your IEP will actually be read and followed by the teachers, the right services will be in place, and the more confident your child will feel in school. Sharing strategies that work at home with teachers and listening to strategies they use successfully in the classroom will also help your child's journey go more smoothly. Remember, each conversation you have with your child's teachers and counselors either strengthens or weakens the bridge you are building to your child's school. The stronger your bridge is, the more likely you are to get what your child needs.

TAKE TIME FOR YOU AND YOUR CHILD

All this action takes extra time and energy. But think of it as an investment in your child. It's important that you know your child's rights, strengths, weaknesses, and how he learns relative to his challenges so you can be his best advocate. But even more importantly, carve out time to connect with your child and do some fun things together that fill you both with positive energy.

....

This chapter has discussed the complex process of advocating for and educating a child on an IEP or a 504 Plan. It's not uncommon for parents to feel paralyzed at certain points in this journey. That's why it's important that you take care of yourself and get a strong support system in place. Your goal is to keep the process moving forward. It won't always be perfect. But if you build a strong bridge with teachers and schools and keep asking questions using the Power of P3, your child will get the support and services he needs. He will make progress. She can and will thrive.

The next chapter focuses on what you need to know to help your child navigate the cruel world of bullying, a world that often, but not always, affects kids with disabilities.

TOP TEN TAKEAWAYS

TO CONSIDER

- To be eligible for an IEP, a child must be diagnosed with a disability, not be making effective progress, and in need of specially designed instruction or services.

- A 504 Plan provides accommodations so your child can better access the curriculum. This does not require a core evaluation or formal diagnosis.

- The relationship you build with teachers and schools around extra support or special education services is just as important as the IEP or a 504 Plan.

TO AVOID

- Don't hyperfocus on the deficit side of ADD; impulsiveness is also creativity; stubbornness is persistence; distractibility is curiosity.
- Don't bury your own feelings in this process. To be sure your child gets the support she needs from you and the family around you, you must also take care of yourself.

TO DO

- Build a strong bridge with teachers and support staff; don't be afraid to ask questions. You are a partner in the process.
- After an evaluation, you should fully understand your child's strengths and weaknesses. Ask questions until you do.
- Listen to your child. A child who feels understood for how his brain learns differently is a happier, more confident child.
- Talk openly and honestly about your feelings, concerns, and ideas with your child, his teachers, and your family. The more sharing and trust there is between parents and teachers, the more likely your child is to thrive.
- Take the time to understand and learn everything you can about extra support and special education services. It will pay off for your child.

CHAPTER 10

The Social and Emotional Realities of Bullying

Kind words can be short and easy to speak, but their echoes are endless. —MOTHER TERESA

Ten-year-old Lauren lies in bed, pretending to be sick. When her mom yells up the stairs for the third time, Lauren's older brother grabs her cell phone in between bites of cereal, types in her password, and tosses the phone to his mom. "Lauren doesn't want to go to school because of all the nasty texts she's getting from her supposed best friends, Mom. It's been going on for a week now."

Shocked by this information, Lauren's mom clicks on an unopened text from Lilly, Lauren's best friend. "You're a loser, Lauren. Don't come near us at recess 2day." She clicks on another text from Mary-my-BFF. "Hey fats. We're done with you. Have fun eating lunch alone." She clicks on a third text from her friend Sara. "Get a life, Lauren." Scrolling further, Lauren's mom finds a string of similar texts.

Feeling like she's been punched in the stomach, Lauren's mother sits down. Her mind races about the meeting she needs to get to at work while guilt and fear about Lauren's situation overwhelm her. "Why did we give her that cell phone in fourth grade anyway? I knew that was a mistake," she thinks. "It looks like she's being bullied and bullying others. I don't even know where to begin!"

The explosion of bullying, texting, and cyberbullying in the past decade creeps into classrooms, cafeterias, buses, recesses, and our children's bedrooms at ages far younger than most adults realize. This chapter discusses the definition of bullying, the hidden emotions that come with it, and how traditional and cyberbullying affects your child, your family, and learning. Whether it's physical or verbal abuse at recess, nasty text messages, embarrassing photos on Snapchat or Instagram, or rude tweets, this chapter gives you the tools you need to address these issues with your children and their teachers in appropriate ways. It's important to know that a child's ability to learn is compromised when he feels threatened or scared. Bullying starts young and can be prevented when the right steps and corrective actions are put into place.

A Community Wake-Up Call

It's difficult to go one day in any school community without hearing the word *bullying*. Sadly, it's taken not one, but many youth suicides and violent acts of retaliation across the country for adults and politicians to wake up to the social realities our children face today. Social networking and its toxic byproduct of cyberbullying remains a constantly changing, hard-to-regulate world—a world that challenges children, parents, teachers, and law enforcers every day. The blame game played out at home, in schools, and on the fields is only natural: "The schools aren't doing enough," "Bullies are bred at home," "Kids will be kids," or even worse, "He's just a bad kid," or "She's just a mean girl." Whether a child is involved in bullying, witnessing bullying, or being bullied, the level of tolerance for disrespect and bullying today is everyone's problem. It infects our children's education, our family life, and the fragile fabric of our communities.

But thankfully, it's also an opportunity to take action rather than perpetuate these roles, a chance to create a culture where bullying is not okay and respect becomes the norm, at home and at school. As adults, we don't need permission to make sure our children are feeling emotionally connected or behaving in socially appropriate ways. Setting boundaries, staying connected, and knowing what our kids are really doing in cyberland or in the cafeteria is not only okay, but it's also our responsibility as parents. Kids get technology but not the impact it can have on others; parents usually understand the impact but aren't as aware of the technology. By working together and instilling good values in our kids at young ages, we can make smart decisions.

But how and when do we do this? What do we do when we don't like what we read in a text or see on the playground? How do we teach our kids to stand up for themselves? When do we get involved? In some ways, it's easier to stay ignorant about what's out there. But the ugly side of social networking and bullying hurts kids, families, schools, and our community. It's certainly a bigger issue than any child, parent, teacher, or coach should have to manage alone. This brings us back to Lauren's mom.

Feeling stressed and anxious, Lauren's mom picks up the phone and calls her husband. After explaining the situation to him, talking through their feelings, and identifying what to do next, they decide that she will take the day off work and stay home with Lauren to get to the bottom of what's really going on. Meanwhile, Lauren's dad handles the Internet research and pulls up the school bullying policy so they better understand what they're dealing with. He also finds a Bullying Prevention/Action Plan (which most schools now have) and shares the information. Mom's next step is to listen to Lauren, to empathize with how she must be feeling and understand her side of the story—what lurks beneath these nasty texts. She heads upstairs, telling herself to listen and be compassionate rather than reactive or demanding.

First Things First: Creating Your Support System

Lauren's mom creates a support system by calling her husband before she speaks to her daughter. While this may seem selfish or a bit odd, it is the best place to begin. She recognizes this is a serious issue that needs to be addressed now, rather than hoping it will work itself out. Dealing with a bullying situation, no matter how your child or your family is involved, is intimidating, difficult terrain—and doing it alone is even scarier. You may find that raw, primal instincts to protect your child come out of nowhere or that old wounds of your own reopen. How you handle the situation with your child and the school is critical to a successful outcome. You'll also be modeling for all your children, whether they are involved or not, on how to handle a problem of this sort in the future. Before you react to your child's situation or contact the school, lean on a spouse, friend, or another family member for emotional support. You will need it, and your child will benefit from that support, too.

Responding to Bullying Information

You know your child best. If something doesn't seem right, try to get your child to open up by empathizing with how she may be feeling or relating it to a situation that you experienced back in school. Don't overwhelm her with questions, but let her know you're there for her: "No matter what happens, Lauren, we're here to support you and we're going to help you get through this." Kids who feel understood are more likely to open up. "I'm not sure what you're going through, but I do know that kids sometimes say mean things, especially at recess, in the cafeteria, or in texts. It hurts to be called a name, to be physically threatened or feel excluded from a group. That happened to me when I was your age." Younger children might need help in identifying or labeling their feelings before they can talk about them. The key is to provide a few thoughts for your kids to think about and let them know you are there for them. Then listen. Once you understand the situation better, it may be necessary to make the school aware of what is going on.

If your child has a cell phone, this is also a good place to look for clues. And yes, you should know your children's passwords and have access to their accounts. Until they are eighteen, I consider this information semiprivate, meaning available to parents on an as-needed basis. If you see a string of texts or sexts (yes, texts with sexual language or graphics are happening as early as fourth and fifth grade), take a screen shot of them and print them out. When you revisit (not react to) the situation with your child, you can use this information to make important points. If the history of your child's cell phone is erased, then you have reason to believe there was inappropriate information being shared.

Resources and software to help you place limits on your child's cell phone and computer usuage can be found at www.theparentback pack.com. Now let's review the definition, signs, and different aspects of bullying, and how to handle them.

Recognizing the Signs of Bullying

Knowing the signs that lead up to bullying or cyberbullying is critical, no matter what role your child may play. One of the most common traits among children being bullied, whether it's in the cafeteria or over a text after school, is the fear that if they tell someone, their situation will get worse. Some have been threatened with retaliation if they snitch, an option that is already taboo in the unwritten code of social survival. So, very often, situations elevate to a significant level before a parent or a teacher is aware. Many kids also feel ashamed to talk about it with their parents or their friends, so they hide their fears and their tears.

Some of the classic signs to look for that suggest social issues may be brewing include a gradual or sudden lack of interest in school or a myriad excuses for staying at home. Over 150,000 students are absent every day because they feel unsafe at school. That's three million kids a month who are afraid to go to school. Other signs include a significant drop in grades, avoiding certain friends, unexplained scratches or bruises, ripped clothing, sleeping problems, becoming moody and angry for no apparent reason, spending a significant amount of time alone, not being able to separate from a cell phone or texting device, or not wearing or carrying a certain material possession because it's a target for a bully.

Facts about Bullying

Bullying affects nearly 30 percent of school-age children every month. Sixty-two percent of students say they either witnessed or are aware of others who are being bullied. While the number of bullying incidents reported in elementary school is higher than in middle school, the severity of the situations increases from sixth to eighth grade, when peer pressure to conform peaks. The word *bullying* is often misused to describe teasing, bickering, social conflict, name-calling, rejection, or physical roughhousing—behaviors that happen on an occasional, infrequent, or random basis. Understanding the real definition of bullying is important for parents, teachers, and kids. Though each state describes it slightly differently, the basic tenets of the definition are similar.

Bullying involves an imbalance of power over another person. It's about control over a target who feels vulnerable and unable to stop the harassment. Bullying violates a child's right to feel safe and secure, either in school or transitioning to or from a school building. It occurs face-to-face, electronically over the Internet (cyberbullying), or through written or typed notes. Bullying takes many forms today, including physical or verbal abuse, threats, emotional intimidation, harassment, or exclusion that intentionally, selectively, and repeatedly harms a person or a person's property. *Intentional*, *selective*, and *repeated* are key words here that distinguish bullying from random teasing or sporadic social conflict. More than one form is often used. In most states, the law now requires that a child be written up for harassment and turned over to the authorities when accused of bullying three times or more. Care must be taken among teachers, administrators, and parents to interpret the law so it accommodates kids who engage in bullying behavior against more than one child as well as victims of bullying who are bullied by different children. This will ensure that steps are taken to stop the bullying before it reaches three times. *Relational aggression*, a term used to describe bullying among girl cliques that I'll address later in this chapter, is also a form of bullying.

Bullying Laws and Policies

Tougher laws dominate school cultures today because forty-nine out of fifty states (Montana being the exception at this printing) now have laws against bullying. Some of these laws are more effective than others in preventing, reporting, and monitoring the behavior. Every school must now have an approved antibullying policy based on these laws. The toughest policies against bullying were passed recently in New Jersey and Massachusetts. Know your school's antibullying policy and prevention plan—it can usually be found online. If you're wondering what's included in your state or school policy, check the anti-bullying state list on my website. The strongest policies and prevention plans include:

- Schools report three or more incidences to the authorities

- Schools report every incident of in-school or cyberbullying to the state annually (for tracking and measurement purposes)

- Counselors, teachers, and staff to have special training on bullying behavior

- An antibullying-designated administrator in each building
- Age-appropriate antibullying curriculum for kindergarten up
- Teacher evaluations that include skills in and commitment to antibullying
- School reassignments for bullied kids at families' request
- Sanctions for parents who protect or regard their child's behavior as harmless

Beyond state laws and school policies, the culture set in a school district on antibullying comes from the top, through a commitment from the superintendent. That carries down to the principals and all staff, including cafeteria workers and bus drivers, who are often present when the bullying occurs. But families at home must also support a positive culture. Setting the stage for tolerance, empathy, and inclusion only happens when these qualities are valued and acted upon by everyone. And that begins with understanding what behavior in a bully, the bullied, and the bystander looks like.

The Child Who Bullies

In many cases, children who engage in bullying behavior (who threaten, intimidate, abuse, harass, or exclude another person intentionally and repeatedly) don't recognize or understand their own emotions or the triggers that lead to their aggressive behavior. Some kids are simply trying out behaviors they've seen, either at home, from other kids, or on one of the many reality TV shows they watch. Other kids lack empathy and tolerance or a close, positive relationship with an adult (as discussed in chapter 8). These kids tend to act out their feelings physically instead of using words, and they often intimidate younger siblings. Kids who bully others seek power or control over another person and feel a sense of satisfaction in hurting others. In their quest for power, they will typically seek out targets weaker than they are on the social ladder. Once they know a target is vulnerable, they have a victim. Some children who bully have low self-esteem, but they are actually more likely to be overconfident, narcissistic, and egotistical. A student who engages in bullying behavior can be a popular kid in school or a more reserved, anxious child who often ends up both the victim and the bully. Some kids who bully are abused at home—physically, emotionally, or verbally—react to their pain by hurting others. Sometimes the bullying behavior is learned from a family member or another influential individual. When questioned, a child who bullies will usually deny his behavior, trivialize the incident (it was just a joke), or blame the victim. Many do all three.

If a teacher describes your child using terms like "aggressive," "overly assertive," "unable to control her behavior," "a leader who's gone too far," or "a child who abuses power or authority," this is code for bullying behavior. Understandably, teachers don't like to accuse or label children, and many don't like using the word *bully*. As a conscientious parent, be aware of what the teacher may be saying about your son or daughter. Ask specifically if he is showing signs of bullying behavior toward a specific person. Ask if she is leading or manipulating other girls to partake in specific controlling behavior. Ask if the behavior appears intentional and repeated. The answers will give you a clear picture of what is going on.

Because the teacher can only legally talk about your child, it's best to keep the conversation focused on your own child's actions and needs. If this is your case, it is a big deal and an important opportunity. Once you learn that your child is engaging in aggressive, hurtful behavior, you have the option to walk away (kids will be kids), hope it gets better, or take action and help your child get on a better track at school and for the future. Ask the teacher what you can do to help your child stop this pattern of behavior.

Teaching empathy, tolerance, and how to recognize emotions and control aggressive impulses are all areas that can be explored through school adjustment counselors, psychologists, and books. Many resources are also available at www.theparentbackpack.com. The important thing to know is that, if your child engages in bullying behaviors, these actions will not stop overnight. A committed, multipronged, and monitored approach needs to be put in place for at least a few months to a year. If your child is on an IEP or a 504 Plan and has been engaging in bullying behavior, a team meeting to discuss the issue and what services can be provided for your child is needed. Many disorders today, from ADHD and autism to Tourette's syndrome and Asperger's involve a lack of social skills and an inability to recognize social boundaries. Bullied–bullies often fall into this category.

The Child Who Is Bullied

Usually more vulnerable than average, a child who is bullied is targeted for one or more reasons. Remember, the goal of a bully is power. A target may appear shy or anxious, be of a different race or religion, look different, have little self-esteem, or be physically small or unable to stand up for herself. All of these traits add up to being easy prey. She may be vulnerable to verbal critiques and become defensive, attack back, or get teary. He may be trying to fit in by acting out or showing off. She may do anything to belong, including being used as the enemy in the group just to feel included. He may respond to being bullied by finding weaker prey and becoming a bully himself.

Bullied kids usually feel a great deal of stress, mentally and emotionally, and they often internalize it. They are afraid. When they're in this state, little learning, if any, takes place. He may get headaches, act out his aggression through video games, or spend time alone and isolated; she may get stomachaches and learn to take back control with her body, as she gets older, through eating-control disorders.

Helping your child build confidence, connection, and resilience—as discussed in chapter 8—with an accepting adult, a buddy, and a competence, will decrease her chances of becoming a victim or a bully. Teaching your child how to stand up to aggressive kids is also an important part of navigating social realities and will be discussed on the following pages. Once you're ready to speak to the teacher about a situation, chapter 5 helps you find the words that are most effective in communicating with teachers. Because so many children fall into the camp of witnessing bullying rather than doing the bulling or being bullied, we'll discuss the bystander role first, then we'll look at what your child can say and do to stand up to aggressive kids.

The Bystanders

Nine-year-old Andrew perceives the social hierarchy in Mrs. Hardy's third grade classroom as most nine-year-olds do. At lunch, Andrew sits with the smart kids, near the jocks and across from the popular kids; on the bus, he has to sit near the back with some of the troublemakers and popular kids, because they live in the same neighborhood. One morning on the bus, Andrew watches a scene with a popular kid's fifth grade brother, big Luke—a scene he couldn't talk about for days.

No one sits in big Luke's bus seat because everyone knows that it's Luke's seat—except for Brian, who just moved in. When Luke gets on the bus that morning and sees a new kid sitting in his seat, he stands over Brian and demands that he get out of his seat. Brain acts confused. "Who says this is your seat?" Luke grabs Brian's backpack, drops it to the floor and kicks it repeatedly under the seat. "Unless you want this to happen to you next, get out of my seat—now." Brian bends down to pick up his backpack and his stuff. As he reaches for a pencil under the seat, Luke grabs Brian by the band of his underwear and picks him up with two hands. As Brian starts to yell out, Luke drops him on the seat and pushes his head into the faux leather. Luke threatens him again. "I said get out of my seat now, or you're going to deal with me every day, punk."

Scared and shaken, Brian gets up and moves to a seat across from Andrew. Afraid to utter a word around Luke, Andrew looks out the window. He finally looks over when Brian gets off the bus and sees the tear slide down the side of his face. For three days, Andrew could focus on nothing but what big Luke did and that tear on Brian's face. "Should I have said or done something?" Andrew thinks many times each day. "But what if Luke comes after me?"

Like most bystanders who witness a bullying scene, Andrew was afraid that if he told the bus driver, or even talked to the victim, that he would be bullied, too. In many ways, bystanders who witness an act of aggression or violence and do nothing about it are also bullied, but in a different sense. An individual has exerted power and control over them because they dare not say or do anything. They are intimidated into submission. Andrew's conscience gnaws at him and he worries that he could have done something: "But, what?"

Coaching Kids to Speak Up for Themselves and Others

The first step in teaching your children how to handle an aggressor, whether they are involved or observing, is to coach them on the reasons why kids feel the need to bully. Children understand right and wrong behavior, and empathy, earlier than we think. Once they have a basic understanding of a bully's need for power, the next step is to coach them on how to respond assertively with the right words. As long as there are others nearby, standing up to a bully in a nonreactive, unemotional way can be very effective. This is much more effective than ignoring the behavior or walking away, which research suggests often makes the aggressor more persistent.

Kids want to feel empowered to stand up to other kids and the earlier you start coaching, the more confident your child will feel in this role. Resist the urge to jump in and come to your children's rescue because they will not feel secure or able to do this for themselves down the road. If the bullying behavior doesn't stop, gets out of control, or puts your child's safety at risk, coach your child to go to an adult or a teacher and explain the situation. If your child isn't comfortable doing this, do it together. This is telling about something important, not tattling about something trivial.

In the case of Luke and Brian on the bus, Andrew might have best diffused that situation by letting Brian know when he sat down that fifth grader Luke likes that seat and inviting Brian to come and sit with him instead. Because Andrew was frightened by Luke's reaction, another effective way for a bystander to make a difference is to approach the victim later and let him know he's not alone. In this case, Andrew might say, "Hey Brian, I saw what happened on the bus today. I thought what Luke did was really wrong and if you want to talk to someone about it, I'll come with you. I think we should tell our parents first."

The more you talk with your children about why kids bully and give them the words to use so they don't feel abused, the better they'll be able to cope in future situations. Kids need to learn how to handle social conflict, teasing, and threats. It will also help them respond as bystanders. In the end, a child who bullies wants power. If your child stands strong, speaks up to an aggressor with other children around him for support, the bully will usually move on and hunt down a weaker target.

Here are some assertive words to teach your children once they understand why bullies do what they do, starting from the youngest kindergarten level and moving up. It's a good idea for your child to look the aggressor in the eye when these words are stated and use the person's name. Notice that the language is assertive, not aggressive, and focuses on the behavior, not the person:

- Jack, we're not supposed to hit in this class.

- Annie, that's not a nice word.

- Sandy, why are you cutting into the line?

- Alex, why are you picking on a little kid?

- Haley, it's mean to grab from someone.

- Rachel, you can use this monkey bar when I'm done.

- Sorry, Ben. I still have ten more minutes on the computer. It isn't your turn yet.

- Sara, I don't like what you did (said). Please don't do it again.

- Jamie, it's not okay to say these mean things. We all want you to stop—now.

- Hey Will, I've had enough of your jokes for now. I need you to back off.

Practicing these words and assertive postures at home with all your children (not just the one involved in a situation) will help turn them into natural responses. Coach your child to use a calm and neutral tone of voice. Overreacting to a kid who bullies is just what the bully wants. All this coaching should be done in conjunction with building your child's confidence as discussed in chapter 8. Once your child understands bullying behavior and how to stand up to it, your child will be ready to learn about cliques and cyberbullying.

Cliques

Cliques are the way in which many girls (and some boys) define themselves from third through eighth grade, the tween through the early teen years. They typically start to wane in eighth grade or high school when teens become more comfortable going against the crowd. The difference between a group of girls that play or hang out together and a clique is that *cliques* are exclusive groups that typically form around a leader. Where a group of friends usually shows equal respect for each other, cliques have an uneven balance of power and often the leader commands or controls other girls in the group. The leader often makes up random rules about who can or cannot join, and the makeup of the group is usually predictable. There is a sidekick, who acts as the leader's right hand, and the gossip, who enjoys using information as power. Then there are associates—cronies or wannabees who follow the leader. Some girls will move from clique to clique through these years. Others stay loyal to one group. Still others will stay on the fringes. In many cliques, there is a scapegoat or an enemy who wants to belong so much she will put up with being bullied.

Sadly, some of this cliquey and mean girl behavior is trickling down to girls as young as six and seven years old. And the leader can appear to hold a lot of power over other girls in a classroom. It's important to talk to your children about what cliques are and what is appropriate and inappropriate social behavior sooner than later. Discuss why it may be better to have one loyal friend than six friends who you cannot trust. Rachel Simmons, author of *Odd Girl Out: The Hidden Culture of Aggression in Girls*, believes some of this early influence comes from reality TV shows (think *Survivor, Dance Moms*, and *Keeping up with the Kardashians*), which kids are watching at younger and younger ages. She writes: "*Survivor*'s rite of expulsion resembles a disturbing ritual in cliques of girls. With little or no warning, a clique will rise up and cut down one of its own. For the targeted girl, the sheer force of this unexpected expulsion can be startling, unpredictable and even devastating."

Be aware of what messages your children are getting from TV. Sit down and watch the shows together and test your daughter's takeaway. If she doesn't recognize that some of the behavior is not just inappropriate but also nasty and devious, she may be too young to watch those shows. In any case, having a conversation about what's okay and what's not based on your family's values will have more influence than you know. And thankfully, TVs come with a wonderful button called Off.

Cyberbullying

Cyberbullying refers to any type of bullying (threats; intimidation; physical, emotional, or verbal abuse; harassment; or exclusion) done intentionally and repeatedly using technology or the Internet to distribute messages to one or more people 24/7. What's important to remember in this electronic aggression territory is that while it's easy to blame the device or the medium for what went wrong—the cell phone, texting, a YouTube video, Twitter, Snapchat, or Instagram—there is nothing inherently wrong with the technology. It's more about the age appropriateness, how it's used, and abused that need to be addressed. We parents are quick to buy our children the latest gadgets and hand them over without talking about how to use them or what the guidelines for using them are. While it's easy to justify a cell phone for safety reasons, or an iPod for music, to not recognize that most cell phones today are actually handheld computers with enormous power, is naive. While schools once shunned these devices and outlawed them in classrooms, they are now more accepted in schools, being used as clickers and assessment tools in learning. What we resist persists. Technology isn't going anywhere and our digital native children are already wired around it (more on this in chapter 11). It is up to us to teach them how to manage it.

WHAT TO SAY AND DO

Giving our kids the tools of technology without training is like giving kids the keys to the car before they know how to drive. You wouldn't do that, and technology is no different. I have summarized eleven tips to teach your elementary kids before you hand over that phone or let them sign up for Instagram or the latest social media. And if they've already done that without you knowing, it's never too late to talk about how to use these tools appropriately.

1. Set Limits. Be clear with your children that if they want the device or the social media, they need to provide you with their passwords and account names. This alone is enough to keep some kids from sending threatening or mean messages.

2. Know what sites your kids visit and what they post. You wouldn't let them play at someone's house unless you knew where they were. The same holds true on the Internet—with much more at stake.

3. Teach them how to take a stand against bullies and speak assertively or approach the victim later, privately.

4. Teach them what respect, empathy, and tolerance means. Model this behavior. Ask "How would you feel if your friend Jamie sent you a message like that?"

5. Remind your kids often that what is put out into cyberland is out there forever. Even when you take something down, it will still exist. Nothing is confidential or private on the Internet. Nothing.

Remind kids to think before they hit Send. Once it's out there, it's out there—forever.

6. Repeat again and again that there is no such thing as "anonymous." Creating a fake name or website so no one catches you doesn't work; you can and will be tracked. It just takes a little longer.

7. Don't ever call the parents of a child who is suspected of bullying or cyberbullying, especially if you know them. This is complex territory that should be handled with the school and local authorities working with both sides.

8. Teach your child that sexts or sexting (talking about or showing anything sexual in electronic media) is against the law for anyone under eighteen and has sent some kids to juvenile jail. Yes, this is happening with fifth graders.

9. Show your children sites that do nice things. "Nicing it forward" or "nice it forward" trends on Twitter and Instagram have recently popped up. Encourage them to follow and imitate this kind of behavior.

10. Explain the difference between "tattling" and "telling" to your children. *Telling* is okay when someone's safety or character is at risk, including your own. *Tattling* on trivial, small issues that can be worked out among kids isn't necessary.

11. Spend as much time as possible as a family to counteract the social networking frenzy that our kids marinate in all day long. Make the time.

School Climate and Prevention

Just as families have a responsibility to teach their children about bullying, schools and teachers also have an obligation to prevent bullying and redirect aggressive behavior before it reaches the level of bullying. In the past five years, most school districts have adopted antibullying policies and plans. Knowing that punishing children who bully won't stop the problem, most schools now include a bullying prevention program in their strategic plans. These programs are typically worked into the curriculum at each grade level a few times a year. The goal with most programs (Dare to Care,

No More Bullying, Peace by Piece, Steps to Respect, and so on) is to raise awareness of bullying behavior, provide teachers with effective responses to situations, and teach respect, empathy, and tolerance to children. Posters spotlighting the antibullying messages are hung around the school, and some plans also feature an all-student program annually (a movie, play, or speaker) that reiterates the messages. If your child's school does not run any kind of prevention program or, worse yet, runs them but doesn't practice what they teach, talk to the PTA/PTO, the principal, or the school advisory board. See the resources section at www.theparentbackpack.com to help you get started.

Some school districts commit to creating caring, respectful communities by going one step further—teaching social and emotional learning (SEL) skills on a proactive weekly basis. Research shows that when schools combine bullying prevention with ongoing curricula for building positive behaviors, self-awareness, and relationship skills, they are able to address some of the underlying issues that contribute to bullying. One such program is called Open Circle, a program developed at the Wellesley Centers for Women at Wellesley College, which provides professional development and curricula for SEL in kindergarten through grade five.

Nancy MacKay, codirector of the Open Circle program, told me in an interview that she places a key emphasis on creating a culture of kindness. "Children can't learn and reach their potential when they don't feel safe in and connected to their school community. Fostering a positive climate of respect and kindness where children feel cared for is a key factor to becoming a successful learner. SEL is time well spent and goes a long way toward helping children to be fully prepared for the tests of life."

After listening to and talking with Lauren, Mom learned that Lauren had felt so excluded from a situation that she retaliated by spreading rumors about the friend who left her out. Then things spiraled from there. This is a very typical scenario and a good learning opportunity for all. Lauren's mom gave her three key messages. First, Mom and Dad will be there to help you through situations like this. Second, it's best to handle hurt feelings with friends by going directly to the person, standing up for yourself, and talking it out with that friend. If that friend isn't receptive to this idea, she isn't really a friend, and it's time to make some new ones. Third, anything you put into a text or online will be out there forever, so think before you hit Send. Ask yourself if you'd like that comment to go out about you. If the answer is no, then don't send it. Lauren promised to apologize to her friend that afternoon in person, and Mom realized she could have been more aware of what was going on this past week for her daughter. It was a big turning point for both of them.

This chapter has given you an overview of the social realities behind bullying. Combined with chapter 1, which discussed the social-emotional part of your child's journey, and chapter 8, which reviewed what it takes for a child to be connected and confident, you are now fully equipped to help your child manage her social and emotional world—a world that gets more complicated every day. Chapter 14 will also provide more ideas on how to coach your child to self-advocate.

The next chapter talks about what you need to know and do so your children grow up as thinkers and learners in a world of technology.

TOP TEN TAKEAWAYS

TO CONSIDER

- Bullying (or cyberbullying) is an imbalance of power. It involves threats, abuse, intimidation, harassment, or exclusion that intentionally, selectively, and repeatedly harms a person or a person's property.

- Giving kids technology without training them on how to use it is like giving kids the keys to the car before they know how to drive.

- If teachers talk about your child's behavior using terms like "aggressive," "hard to get along with," "overly assertive," "a leader who's gone too far," it is code for bullying behavior; some kids who feel bullied become bullied bullies.

TO AVOID

- Don't overwhelm your children with questions. They may be afraid to get you involved, so assure them you are there to help and you'll get through this together.

- Don't give your children a device (cell phone, tablet, or other electronic device) or access to social media without getting their passwords and account names and giving them some coaching on how to use it.

- Don't blast the teacher with an email blaming the school for not stopping a bullying situation. It takes families, schools, and communities to prevent bullying.

TO DO

- Teach your children how to stand up for themselves using assertive language as early as kindergarten so they don't become a target. It's never too early for them to learn about cliques, real friends, and why kids bully.

- Let your children know you will always be there for them when they feel hurt or rejected. Empathize with how they might be feeling and listen to their stories.

- Know what your kids are doing online and where they are playing. You wouldn't let them play at a house you didn't know; the same holds true for the Internet.

- Remind your children that every word and image sent via text message, Instagram, Snapchat, or Twitter becomes a permanent part of the Internet. Nothing is private, ever. Teach them to think before they send.

Thinking, Learning, and Technology

The teacher who is indeed wise does not lead you to enter the house of his wisdom. But rather leads you to the threshold of your mind. —KHALIL GIBRAN

Whispering to himself, William stretches his left arm across the desk, rests his head on his shoulder, and writes down the answers to the pretest questions. Ms. Joslyn, William's fourth grade teacher, stops at his desk to ask him a few questions. She had created a mock battle of the Revolutionary War in class and was excited to gauge her students' takeaway. When she asked William why the redcoats were charging, his response was discouraging, "Um. . . I don't really know why, Ms. Joslyn. I'm just trying to memorize the names of the battles and bunkers so I can get an A on the test tomorrow."

Herein lie the crucial questions in education today: How do we raise the bar for schools and students without surrendering to the realities of testing facts and lower-level thinking? How does genuine learning stay a top priority when incentives are given to schools to improve test scores, a move that by default encourages teaching to the test? The questions continue: How can kids and parents keep grades in perspective when societal pressures say do more, study harder, earn an A? What can parents do to bridge the gap between the skills and qualities employers are looking for when they hire and what our schools are forced to teach? How do we integrate technology into teaching to optimize learning?

This chapter provides an overview of the skills our kids will need to be successful, what parents can do to help their children acquire these skills, and the role of technology in educating our digital natives. While using some of these skills may seem a ways off for elementary-age kids, the roots of these skills take hold and are heavily influenced in the early elementary years.

From Three Rs to Four Cs

The tools of technology have propelled the world of teaching and learning to a new level, whether your child's school embraces them or not. It's no longer about what facts kids know today because our children have or will have access to every fact they could ever need—literally at their fingertips—from the moment they can read. Memorizing, while less important than integrating facts into higher-level thinking, still plays an important role, especially in elementary schools, to provide foundational knowledge that is later built upon. But what's also important is what students do with the knowledge they have access to, how well they understand it, manipulate it, and apply it to the next level of thinking and doing. As we morph from the information age into the age of innovation, schools must manage the blending of learning and technology.

For the past decade, many educators, researchers, and corporations have worked to identify the skills that students need to succeed in our digital world. The good news is that all sources point in the same direction, which is a rare occurrence in the field of education. Various groupings of skills have been proposed by leaders in the field, including Dr. Tony Wagner, author of *Creating Innovators: The Making of Young People Who Will Change the World*, who spent years interviewing educators in Finland and CEOs of successful companies, and Benjamin Bloom, a theorist of logical reasoning and thinking who is best known for Bloom's Taxonomy, a classification of learning objectives.

The Partnership for 21st Century Skills (P21), a think tank focused on the future of education, has also identified four core skills that students need to succeed in this millennium. These skills are based on our nation's Common Core goals of readiness for college, career, and citizenship: creativity and innovation, critical thinking and problem solving, collaboration, and communication.

Outlined below are the traits that support these skills and what we parents can do to develop them in our own children, down to the youngest kindergartner—the i-generation five-year-olds, many of whom have already been playing on computers for two to three years.

CREATIVITY AND INNOVATION:
THE ABILITY TO THINK OUTSIDE THE LINES

Discovering new and different approaches to solving problems is a critical life skill that your child needs to succeed in this millennium. As computers continue to replace our left-brain skills on a daily basis, our right brain, the creative hub, remains the most underutilized part of a human being. Creativity stems from a child's curiosity and imagination, and the best way to develop this important attribute in your child is to make time for unstructured play. Let your children discover. Throughout the elementary years, imaginative play is critical for nurturing creativity. Let them play outside and unearth the extraordinary ways that nature takes care of nature. Did you know Velcro was inspired by nature decades ago when a Swiss man observed how burs clung to his clothes after a hike? Nature was also the impetus for the latest discovery of a life-changing antibacterial plastic. If you have a child who spends hours building, let him build. Kids who are curious are more likely to love learning.

Provide opportunities and time for your children to wonder, play, and discover. Letting your kids read and explore whatever subject sparks their interest will also feed their creative side. Keep LEGOs, paper, markers, or crayons handy in the car and during downtime so your kids don't automatically default to screens and buttons that do the work for them. Reading to your children regularly throughout their elementary years will fuel this attribute, too. Being able to brainstorm, free associate, and connect unrelated categories sparks creativity, and kids do this better when they have time for free play. Bring them to science fairs and museums and encourage them to participate in hands-on activities. Many cities offer rotating programs in their science museums that present interactive and engaging ways to spark your child's interest and curiosity.

The arts and music are critical pieces of your child's education because they encourage creativity and innovation. This is also why it's important to advocate for these programs in your school. Find creative ways to fundraise for them, if necessary.

CRITICAL THINKING AND PROBLEM SOLVING: TURNING OUR KIDS INTO THINKERS

Thinking critically involves the use of logic and reasoning skills such as comparing, analyzing, synthesizing, hypothesizing, and critiquing. Many of these skills were once taught only in middle school years and above. While a child's brain development triggers more abstract thinking as they hit adolescence, we now know that elementary children are very capable of thinking about outcomes, deducing, and analyzing cause and effect at a very young age. I read somewhere that finding a detail in the flood of information from the Internet is like trying to get a sip of water from an open fire hydrant. Our children may be faster at accessing the information than we are, but learning how to find the right details or how to synthesize and summarize the relevant data is an entirely different skill. Schools need to teach kids how to access and identify legitimate sites and how to synthesize data on the Internet from grade three and up—and many are starting to do this.

How do we turn our kids into thinkers? We ask questions. Challenge your kids to look at difficult everyday situations and figure out how to analyze and work through them or around them. Answer questions with questions: What else can you do to solve this? How could you share it so both of you can use it? What else do you need to know to make a decision? I wonder, is there another way? We also expose them to experiences that encourage thinking.

Another way to help children evaluate and critique information is to involve your kids in researching and planning a family vacation, finding a fun activity, or comparing choices when making a big purchase. All these types of activities teach kids how to access information, compare, analyze, and summarize it. Another way to get kids thinking critically is when you're watching TV together. Ask your child what a commercial is trying to do. What are they selling? (It's not always a product—sometimes it's an emotion.) What parts of the ad are believable? What might be misleading? While much of a school's curriculum and standardized tests don't prepare kids for this level of thinking, the best schools are integrating project-based learning into their curriculum—where students are given a problem to solve and work together in groups to come up with a solution.

Critical thinking and problem solving are about sizing up the situation and trying out new ideas—taking risks, climbing the monkey bars without Mom underneath ready to catch you, answering the question even if you're not sure it's the right answer. The key for developing these skills is nurturing kids who are not afraid to fail, who understand that learning comes from making mistakes, and who are comfortable making them. That's why rewarding effort is so critical, as outlined in chapter 8. Given our culture's overreliance on structured play and organized activities for children, this skill will be tough for many kids to develop unless they're given some freedom to deal with what comes up in their school, peer, or sibling world without parent interference.

COLLABORATION:
WORKING WITH OTHERS EFFECTIVELY

Collaboration requires that kids transition well and adapt to new situations. Technology is changing our world so fast that our children will likely have a new job or require new skills every three to five years. Take a walk on most any college campus today and you'll discover that your kids' future peers and colleagues will be from China, India, Finland, and Japan. Kids need to understand different cultures and have a healthy appreciation for them. This is why teaching diversity through group projects in public schools has become so important. Project-based learning is becoming a best practice in schools today to encourage this skill and meet the Common Core requirement of collaboration. Teachers often use peer-based evaluations (students grading students) and take these into account in final grades. Encouraging kids to read books with multicultural or working-together themes can also help. (Ask your local children's librarian for suggestions.)

To be collaborative—to be able to work and think together to reach a goal—kids also need to recognize and respect differences in people and cultures. They need to be flexible to changing ideas and open to different ways of thinking. While kids whiz quickly around video games, social media, and the Internet, adapting within face-to-face social environments is different. Help your children learn how to connect with others and be cooperative by making sure they get enough playtime and face time with other kids, without a screen in between. One simple way to teach collaboration is to let siblings and friends work out their differences. Intervene only when absolutely necessary, and revisit situations later to give guidance on how to do it differently next time. The best way to help kids who are slow to warm up or who fear an unfamiliar situation is to place them in new situations with the right support around them. Teach your children to be prepared for possibilities by talking about "what ifs." Having a "let's talk it through and solve this problem as a family" attitude will also help.

Destination Imagination (DI) is a team-based program that gives students the chance to experience the creative process, from imagination to innovation, and have fun while doing it. Students experience creative problem-solving through project-based, open-ended challenges. While kids are told what to do and how to do it at school and in most of their organized activities, DI provides a fantastic opportunity for students to learn how to think and to work collaboratively on a team. During the challenges, neither parents nor team managers can contribute to solving the challenge.

DI is offered in schools, as an after-school program, in homeschool programs, and through community groups in forty-eight states. Aligned with STEAM standards (science, technology, engineering, arts, and math), DI is project-based learning at its best. While many people think that DI is only for gifted students, it is actually a program that benefits children across the spectrum, including those with learning disabilities.

Michele Easter is a mom in Arkansas with two children who have participated on DI teams for the past few years. She's been so passionate about the program and what it has done for her kids' confidence, school performance, and leadership abilities that she got involved as a DI volunteer. Michele was recently recruited to become a state director and expand DI into new schools. "DI is one of the best programs you could ever get your kid involved in," Michele told me when I interviewed her. "It's fun, challenging, and so rewarding. Volunteering with DI is also a great way to connect with your kids. My extended family loves it so much that we have five kids on teams, two volunteers, and a cheering section at all tournaments. We all love it!" For more information, visit www.destinationimagination.org.

COMMUNICATION:
WRITING, LISTENING, AND SPEAKING WELL

As students learn how to analyze and synthesize, think creatively, and work collaboratively, they must also learn to listen, write, and speak effectively—skills most employers say are sorely lacking in young hires. Writing is a skill that's particularly in demand to create persuasive documents that use evidence-based data for corporate presentations. Synthesizing research sources or information on the Internet and communicating a position succinctly is a critical twenty-first-century skill for most employers. Some elementary schools have a writing curriculum, such as the 6 Traits Writing Program, but many do not. Some teachers feel intimidated by writing and either don't have time to teach it or lack the skills to do so. Writing is hard work, and teaching writing is even harder. But the best time to establish good communication skills is during the elementary years.

Allowing children to write freely encourages kids to enjoy writing and improve their communication skills. Because writing is a critical component of literacy, and a skill needed for both college and career, the Common Core has increased the number and level of research papers required in the upper grades. This in turn requires that elementary students know how to do inquiry-based learning. Inquiry-based learning is a model of teaching where students learn about a subject they are passionate about by asking questions. Kids dig for answers on the Internet and elsewhere while teachers serve as coaches and facilitators, guiding the search and asking more questions. The theory behind this model is that kids are more motivated to learn when they are doing their own research about a subject they are really interested in. This kind of online research, analysis, and follow-up replicates modern skills needed in the workplace. Once the kids have answers, they are then challenged to put their information together in a well-organized, persuasive document.

If your kids aren't writing full paragraphs and full-page responses to fiction and nonfiction reading in English and social studies, researching, journaling, and developing persuasive points of view in the last three years of elementary school, talk to your children's teachers. If that isn't sufficient, visit with the curriculum coordinator, the school board, or the principal. Many schools are also starting writing centers, particularly in the upper grades, where students can come after school and hone their research and writing skills.

Here are a few ideas for how you can help your children develop communications skills at home: beginning in kindergarten, consider making thank you letters mandatory in your family for every birthday and holiday. I know it's not always easy, but it will provide your children with opportunities to express themselves and begin to find their voices. Ask them to research a product or service that they want you to buy and convince you that it's a good purchase. This works great with cars, electronics, or even the latest movie. Have your kids summarize one or two TV shows they watch each week. Start doing this when they're young and they'll get pretty good at identifying the main idea, themes, and the conflict in each show. Any opportunities we give our kids to practice writing and communicating will pay off.

Speaking is another skill that is highly important now and underdeveloped in our education system simply because we don't give our children enough opportunities to speak in front of others. Often there isn't enough time in the school day to make this a priority. Some teachers incorporate a current events presentation in their classrooms where kids report on something happening in the news either daily or weekly. Others enlist a student to deliver the weather report to the class each morning. If there isn't a debate team or club in your child's elementary school, grab an interested friend or teacher and look into starting one. All you need are six to eight kids, a teacher who values public speaking, and a few interesting or controversial topics to choose from.

....

Developing the four Cs in our children begins as early as kindergarten. Creativity, critical thinking, collaboration, and communicating effectively are four skills our kids must have to succeed in our digital, international world. They need our help and guidance in developing them.

Now let's turn to tools of technology and how they impact our children's education.

Teaching and Technology

It's Open House night at Milford Elementary, and Stu and Caroline Emery are visiting their fourth grade daughter's classroom. The teacher, Ms. Buford, welcomes parents to her classroom—a place where "my young explorers learn to think, to get along, and to problem solve." She emphasizes technology and demonstrates her interactive whiteboard with Internet capabilities and the latest "one-to-one technology." Ms. Buford shows parents a device that gives each student the means to relay ". . . instant feedback on comprehension levels. It taps a medium that these students connect with and understand far better than we adults ever will."

On the way out, Stu runs into a friend who's quite impressed with the teacher's approach and tech skills. "Amazing stuff isn't it, Stu?" says the friend. Stu doesn't hold back. "Are you kidding me? These kids need their heads back in books so they can get a real education. They've got enough Internet and bells and whistles at home to distract them. They don't need any more of it in school; all this technology is just a crutch and another line item to add to the budget."

The questions of if, how, and when to integrate technology into our children's education is a key issue for many educators today. While many middle and high school students are already engaged in various levels of technology in the classroom, bringing it to the elementary level is more controversial. Some early-adapter teachers have been experimenting with tools of technology for over a decade, but other teachers resist a laptop, a board that's considered smart, or a one-to-one technology because it gets in the way of their preferred traditional lessons and testing. Meanwhile, children under the age of twelve is the fastest-growing segment of mobile technology in the United States and experts believe (and brain scans prove) that our children's brains are being rewired in multiple ways—in processing, memory, neuron connection, and patterns from the moment they are born and connect to the digital world. Interestingly, generational lines don't always divide the early-adapter teachers from those who don't embrace technology. I've seen veteran teachers with twenty-five years of experience lead the way in using technology devices and training other teachers, while down the hall novice, young teachers reject laptops or other tools that integrate teaching with the digital world.

Amid all the controversy over whether technology will or will not be part of the elementary classroom, the one thing I've learned is that technology in schools is merely a tool. It doesn't transform teaching and learning as much as it elevates it to another level. And it only does that when teachers receive the training and development they need to recognize the value of the technology and make it work for teaching and learning. The tools of technology are a means to an end, not the end itself. How we use them and integrate them in our children's learning is more important than what they are or what they do.

Understanding Technology in Schools Today

Ian Jukes is a famous technology education expert. He reminds us that our children are "digital natives" who speak digital as a first language (DFL). They are "screen-agers," born with a tablet or a cell phone in their hand. We parents, on the other hand, and most teachers, are "digital immigrants"—or DSLs, who speak digital as a second language. Thus the digital divide. To educate our children outside their first language, their digital world of tech-speak, means that they miss out on a world in which they live and thrive. Our children's brain wiring is changing faster that we know or understand. As we observe this changing digital world and the intersection of learning, technology, and children's rewired brains, the only thing we can be sure of is that these tools of technology will change and evolve in numerous ways.

But beyond the digitial divide we may experience between our children and ourselves, we also have a tremendous digital divide in this country (only 59 percent of households have Internet) with limited bandwidth in many towns and school districts that restrict what can be accessed and required in public schools. One standardized test administrator wants all of their tests to be conducted via computer by the year 2015. Whether our school systems and students can reach that goal will soon be determined. As parents, it helps to understand some basic terms so we can talk with our kids about their learning and technology. To that end, I offer you some explanations of what's what in the ever-changing world of education technology and twenty-first-century skills, where they came from, and how they might evolve. Keep in mind these are tools or areas of focus, and they are only as effective as the teachers behind them. Since this book's printing, many new devices, gadgets, and software have been launched that may not be captured here. The resources section at www.theparentbackpack. com will help keep you current.

STEM AND STEAM EDUCATION

STEM refers to education and careers within the science, technology, engineering, and mathematics world. *STEAM* refers to STEM plus arts under the argument that the arts push the creative and right side of the brain to be more innovative and creative with STEM. Music is considered an important part of the arts and it's proven to increase comprehension in math. The latest research also suggests that playing a musical instrument for at least fifteen months leads to enhanced working memory. For this reason, encouraging your child to play an instrument has value beyond learning music.

Policy makers and education leaders have pushed for more focus on STEM in our schools for the past two decades for three reasons: (1) jobs in the STEM fields are growing three times faster than any other career fields today; (2) they are the most lucrative jobs; and (3) we suffer a shortage of graduates with skills and interest in these areas. High school graduation requirements are beginning to change with many high schools now requiring four years of math and three years of science to graduate. All this trickles down to an opportunity for elementary schools and parents to instill curiosity and seed the skills for our future engineers, scientists, and computer programmers. These skills will also lead to careers in other areas: people will be needed to run plants with robots, manage computer facilities, invent new green products, and create biomedical solutions for our health-care industry. And, undoubtedly, there will be endless careers that we can't yet imagine.

Our abysmal standing among competitive countries in the latest international testing (the United States ranks in the bottom half of developed countries in both math and science) continues to fuel the push for STEM and STEAM. Second through fifth grade are peak curiosity years, key years to inspire children who show even a sliver of interest in these areas. If your children show this interest, encourage them to get involved in the school science fair, participate in Destination Imagination (DI), or join a

LEGO group. See the topic of "science" in the resources section on my website. Even watching and discussing a show on the Discovery Channel together fuels interest. If your child isn't ready to participate in the science fair, bring her to the public opening and let her observe, explore, and learn from other kids. This is a great way to seed ideas for next year. While not all kids are cut out to be engineers, every child needs to be STEM literate and that begins with asking simple why or how questions.

BLENDED LEARNING

Blended learning refers to merging what teachers and technology bring to instruction and learning. It's about leveraging technology and using teachers as coaches so students are empowered to manage their own learning. Depending on their age and grade level, some students will be better at this than others. And that range of ability continues from first grade through high school. In some situations, blended learning uses technology to individualize instruction; in others, it uses technology to broadcast a lesson to the entire class, and then the teacher uses technology in a more targeted way. For example, in a math lesson, students may watch a video online about the order of operations in algebra, while the teacher prepares problems for the kids to test their new knowledge using a one-to-one device. Because the test data comes in immediately, the teacher can reach out to students who need redirection or a reteach of the lesson and challenge students ready to move on with higher-level problems. Some high schools now require that students take at least one class online to prepare them for what is ahead in college and future training and development seminars. Some charter schools are experimenting with blended learning methods. Time will tell if these are effective and whether technology in elementary schools is necessary to prepare our kids for this learning.

WHITEBOARDS

The first "child" of the chalkboard, this is a supersized, wall-mounted glossy whiteboard, also called a dry-erase or marker board. Teachers use colorful markers without the chalk and dusty cleanup caused by erasers. Many elementary teachers use a whiteboard in conjunction with a projector while some still prefer to use the good old-fashioned chalkboard. Many schools now give kids their own mini whiteboards, instead of paper and pencil, to work out problems at their desks and then wipe clean. Whiteboards do, however, come with a cautionary note because dry-erase markers contain a chemical called xylene. If inhaled directly by kids for too long, this toxin can produce headaches or nausea, and is hazardous waste when disposed of. But many dry-erase markers on the market now come in low-odor or odorless versions. When you buy them, look for brands with the new Certified AP Nontoxic symbol and the words *Conforms to ASTM D4236 or LHAMA* on the marker to ensure your kids are using safe products. And show your children how to replace the cap with a snap so it doesn't dry out or leak fumes. This is good to know for home use, too.

INTERACTIVE WHITEBOARDS (IWBs)

The grandchild of the chalkboard, this is a high-tech, digital interactive whiteboard (also known by its trademarked name, SMART board) that is also wall mounted and works like a giant touch-screen monitor. Hooked up to a computer and a projector, an IWB—with a trained teacher— provides audio and video presentations, interactive lessons, Internet access, and, in a growing number of schools, remote clickers that provide teachers with immediate one-to-one feedback on student comprehension and tests. Although used more often in middle and high school, *clickers* are smart phones or other devices that sync up with whiteboards and test questions. Students read the test problem on the whiteboard, choose the correct answer on the clicker, and hit Send. Within minutes, the teacher has a summary of who understood the lesson and who needs a reteach.

An interactive whiteboard brings curriculum and instruction to life with highly individual lessons, ideal for young visual and tactile learners. For example, for a fourth grade social studies lesson in continents, a teacher can access Google Earth and visit that continent with all its terrain, weather, cities, and people on Tuesday afternoon at 1:17 p.m. while your son sits in his seat, motivated and attentive. For a second grade math lesson introducing geometry, the teacher can illustrate two- and three-dimensional shapes and have students come up to the board to design and manipulate their own shapes. In a third grade science unit on the human body, a teacher can show what veins and arteries of the heart actually look like and spark your daughter's curiosity.

The key for an IWB board to be smart, of course, is teacher training. Some early problems with calibrating the interactive boards turned some teachers away from this high-tech teaching tool, but many teachers embrace the opportunity to experiment and eventually master its many features. Initial research on IWBs in the elementary grades show that it increases student motivation and participation, attracts the more reluctant learners to get involved, and shows a high level of student competence in using the boards (for example, finding and changing settings, despite never being taught)—no surprise there. As long as the focus stays on the child and the learning, not the technology, IWBs provide a rich and productive learning experience. New technology has emerged making the IWB technology less costly and easier to operate.

FLIP INSTRUCTION

When you take a traditional teaching model used in the classroom and turn it upside down, you get *flip instruction*. Instead of a class lesson, followed by some discussion, then practice and homework to be completed at home, flip instruction assigns a lesson to be watched for homework the night before the class and then uses class time to discuss the material and practice work in the classroom when the teacher is present. The lesson may be a screencast, instructional video, or podcast found on the teacher's website or another online source of learning assigned by the teacher. In elementary school, this applies to fourth grade and up. The benefits of flip instruction are that it allows more time for the teacher to individualize instruction and focus on higher-order thinking skills and it takes the pressure off intensive homework at night when kids are tired. A major problem with this approach is that students without regular access to the Internet are at a disadvantage.

ONE-TO-ONE LEARNING

A one-to-one learning initiative is a school program that provides students with their own individual device (a laptop, tablet, or other portable device). The benefits of one-to-one learning are that it individualizes the curriculum, increases kids' interest and engagement in the material, and improves self-initiation and independence. It also gives teachers real-time assessment—immediate feedback on each student's comprehension level—in a more private way. All textbooks are delivered online and students receive assignments tailored to their own ability levels. School districts in Maine, New Jersey, Virginia, Kentucky, and Indiana have paved the way for one-to-one learning in the past decade and many other states and districts are pursuing similar initiatives. However, the cost, required tech support, and teacher resistance prohibit some districts from moving forward with one-to-one learning.

BRING YOUR OWN DEVICE

Bring Your Own Device (BYOD) is a program some schools have adopted to bring technology into the classroom. Teachers allow kids to bring in their own cell phones, tablets, readers, or other devices that can be wirelessly connected to an IWB. When students use their own devices as clickers, teachers have an efficient way to assess kids, personalize the lessons, and get immediate feedback from students. Parents against the program argue that they don't want expensive devices being played with in the classroom and it puts students who don't have the same level of device at a disadvantage. When this occurs, kids share. This territory will continue to be negotiated in classrooms for the next few years as technology evolves.

TABLETS IN ELEMENTARY SCHOOL

Amid much debate around whether tablets provide nothing more than a digital worksheet for a child or a more stimulating learning environment, many schools are beginning to embrace touch-screen technology in kindergarten through grade five classrooms. On the pro side, tablets are proving to be a more engaging, personal tool for kids to learn from. They help to deepen kids' curiosity, encourage them to explore, challenge them to ask more questions and dig for answers, and push learning beyond the four walls around them. The breadth of audio and video tools creates visually appealing presentations, publishing centers, and many opportunities to create and extend learning. Because so many apps are available, students and teachers have a variety of ways to explore information and subjects.

On the con side, some argue that limiting hands-on touching and manipulating of digital devices at such a young age is a mistake. Others claim that tablets serve as a great way to engage kids in new lessons but then the novelty wears off and the distractions set in. Whatever the decision may be, there's no doubt that tablets and all the tools of technology available today (and those on the way) are rapidly changing the way teachers teach and how children learn.

....

The issue of integrating technology with learning in schools is not a question of if, but of when and how. And what are the best tools to use with five to ten year olds? Over the next decade, schools and teachers will experiment with a range of technology tools that bring learning to another level. Getting our kids ready to work in a digital world demands that we teach them the skills they will need.

The next and final section of the book gives you tips and tactics to support your child's learning at home. You'll learn how to end homework meltdowns, fuel your child's mind and body for optimal learning, and help your kids organize themselves and become self-advocates.

TOP TEN TAKEAWAYS

TO CONSIDER

- The four Cs—creativity and innovation, critical thinking and problem solving, collaboration, and communication—are critical skills our kids need to succeed in our new digital world.

- The tools of technology in schools are just that—tools. How effectively they are used by teachers and integrated into our children's learning is more important than what they do.

- Writing and research will be a bigger focus in the Common Core curriculum and the best time to start this is in the elementary years.

- Playing a musical instrument has been proven to enhance both math skills and working memory.

continued

TOP TEN TAKEAWAYS, *continued*

TO AVOID

- Don't focus only on core subjects and grades; thinking, creativity, and the ability to collaborate with others are equally important skills.

- Don't dismiss technology in schools outright; our children's brains are being rewired through technology, and schools are trying to tap that learning potential.

TO DO

- Make time for your kids to play in unstructured ways to help them develop skills in creativity, critical thinking, and collaboration. Let them discover, create, build, and take risks.

- Ask questions to help your kids become better problem solvers rather than solve a problem for them. "I wonder if there's another way?" "What other information do we need?" "What else can we do to solve this problem?"

- Give your kids research projects to do at home that teach them to think and be resourceful, such as figuring out the best dog for your family and why.

- Keep an open mind about one-to-one learning in schools; our children's future college years and careers require a mastery of technology—a skill they are wired for.

PART THREE

Supporting Your Child's Learning at Home

CHAPTER 12

Guiding Homework, Projects, and Studying

It is not the answer that enlightens, but the question.
—DECOUVERTES

"No, Dad!" yells Sam. "That's not how we learned it. If I do it that way, Mrs. Morris will mark it wrong!" Sam's dad uses the last ounce of patience he has to explain how to convert fractions to decimals to his fourth grade son. But it's no use. Sam grabs the worksheet, crumbles it into a ball, and flings his math book off the table. "I hate this stupid homework," cries Sam in tears. "Mrs. Morris didn't explain it and I don't even care if I get a zero. I'm not doing it."

Homework meltdowns. It's a familiar scene for many families: too much homework tackled by tired kids in millions of homes every night, and too much—or too little—coaching from frazzled parents trying to do the best they can with the little time they have.

School districts and parents across the nation are starting to question homework practices: Where's the balance? What's the point? Would we be better off just having elementary kids read for thirty minutes a night? But amid the debate, homework is still being assigned and needs to be done. Schools have ramped up homework levels in elementary through high school for the past two decades since the *A Nation at Risk* study revealed that American kids lag far behind students in other countries in homework (not enough assigned, not enough hours). Fueling this trend are new and higher Common Core standards leaving teachers with more to cover than ever before. That means more of that work is coming home after being newly introduced, but not yet learned.

This chapter guides you through everything homework: its role and the benefits to your kids' education, what the appropriate amount of homework is by grade level, your role in supporting, guiding, and making sure it's done (versus actually doing it for your child), and what to do when the overload factor becomes too much. It also coaches you on how to help kids organize for projects and study for tests.

How Homework Benefits Your Kids

There's lots of research on the pros and cons of homework. I believe homework in the elementary years serves a number of worthy purposes, as long as it's not busy work, it can be completed within the grade-appropriate amount of time, and parents make it a priority for their children.

IT FOSTERS DISCIPLINE AND RESPONSIBILITY

Homework establishes good work habits at an early age. Your child learns how to follow through on a regular commitment, complete an assignment, and do the best work he can on that day. Kids also learn that it's not just about doing the work; it's also about getting it back to class the next day—often the hardest part—four to five times a week. Homework instills responsibility and accountability.

IT IMPROVES CONFIDENCE AND COMPETENCE IN KEY AREAS

Homework provides an opportunity to practice subjects that need repetition and reinforcement before they can be mastered—math, reading, and writing. Only practice improves the automatic recall kids need for math facts and formulas. In a subject like math, which builds year upon year, this foundation is critical. And much of that practice and repetition needs to happen at home so teachers can utilize valuable class time to teach new concepts. Reading passages and answering questions supports skills in reading fluency, comprehension, and writing. That is why the fifteen to twenty minutes of nightly reading ritual assigned by most elementary schools today is critical for developing fluency in reading. And writing only gets better with practice.

IT GIVES TEACHERS VALUABLE FEEDBACK

Homework lets teachers know what your child knows. This is important for standards-based grading, but it's even more important because it allows the teacher to give your child clarification on concepts she doesn't understand or challenge her more in the right ways. Homework assignments also provide teachers with information on how a class lesson was understood or how their instruction needs to be modified. If you do your child's homework instead of guiding your child in doing it herself, it gives the teacher a false impression and deprives your child of the additional instruction he needs. Teachers track on a daily basis where their kids stand. They can usually recognize when you're doing your child's work.

IT GIVES YOU A WINDOW INTO WHAT TO REINFORCE AT HOME

Studies show that the more connections children have to the concepts they are learning, the more likely they are to retain the information. Your child's homework clues you into what your child is studying so you can reiterate these ideas at home. When my youngest daughter was introduced to measurements of volume, I had her help me cook dinner every night for a week. She also made cookies one night. By the end of the week she had learned how many teaspoons are in a tablespoon, the number of quarter cups in a cup, and the number of ounces in a pound—from doing, not only reading. For other simple ways to connect to your kids' learning, see chapter 3. The more connections we can make at home to what our kids are learning in school, the deeper and more relevant their learning will be.

IT LEADS TO BETTER GRADES

Research also shows that kids who complete homework assignments on a regular basis usually get better grades on tests and report cards. Establishing good work habits in elementary school also leads to more success through the middle and high school years. Teaching a seven-year-old child the importance of homework and reinforcing good habits now is much easier than trying to convince a seventh grader when homework accounts for 20 percent of your final grade.

The Right Place and Time for Homework

Many teachers and parenting books (some friends and relatives too) will advise you to find a place in your home where your kids can do homework, preferably at a desk in a separate room, away from distractions and activity. I agree with this advice when kids are in middle and high school, but not in elementary school. If you have one of those kids who gets home and wants to finish his homework before he does anything else, this approach may work. But for the majority of kids, it won't. I find most children between the ages of six and ten want to reconnect with family after school. They've been away all day, shuffled from place to place, during and after school. Most kids crave your attention, and this often plays out at homework time. As parents and family members hustle around getting dinner, shuttling kids, or running off to evening commitments, homework often becomes a sidelined activity to hurry up and finish rather than a valued priority in the family—unless you establish some guidelines.

TALK TO YOUR KIDS ABOUT THE IMPORTANCE OF HOMEWORK

Reiterate why homework is a priority in your family (see reasons above). Make sure your children understand it will happen four nights a week and that it's their responsibility to complete it, do their best work, show it to you when they're done, and turn it in the next day. Include any other parameters around homework (comes before television or electronics) that are part of your message. Explain that your responsibility is to supply whatever they need to get the homework done, to help when they have a question, and to make sure they do the work. Engage your kids in a homework discussion. Give them choices about where and when they do their homework, and then keep the routine consistent. Kids thrive on routine. You'll be surprised how much kids appreciate being involved in decisions and what ideas they come up with. Some families actually create a homework contract that parents and kids sign.

THE RIGHT PLACE AND TIME TO DO HOMEWORK
WILL DEPEND ON YOUR CHILD

Your child's temperament, learning style, and most likely, what day of the week it is in your family schedule, are all factors that need to be considered in creating the homework schedule. Some kids can come home from school, grab a snack, and pound out their homework in thirty minutes without taking a break. But many kids need to decompress from a long day, step away from structured activities, and just play. This is how they process their day. Once they do that, they can move on to the next thing. Homework battles often come about because parents push kids to do homework when it's convenient for them, not when it's the best time or place for the kids. Ask your kids what they think: when would be the best time to do your homework and where? A child eight years old or older can probably think logically about this question and come up with a great plan. Six- and seven-year-olds will need more guidance from you.

Some kids will do homework at the kitchen table or counter with an adult in the same room (doing other work at the same table or in the kitchen) either before dinner with a snack or immediately after dinner. Others create a homework area off a main room with an adult close by. Little-used dining rooms often serve this purpose. The point is that making sure your child understands that homework is a priority is just as important as where and when it's done.

CREATE A "HOMEWORK TIME" BASKET OR CADDY

Have your kids help create a homework basket filled with all the supplies they'll need. This will help avoid frustrations, keep kids focused on getting the work done rather than looking for something they need to get it done, and help them understand the importance of organization. Keep the basket well stocked and separate from the supplies in your child's backpack to designate the importance of homework time. At the start of each year, you will get a sense of what is needed for each grade, but some good basics are pencils and colored pencils, a pencil sharpener, an eraser, a red pen for editing, glue sticks, scissors, a ruler, and a calculator. A clock will also help you monitor how much time is spent on each homework assignment. As your child gets older, more homework will be done on a computer or a digital device, so your child may need

Internet access to connect to a teacher's webpage, Google docs, or a school portal.

How Much Time Is Too Much?

Most educators agree on the amount of homework time that is appropriate for your child's grade level. The general rule of thumb is ten minutes per day multiplied by the grade, with daily reading assigned as an extra. This is an accepted norm under the National Education Association and the National PTA. So a second grader will usually have twenty minutes, a fourth grader forty minutes. First graders are sometimes given fifteen minutes, and kindergartners only when necessary. Grade five homework assignments go up to sixty minutes per day in many schools to prepare them for middle school.

Given that some kids look like oversized jumping beans doing homework, it can be difficult to gauge how much time your children have actually been working. But it's important to monitor this issue and alert the teacher if they are spending more than 10 percent over the recommended homework time on a regular basis—minus, of course, the up-and-down time of getting another snack, taking a bathroom break, or playing with the dog. Enlist your children in the process of monitoring their time. Get an easy-to-read face clock and ask them to begin an assignment when the big hand is on a number. Depending on the age of the child, as they finish, they can check the clock, add the minutes up, and write them down lightly on the back of the paper. This keeps kids focused on finishing their work. It also builds skills in telling time and addition. When homework is going smoothly, this activity works well. If your child is struggling with homework, put the clock aside and get more involved.

A Parent's Role with Homework

"Allie, how many times do I need to tell you to please sit down and finish your homework?" says Allie's grandmother as she chops broccoli on the cutting board. "No more bathroom, no more checking your backpack or drawing on your notebook with those smelly markers. Just finish it up so I can get your dinner on the table."

"Nanny," says Allie holding her head in her hands. "I don't understand these math problems. My teacher didn't really teach us this yet. I have no idea what I'm supposed to do. I don't even like math."

"I know, honey, and I'm sorry I can't help you either. That new fifth grade long division is way over my head. I don't think your mom is any good at it either. Your daddy can help you when he gets home later tonight. Now, let's eat dinner."

....

Our role with our kids' homework is to be the consultant, the positive facilitator. We guide, coach, organize, and encourage, but we don't jump in and do. We help connect the dots. There's no place this is more crucial than with homework. I've experienced my share of homework meltdowns and I know supervising homework is not easy. Here are ten golden rules that I picked up along the way that I wish I had had at the beginning. If you can make these happen in your house—on a consistent basis—you'll say good-bye to those draining homework battles and meltdowns.

CONVEY A POSITIVE ATTITUDE

If kids know that homework is a priority in their family, they'll eventually make the best of it and adopt a similar attitude. They'll want to master it. But when they hear a parent or relative talking negatively about homework, an assignment, or a teacher, it's hard for them to reconcile their mixed feelings. The vast majority of kids in elementary school want to please their teachers. Take advantage of their positive mindset. It will pay off in later years.

SPLIT IT INTO SECTIONS

Many kids get paralyzed when they think of all the homework they have to finish. Helping them break it into sections is a key role for parents to play. Homework is typically assigned in math and literacy work, which makes two sections. If one part is reading and the other part is answering questions, divide that into two separate sections. Kids like to categorize at these ages. Then get out the clock. Encourage them to identify and start with the hardest section first when their brain is the least tired. This may take some convincing, but it's important. Tell them that you'll work alongside them and pay some bills for ten minutes or empty the dishwasher while they do their hardest part. This also helps them see how much they can accomplish in a short time.

TAKE BREAKS ON THE DOWNHILL

Some nine-year-olds can sit for forty minutes doing homework without a break. Some can't. Teach your children how to take a break just when they figure things out or they're at an easier section. This may seem counterintuitive, but it will get them back to the work faster. They won't dread it. Remember, kids like to conquer work. They want to feel competent and repeat it until they master it. If they break at a difficult point, you'll spend more time than you want to cajoling them back.

CHECK IN WITH THEM

Checking on your kids' progress, rather than them coming to you or calling out to you regularly, keeps them focused on their work rather than getting you over to their side. If your child is seven, tell her you'll check back in seven minutes; if your child is nine years old, make it nine minutes. And then honor your commitment. This lets them know that you're paying attention, and it keeps you focused on when to check in. First and second graders will need more guidance than fourth graders. By fifth grade, kids need to be doing homework almost independently. Your eleven-minute check might become a twenty-minute check instead.

STAY NEUTRAL

They call it "home work" for a reason. It's tough to stay unemotional when it's your child, you are both tired, or homework brings up natural feelings that you have on specific subjects, especially when it comes to math, as we saw with Allie's grandmother. Women have a tendency to downplay their skills in math and science and turn that subject over to the men in the family. This sends a very negative message to our girls about their abilities. The same is true for grammar or handwriting with boys and their dads. It's tough, but try to stay as neutral as you can on subjects, even when it isn't your favorite.

GUIDE, DON'T DO

This is hard, especially when kids struggle. The easy way out when things get tough is to just do it yourself. This is tempting because everyone's tired. But it only hurts your child. If he needs a reteach, he won't get it because the teacher sees his homework completed and gets a false impression of his understanding. If your child doesn't understand something from the beginning, play school and ask questions. "Teach me what you learned today in this lesson." Many kids understand a concept better once they try to teach it themselves. If that doesn't work, split a question or a problem into sections and take them one at a time. Ask questions. Resist giving the answer because your child won't learn from that. Take a "let's figure this out together" approach. Try an online resource to help find the answer. (See the resources section on my website for suggestions.) Encourage your kids to stay after school for extra help; all teachers have to stay in the classroom for at least twenty minutes at the end of the day. And let the teacher know if your child is struggling regularly when doing homework. This information gets your child the help he needs.

PRAISE THEIR PROGRESS, NOT THE RESULT

Knowing that kids build on their competencies, praise their effort as much as possible, not their smarts. And remember, kids learn lessons from making mistakes. Keep the praise specific and focused on what they can control such as handwriting, showing their work, or giving their best effort. You can always find something good in what they've done. A child who believes she is hardworking is more likely to complete her homework with a positive attitude and not get frustrated. More details on this idea are in chapter 8.

MAKE CONNECTIONS TO WHAT YOUR KIDS ARE LEARNING

This is one of the most helpful things you can do. The more ways a child sees or hears information, the more likely he is to retain it. If your child is learning measurement, have him measure different toys and compare them. If his class is doing a unit on space and our galaxy, go to a planetarium or get a book at the library about an astronaut to help him connect the dots and bring it to a human level. Chapter 3 shows you lots of other ways to connect to learning.

SET YOUR CHILD UP FOR SUCCESS

If you're late coming home from a practice, stop to grab dinner, then have to run an errand while the kids eat in the car, and don't get home till eight o'clock at night, don't expect your child to come home, sit down, and crank out the homework. Know your child's limits and learning style. (Chapter 1 will help you figure this out.) If your child is more of a kinesthetic learner (a hands-on learner), don't force her to sit in a chair for forty minutes or she's punished. That's a battle no one wins.

COMMUNICATE WITH THE TEACHER

This is critical, especially when your child is struggling. Teachers appreciate a heads-up about homework, sooner rather than later. Send in a short note with your child on the actual homework or via email to let the teacher know your child isn't getting the concept and needs some extra help. Or let the teacher know that your child spends much more time on homework than the allotted amount. This lets the teacher know that addressing the issue of homework length needs to be a priority for the day; it also lets the teacher know that you care. It helps build your bridge of communication, too. (See chapter 5 for more on words that work for communicating about homework. Chapter 14 offers ideas on how to help your children advocate for themselves around homework.)

So now that you understand how homework benefits your child and you know how to help end those homework meltdowns, you're ready to become a guide on projects.

Managing Projects

As Shawn drives his twins home from a hockey game late on Thursday night, he scans his rearview mirror: Todd is half asleep. Scott is completely out. It was tough keeping their schedule together in the spring. School is a priority, but the boys love their hockey, too. He hated to ask the homework question—out of fear that it wasn't yet done—but as soon as the car pulled into the driveway and the boys woke up, he did.

"Umm, well," replied Scott, still half asleep. "My homework is done, but I kind of forgot that my big solar project is due. Remember Dad, the one I mentioned a couple of weeks ago and I think you said we'd start it next week and we forgot about it?" Shawn held his breath as he braced for the bad news. "WHEN is it due, Scott?"

"The guys on the team reminded me that uh . . . it's due . . . umm, tomorrow."

....

As schools move more into teaching kids how to think versus getting the right answers on a test (as discussed in chapter 11), project-based learning will continue to grow. This means individual and group work that may or may not involve building something that needs to be done on a schedule. There is a way to get kids to take ownership of projects so you don't have to. An elementary teacher taught me this approach and it worked with my kids every time the word *project* came through our door. In full disclosure, I was taught this after one of them missed a big deadline, a great lesson for all of us.

RESIST THE TEMPTATION TO DEAL WITH THIS NEXT WEEK

Procrastinating will only get you and your child into trouble. As soon as your child mentions a project or you read it in the newsletter, help your child get organized. Look at this as a training session where any child from grades two through five can learn how to manage this project and others in the future so you won't have to. Ask your child what he has in mind for this project. It most cases, the teacher has discussed this assignment in class and the kids' imaginations are running.

SIT DOWN TOGETHER AND MAP OUT A SCHEDULE

Praise your child for telling you in advance about the project; some parents don't hear about it till a night or two before it's due. The most important step to turning a project into a reality is to set up a time with your child in the next twenty-four hours to organize it. Take out a calendar, or make a copy of the current month, where your child can mark up each day. Do it with all your kids watching so they learn too. Let them know this is how you create a project timeline for every project you are ever assigned in school or and in life.

BEGIN AT THE END

Ask you child what she sees herself doing on the day it's due. Hopefully, she'll respond with "Duh . . . bring it to school." Have her write that down on the due date. Next, ask your child to name three things that she'll need to do to create this project. Many teachers will have written steps or what elements students will be graded on, which is called a *rubric*. Ask her to review that and help her understand what to buy, how to make it, and how to label it (most projects include labeling as part of the graded assignment).

HELP YOUR CHILD MAP OUT WHAT STEP HAPPENS EACH DAY

Work backward from this "bring it to school" date, based on what's needed for the project. For example, the day before it's due might be "check over final labels and put in box to carry." Labeling will be the last couple days: one day in pencil, the next in marker. "Build project" will take the bulk of the time and needs to cover a number of days, breaking down each section of the project by day. Don't forget to include time to go to a supply store and get what you need. The day before that day is "make the list for what supplies I need" day. The day before that, figure out what supplies you have at home. As each day passes, have your child cross off the day and mark the progress.

He may not complete every task exactly as mapped out, but it's a guide and a place your child can turn to each day until the project is due. You can say, "Let's check your calendar today to see what needs to be done on your project." Your job as parent is to guide the timing rather than do the project for your child. Teachers know instantly when a parent has taken over a project. If you do the work, your child has lost a chance to learn some good lessons and the final grade will show that.

If you take the time to map out a schedule with your child and help keep him focused on the next step on the calendar rather than doing the project for him, you've taught your child how to manage a project. Next time, it will be much easier (on both of you), and you'll have more time and energy to help your child in other areas.

Teaching Your Child How to Study

Lilly sat at the dining room table hunched over her test-review sheet. After filling in the last answer, she wiped away the eraser shavings that covered her paper and her desk. Lilly was nervous about this English test tomorrow because her teacher said they would need to study hard. Lilly handed the paper to her dad and asked him to check to make sure it was "right."

Ten minutes later, Lilly's dad handed the review sheet back to Lilly. "Did you include every example you could think of on each of these questions, Lilly?" Lilly thought for a moment, "Well, maybe not on number five. Is that one wrong?" Lilly's dad asked her to bring it back when she had done her best work.

Lilly came back ten minutes later. "I fixed number five, Dad. Can you check that one now? Are the rest okay?" Lilly's dad was silent for a moment. "Lilly, have you done your very best thinking on this review sheet? Have you thought through each question as much as you can?"

Getting frustrated, Lilly stomped her feet. "YES, Dad. I want to do well on this test. Can you just tell me if they're right or not?" Lilly's dad looked at Lilly and waited.

"Well, maybe on that last one," said Lilly, "I could have talked more about the ending and how it relates to the beginning of the story. But it doesn't matter, Dad. That won't be on the test." Lilly walked away with the paper, ready to do another revision.

When she returned, she said "Dad, this is the absolute best, best work I can do. Now can you please just finish correcting it?

"Great. That's what I wanted to hear, Lilly. Your best thinking is most important whether you're reviewing for a fourth grade test or a college test," said Lilly's dad. "Now, I will read it."

. . . .

In an era of standardized tests, it's easy for our kids to get caught up in memorizing data and responding with rote answers instead of really learning concepts. This is especially true at the elementary level. While there is a place for rote memorization and many concepts require that certain facts be recalled to understand the bigger idea, the goal is to have our kids think about a question and genuinely understand and discuss the concept, rather than play back a rote response.

At the elementary level, kids don't always equate studying for a test with homework. Unless the teacher writes "study for test" for homework, kids don't categorize it as work to do at home. Unfortunately, teaching kids how to study is not in the kindergarten through grade five curricula. Unless a teacher decides to take on "study skills," the onus often falls on parents. The good news is the newest research on mind, brain, and education shows that studying in the right ways can actually improve comprehension and retrieval.

GET READY FOR TESTS

When are the tests? Watch the teacher newsletters so you know dates, and make sure your kids feel comfortable talking with you about upcoming tests. If they believe you will be encouraging and helpful in the process, they will share information; if they are scared you will put too much pressure on them to get a perfect score, they will be less inclined to tell you about upcoming tests. Most are announced a week to ten days in advance. Depending on the subject being tested, there are different ways to study.

HOW TO STUDY FOR MATH

Research shows that, in math, the more repetition, the better. Encourage your child do as many practice problems and practice tests as she can. This is particularly true for math facts. Automatic recall of these is critical, and it takes drilling and practicing again and again to master them. Accuracy and speed are critical. But she also needs to understand the concepts behind adding, subtracting, multiplying, and dividing. Research shows playing board games with kids ages five through ten has a significant impact on math achievement. Most games with dice or a spinner strengthen the understanding behind math, so find some favorite games and play. Sorting and categorizing socks—sorting them by color or pattern—reinforces math concepts, too. Practicing math facts in the car is another great way to reinforce them.

Most schools will use an incentive program for getting through all the times tables from zero through twelve. This is one of the few times I think a rewards program makes sense. If you child is a visual learner, flash cards that show both the number and the number of elements will help; for example, a card that shows $4 + 3 = 7$ on one side and four dots and three dots on the other, helps kids better understand the concept. If your child is a kinesthetic learner, get out pennies, nickels, and dimes and start sorting and counting. A quality toy store or bookstore will help you find what works for your child. Let your kids test out different games and activities. There are also many good apps that reinforce math listed in the resource section at www.theparentbackpack.com.

HOW TO STUDY FOR OTHER SUBJECTS

When it comes to studying for reading, science, and social studies tests, the key is that the review and studying time is active rather than passive. Passive means reading over the chapter and reviewing the questions and answers. Active means using our brain to retrieve information. Every time we actively tap our memory to recover information, we are making it stronger. The harder we work to get that information, the more likely we are to retain it later. A child will learn more by fixing a sentence that has five grammar mistakes than by reviewing the grammar rules that will be on the test. Also, the more a review has problems or questions out of order, the better a child's brain learns the material. For example, with spelling words that are usually categorized, give a practice test out of order. Your child will resist, but let him know it will make it easier to remember them on test day. Meaningful understanding means comprehending the concept, not just the words on paper.

Countdown to Test Day

Once kids hit third grade, they are reading to learn and are tested regularly. The best way to help your children study for a test in an active and meaningful way is to guide them to begin three days out. Kids need to understand that studying for a test happens in stages and just reviewing the material the night before doesn't usually work. I always used questions and a note card method to teach my kids how to study. First they read about the subject that will be tested and discuss it in class. Then they write down in their own words the answers to key questions and concepts on note cards: *What is . . . ? How does . . . ? Why did . . . ?* Let's look at how this process works in more detail.

STEP 1: THREE DAYS OUT

Encourage your child to create note cards for each part of the concept or question she is learning. Writing these out is the first active step in studying. Concept or question on one side, answer on the other. If your child is learning about the life cycle of a plant in science, for example, begin by actually looking at a real plant and talking through the stages. Moving away from the text book into a real life situation helps a child connect with the subject. They will probably identify seeds, roots, plants, leaves, sun, water, flowers, pollination, and germination. If you don't have a green thumb and your child is a visual learner, encourage her to draw a picture or find one online. Note cards now come in different colors and can be categorized if needed. Our role as parents is to buy the cards, encourage our child to make them at least three days out from a test, and quiz her on them later on. Some kids will make them as they go along in a unit. Either way is great, but the key is, your child makes the note card—not a parent, not a tutor, not a teacher. The process of writing down the questions and answers in their own words helps their brain process the information.

STEP 2: TWO DAYS OUT

Two days before the test, show your child how to review the concepts written on the cards and try to answer them. Those he knows go into one pile; those he doesn't know go into the other pile. On the don't-know pile, encourage your child to reread materials that explain the concept. Ask him questions. Go back to the plant. If he's still stuck on germination or pollination, guide your child to write a sentence out on the card that uses this idea. This is tapping his working memory and will help him retrieve the information later. This pile of don't-know cards can be frustrating for your child. Be sure to praise his hard work, all the notes he's made, and the progress made. Then have him review the don't-know pile again, which will probably be smaller. If he still doesn't understand it, encourage him to watch a YouTube video that explains the life cycle of a plant. This always works better than an explanation from mom or dad. Continue to praise progress and good study habits. Encourage him to ask the teacher for help if he cannot grasp it on his own.

STEP 3: THE DAY BEFORE

The day before the test, tell your child you're happy to quiz her when she's ready. If there are some concepts that end up in the don't-know pile, reinforce how many questions and ideas your child does know. If a child is in fourth grade or higher, sometimes studying with a friend can help. Or bring another adult into the mix. Either way, going through this three-step process for studying will help your children absorb, retain, and apply the knowledge they now have in meaningful ways. Help them sum it all up. "So tell me again how a plant grows?" Kids like to teach what they've just learned. Play school if they like to do that. Ask them if they've done their best to study for the test. Is there anything they wish they knew a little bit better? You'll be surprised how well kids know what they know. Once they answer yes to these questions, they are ready for the test. The grade doesn't matter because they've done the best they can do. What matters more is that they learn how to learn and do their best.

So now you've learned everything you need to know about homework, projects, and studying. The last two chapters will focus on what you can do at home to fuel your kids' bodies and brains well, help them get organized around school, be accountable for their schoolwork, and start advocating for themselves.

TOP TEN TAKEAWAYS

TO CONSIDER

- Doing homework fosters good work habits, discipline, and responsibility, which lead to better grades through the school years; it also instills confidence and competence, and reinforces learning.

- Teachers use homework to understand what kids know and don't know. It also gives them feedback on how well a class lesson was understood.

- Our role as parents is to help kids organize their time and plan for projects, homework, and studying for tests; teachers and schools don't teach kids how to study; this is a big part of our job as parents.

- Keep the attitude about homework positive in your home; it's hard for kids to reconcile their beliefs and behaviors when they hear conflicting messages and want to please both their teachers and their parents.

TO AVOID

- Don't do your child's homework or give him the right answers. This gives the teachers a false impression and hurts your child because he won't get the support he needs.

- Discourage your children from studying only the night before a test; the study habits they form now will make a difference later in middle and high school.

TO DO

- Our role as parents in our children's homework is to support and facilitate, help organize the work, break it into sections, and ask questions that encourage our kids to think.

- Use homework as a lens into what your child is studying and make natural and personal connections to that learning every day—at home, in the car, or on vacation.

- Guide your child on how to organize a project: this involves mapping out together each step on a calendar, buying supplies, and helping your child manage the schedule.

- Teach your child how to study for tests beginning three days out using note cards and questions about a concept.

CHAPTER 13

Fueling Your Child's Brain and Body

It's bizarre that the produce manager is more important to my children's health than the pediatrician. —MERYL STREEP

Matt and Luke are studying together for their big math test. Their fourth grade teacher, Mr. Bentley, warned it would be difficult. In between practice problems and quizzing each other on decimal to fraction conversion, metric measurement, and long division, the ten-year-olds reward themselves with a short round of video games. After lots of studying, they decide they are ready. Both moms agree they're good study buddies and helpful to each other.

The next morning, Matt's mom gives him a special treat before the test for all his hard work: his favorite Cap'n Crunch cereal, along with yogurt and strawberries. Matt gulps down two big bowls, slurps the leftover milk, tosses the strawberries in his lunchbox, and leaves his yogurt untouched. He could have eaten a third bowl of cereal, but time ran out. On the other side of the street, Luke's mom insists Luke eat a nutritious, balanced breakfast. "Eat your best, get plenty of rest, you'll do well on the test," she claims. Luke's mom serves him two poached eggs on whole-wheat toast and cut up fruit on the side.

That evening, the boys' moms check in on how the test went. Luke says it went great. "I think I aced it. We studied a ton and I knew everything." But Matt doesn't feel as confident. "I don't know what happened. I knew it yesterday, but I couldn't remember a lot of it today. I think I was just tired."

You've probably heard the statistics about children's health these days—more than one-third of American kids are obese or overweight, diabetes among children is skyrocketing, and most children don't meet the government recommendations for a balanced diet. At the same time that we grapple with childhood obesity, brain research is proving that diet, sleep, and exercise impact children's learning and how well they behave in the classroom in profound ways. When we put our kids to bed and what we feed them for breakfast, lunch, dinner—and all those snacks in between—effects their ability to process, learn, and retrieve information—in significant ways.

Cap'n Crunch tastes about as good as it gets when it comes to cereal; I have to agree with my kids on that one. But it tastes good because over half its calories are added sugar. Cap'n Crunch is considered a simple carbohydrate, like refined table sugar and many other processed foods. So eating one bowl is actually the equivalent of 24 grams of sugar. Don't let those short-on-serving-size nutritional labels mislead you: a typical-size bowl of cereal is usually 2 ounces, not the 1 ounce that most nutritional labels claim equals one serving. Add milk—13 more grams of sugar for every 8 ounces of low-fat milk—and that's well over the recommended sugar intake of 25 grams for a child aged five to ten for an *entire* day.

But Matt didn't eat just one bowl of Cap'n Crunch that morning. He ate two bowls for a total of 48 grams of sugar. That's the equivalent of eating twelve teaspoons of sugar. (Divide total sugar grams by four to calculate number of teaspoons.) Add to that the sugar in the milk. It's no surprise that Cap'n Crunch is tied for first place on the least nutritional cereals on the market. Right up there with it are Froot Loops, Corn Pops, Lucky Charms, Trix, and Reese's Puffs. In fact, children's cereals contain 85 percent more sugar, 65 percent less fiber, and 60 percent more sodium than cereals aimed at adults. And many of them are advertised directly to kids ages three and up; $156 million is spent per year on kids' television commercials alone. Parents who want their kids to get the best education possible need to teach good nutrition and be the gatekeeper on what kids eat. But many of us are just not aware of how much sugar our kids are getting. Let's take a look at why the right food is so important to learning and the brain.

The Food-Brain Connection

The human brain runs on a chemical in our body called glucose, like a car runs on gas. Glucose, or the sugar level in your blood, is the only energy source used by brain cells. Because our brain neurons cannot store glucose, they rely on the bloodstream to carry the right balance of sugar to the brain at all times. Billions of brain neurons need this regular supply of glucose to produce energy and connect to other neurons. When these neurons are depleted of glucose for even a few minutes, they begin to die.

Glucose is made from simple carbohydrates (processed foods, sugar) and complex carbohydrates (grains, fruits, and vegetables). When the body receives an overload of simple sugars—like it did with Matt's cereal injection—it depletes its glucose supply before it gets to the brain and compromises a child's ability to concentrate, remember, and learn. The better quality of carbohydrates you eat, the more balanced your glucose levels are. This means more glucose goes to the brain to fire up neuron connections, which spark learning. Our brains are made up of fat and protein cells. Amino acids from protein help to fire up those brains neurotransmitters that trigger memory, retention, and retrieval, like a spark plug in a car. Our brain needs some sugar to run normally, but too much sugar is like adding toxins and water to the gas you pump in your car.

SIMPLE CARBOHYDRATES

Unlike complex carbohydrates, simple carbohydrates—sugar cereals, white bread, juices, candy, donuts, white rice, soft drinks, cookies, and most packaged junk food—are processed quickly through your stomach rather than your blood. They are reduced down to their simplest form and then further processed to make them taste good. In order for your body to process a big boost of sugar, the pancreas produces extra insulin that triggers cells to steal glucose from the blood to store all that sugar. That means less glucose goes to your brain. The brain becomes moody, confused, and tired within a short time, and your child's ability to concentrate and retrieve information stored in the long-term memory center is significantly compromised.

Mental activity takes a lot of energy. In fact, brain cells require two times more energy than regular cells. So now you understand why Matt had trouble on his math test. The 70-plus grams of sugar he inhaled that morning drained the glucose supply to the brain and compromised his ability to do his best on the test. Sugar comes in many forms now, including sucrose, dextrose, corn syrup, high-fructose corn syrup, fructose, maltose, barley malt, mannitol, sorbitol, corn sweetener, evaporated or crystallized cane juice, fruit juice concentrate, and its newest disguise, "sugar alcohol." It's added to food to improve the flavor, add color, and act as a preservative. It's important to know that kids' juices are loaded with sugar. Look for less sugar on the nutrition labels or switch to water.

Don't be fooled by claims on kids' cereal boxes. They're mostly sugar—simple carbohydrates that release into your child's blood stream immediately, causing blood sugar spikes and a lack of nutrients to the brain. Be a detective when it comes to cereal box nutrition labels: no more than 6 grams of sugar per serving and at least 3 to 5 grams of fiber is ideal. For more information on reading nutrition labels, go to www.realsimple.com and input "how to read a nutrition label" in the search bar. The most important thing to note on any nutrition label is the serving size. The facts are given per serving size, not per package, and many packaged products contain more than one serving. Cereal servings are usually ½ cup, which is about half the size of a typical cereal bowl.

COMPLEX CARBOHYDRATES

The easiest way to remember the difference between a complex and a simple carbohydrate is that complex carbohydrates are usually natural and colorful versus processed or packaged. Complex carbohydrates include fruits, vegetables, beans, and whole grains. Because they have longer food chain molecules, they are processed slower. That means they enter the bloodstream and raise blood sugar but over a longer period of time because they contain natural sugars and a lower glycemic load (this is the term used for how long it takes a particular food to raise blood sugar). Complex carbohydrates keep the glucose levels balanced so your child's ability to think and remember is optimized, not compromised by an influx of sugar processing. The micronutrients from fruits and vegetables also help to maintain the right balance of oxygen in your brain (keep the gray matter safe from dysfunction) and they balance the immune system to keep your kids healthy.

A HEALTHY START IN THE MORNING

Now, I'm a mom too, so I know that mornings are hectic. There's breakfast to get, lunches to pack, socks to find, buses to catch, schedules to keep, and jobs to get to. Convenience is paramount when you're trying to get out the door, and cereal is often the easiest breakfast to serve. I'm not saying don't serve cereal. I'm saying to think about what kind of cereal you buy and make the best choice you can so that you give your child the best possible start to the day. There are healthy options. Here are the kids' cereals that *Consumer Reports* rates "very good in nutritional value." Note that they have no more than 6 grams of sugar and have at least 3 grams of fiber: instant oatmeal, Cherrios, Honey Nut Cherrios, Kix, Life (Mikey didn't lie), Barbara's Oats, Kashi Sunshine, and Wheaties. When you throw a handful of blueberries or strawberries into that bowl, along with low-fat or skim milk or yogurt, you will serve your kids a healthy breakfast that will leave them ready to learn. On mornings that aren't so hectic, or if you can find a few extra minutes, yogurt smoothies, waffles (whole wheat are even better), oatmeal, French toast, and any kind of eggs bring a little flavor to the morning routine and fuel your child's brain well.

WHAT IS THE RIGHT BALANCE?

Michelle Obama's Let's Move! campaign played an important and much-needed role in changing the government recommendations for a balanced diet, particularly for children. Below are the recommended daily nutritional guidelines for children ages six to eleven based on the updated USDA MyPlate initiative (www.choosemyplate.gov). I would be remiss if I didn't mention here that a conflict of interest exists with the USDA (United States Department of Agriculture) subsidizing dairy farmers in this country while it is also charged with promoting good nutrition. The rule of thumb is every meal you serve your children is ideally 50 percent fruits and vegetables. Fill them with good carbohydrates (whole grains, fruits, vegetables) and protein every two to three hours to keep their brains and bodies well fueled for learning. Here's the approximate breakdown of recommended nutrients for children aged five to ten with examples for each:

Dairy: 3 cups per day. For example: eight ounces of yogurt equals one cup, one cup low-fat or skim milk equals one cup, one slice of processed cheese equals $1/3$ cup; one slice of hard cheese equals $1/2$ cup.

Fat: Experts say kids should get about 30 percent of their calories from fat. Fat is an important part of a child's diet to optimize brain cells and the nervous system. Two slices of bread equal 13 percent fat. Two tablespoons of peanut butter is 75 percent fat. One cup of 1 percent milk is 18 percent fat, and fruits have no fat. Try to avoid trans fats and saturated fats.

Fiber: A child's age plus five or up to 25 grams per day. For example: one apple or pear equals 3 to 4 grams; 1/2 cup banana, strawberries, blueberries, or similar fruit is 4 to 5 grams; 1/2 cup peas or avocado equals 5 to 6 grams; 1/2 cup beans equals 10 to 12 grams; 1/2 cup of bran cereals equals 5 to 8 grams; 1/2 cup of Cheerios equals 3 grams.

Fruits: 1 1/2 cups (the equivalent of two to three pieces) per day. For example: eight strawberries and one plum; one orange and one peach; one apple and one banana.

Grains: 5 ounces, with half of that whole grains. For example: one slice of bread, one ounce of cereal, 1/2 cup rice or pasta equals one ounce; one large bagel equals four ounces, one mini bagel equals one ounce. One pancake or one waffle equals one ounce. Whole grains are defined in the "Be Claim Cautious" section on page 250.

Protein: 4 to 5 ounces per day. For example: one ounce equals one slice of turkey, one tablespoon of peanut butter, or one egg. Three ounces equals one small chicken breast, one medium burger, or one small piece of tuna or salmon. There's more on protein as brain food below.

Sugar: No more than 5 to 15 percent of calories from sugar or solid fats, which translates to 120 calories per day from sugar or 25 grams of sugar per day. The American Heart Association approaches this by recommending no more than half a child's discretionary calories come from sugar or 100 calories per day (25 grams).

Vegetables: 1 1/2 to 2 1/4 cups per day. For example: one cup equals one cup of beans, one cup of potatoes, one cup of peas, one cup of carrots, or two cups of leafy greens. This is the toughest area for kids to hit and one of the most important.

It's easy to see from these guidelines that most kids don't get enough fruits, vegetables, or whole grains. And all that packaged junk food we stock up on for school lunches and snacks? Most of it falls under empty calories and many contain fat or even trans fats. They have little nutritional value, unless you see a few grams of fiber, protein, or whole grains on the nutritional label. Fiber is an important part of the equation. In addition to making you feel full, it also slows down the absorption of carbohydrates and sugar so that energy from food lasts longer and your brain gets a healthy balance of glucose. Adding a handful of fruit to cereal or yogurt makes it that much healthier.

And finally, about sodium. Most kids consume more sodium than the recommended amount due to processed food. For kids in kindergarten through grade five, the recommended level of sodium averages no more than 1,500 mg per day. That's nearly the sodium level in just one Lunchables meal. Limit lunchmeats, use real—not processed—cheese, and check sodium levels on chicken nuggets.

BRAIN FOOD

Perhaps you've heard that certain foods actually boost your brain cells. It's true and this is where the protein piece comes in. That gray matter known as your brain is made up of lots of fat cells. Maintaining the right balance of essential fatty acids (EFAs) is key to maintaining a healthy brain. You may have heard that fish is good brain food. While this link hasn't been completely proven yet, it has been proven that two fatty acids found in fish—omega-3 and omega-6—boost memory, intelligence, and overall brain function. It's also been proven that omega-3 helps hyperactivity symptoms, which is why doctors often prescribe omega-3 supplements for children diagnosed with ADD.

Your kids can get omega-3 through flaxseed, walnuts, leafy vegetables, salmon, and other cold-water fish such as trout. Some eggs are fortified with omega-3. It can also be found in fish oil supplements, if you don't feel your kids get enough. Another nutrient that protects the brain, improves learning, and keeps it active is choline, which is found in egg yolks. The complex vitamin B12 in an egg also helps maintain the structure of brain cell membranes. Eggs do all this for only 50 calories each. Research also suggests egg yolks guard against senility and old age. (Perhaps it's no coincidence that my grandfather-in-law, who was infamous for eating at least one soft-boiled egg every day for breakfast, lived to be 109.) And no, the egg association isn't paying me for sponsoring this message. Eggs are good for the brain, yet another reason why the egg is considered to be a "perfect" food.

Let's take a look now at some other foods known as "superfoods." These are also considered "brain foods."

POWER SNACKS AND SUPERFOODS

Superfoods are foods that are extra good for the brain and body. They include complex carbohydrates, proteins, and fats that have a lower glycemic load. Superfoods include avocados, blueberries, broccoli, beans, fish, oats, oranges, salmon, soy, spinach, sweet potatoes, tea, tomatoes, turkey, walnuts, and yogurt. If you can get at least two servings of these into your kids every day—and educate your children on how they help the brain and body function—you'll be on your way to optimizing your child's food-brain connection.

Here are a dozen snack ideas that provide lots of nutritional value and help fuel the brain for school. They also work wonders to keep homework meltdowns to a minimum. Some of these ideas will also get you out of the PBJ (peanut butter and jelly) doldrums:

- Veggies and dip (peppers, zucchini, celery, cucumbers, carrots with hummus or a low-fat dressing; the key is to cut them up before and leave them in fridge so they are ready and waiting)
- Turkey twirls (turkey, cheese, and lettuce rolled up, cut into pinwheels)
- Smoothie (yogurt, fresh fruit, and throw in some flaxseed if you can)
- Yogurt with granola or topped with fruit
- Ants on a log (celery topped with peanut butter and raisins)
- Oatmeal cookies (even better with nuts and fruit)
- Cottage cheese and fruit (for kids not sensitive to texture)
- Toothpick fruit kebobs (make a bunch up a couple times a week)
- Zucchini or banana bread (made with whole wheat or oatmeal-based flour)
- Fruit dipped in dark chocolate
- Peanut butter and banana crepes
- Hard-boiled eggs (they last seven days in the fridge)

Any kid favorite sandwich is even better for the body and brain if you make it on whole grain or wheat bread. Hint: to avoid "the jelly made my bread soggy," spread peanut butter on both sides of the bread, then put the jelly or jam on top of the peanut butter so the jelly doesn't leak through.

BE CLAIM CAUTIOUS

When you only look at the outside packaging of food items (particularly breads and cereals), it would appear from the claims that many are made with whole grains or provide a good percentage of dietary nutrients. But if you turn to the nutritional information label of those same products, you will see that is often not true. The most important thing to know is that whole grains are better for your body and brain. Because they are only partially milled, whole grains contain more fiber, keep their vitamins and minerals (especially vitamin E), and have a lower glycemic load so they do not spike blood sugar. They also help prevent obesity, heart disease, and cancer. Foods with higher contents of fiber, protein, and fat also help to keep blood-sugar levels balanced.

When the packaging on bread claims "Made with whole grains," it may not be a whole grain bread; they just want you to think it is. Check the nutrition label. The first ingredient listed designates whether it's whole grain or not. If you see "100% whole wheat flour," oatmeal, bulgar, brown rice, or whole corn-meal as the first ingredient, it is considered a whole grain product. But, 100% wheat flour, unbleached flour, or processed wheat flour are not whole grains—they are still simple, refined flours and less healthy for the brain.

Remember, *whole grains for better brains*. Many claims on packaging are misleading because the FDA has not yet come to a consensus on what manufacturers can or cannot say. A few manufacturers now market an authentic whole grain white bread that looks white to the kids, but it's made with whole grain so it's better for the body and the brain. But these breads are hard to find. Be aware of breads that claim to be "whole grain white." Ignore the claims made on packaging and read the ingredients on nutrition labels instead. Make sure the label says *whole grain*. If your local supermarket doesn't carry a real whole grain "white" bread yet, put in a request. Many will try a new product out at a customer's request. Then be sure to tell all your friends to buy it when it hits the shelves.

One other tip: jam spreads better than jelly and it usually contains less sugar. Here are a few more alternatives to PB&Js:

- Almond butter and honey or fruit
- Peanut butter and dried cranberries or pickles or bananas or whole grain potato chips
- Cream cheese and cucumber
- Cream cheese and jam
- Tuna salad (put in container; let the kids spread it themselves)
- The Laughing Cow Cheese with crackers
- Turkey and cheese roll ups (toothpick holds it together)

Now that you've got the home piece figured out, let's move to the school cafeteria, where it gets a little more complicated.

The School Cafeteria and Vending Machines

A healthy school environment supports consistent and healthy messages in the classroom and the school at large. But these two points are often at odds with each other in school districts. It's no surprise that soft drink consumption has jumped 500 percent in the last fifty years. In the same time period, childhood obesity increased 54 percent for six- to eleven-year-olds and 40 percent for adolescents, thanks in large part to highly profitable soft drink vending machines installed in schools. From 1989 to 1995, soda consumption increased by 41 percent among children ages two to seventeen. Aside from the bad effects soft drinks have on a child's brain due to the high sugar content (usually ten times the daily amount of sugar recommended for a child), soft drinks also contain a high level of phosphoric acid, which leads to loss of vital vitamins and minerals in a child's system. All this impacts your child's ability to think and learn.

The good news is that a few years ago, policy makers finally heard the message that vending machines in schools were a big part of the sugar and obesity epidemic with kids. About forty states banned soda from cafeterias and in school vending machines. The bad news is that due to heavy lobbying, many vending suppliers just replaced soft drinks with sports drinks and vitamin water, which in fact can be just as bad for kids. Some replaced half the machines with plain water. A recent study of fifth graders across those forty states found that their consumption of sugary drinks didn't go down; it just shifted to other sources. In schools that did replace both sweetened drinks and sodas with plain water, many kids brought in sugary drinks and juices from home.

The reality for most school cafeterias is that they need to at least cover their costs. If they don't, the deficit comes out of the general budget, and no superintendent, who is in the business of educating, not feeding kids, wants to cut staff to make up for losses in food costs. Most public schools participate in the National School Lunch Program. For each free and reduced lunch offered to lower-income students who qualify, schools receive a government reimbursement for every meal. But this typically covers only a portion of the cafeteria expenses. The rest comes from kids who buy their lunch. And let's face it, kids buy what tastes good, if given the choice, which is easy to do because parents are not there to guide or overrule them. The latest wave of technology, however, allows kids to have their own account in the cafeteria that parents can fund and view what their kids are actually eating. This technology, along with the good old-fashioned lunch menu listed on the school website or in the local news-paper provides parents the opportunity to monitor and steer their kids to make the best choices for lunch.

In hopes of boosting the number of lunches sold, many school districts are turning to local fast-food chains to bring in branded

IMPROVED SCHOOL NUTRITION STANDARDS

To mitigate the childhood obesity problem, nutrition standards have been raised for all schools under the National School Lunch and School Breakfast Programs for the first time in fifteen years. These standards are now more in line with the Dietary Guidelines for Americans. Specifically, the new stan-dards increase availability of fruits and vegetables, whole grains, and fat-free and low-fat milk. In many schools today, chocolate milk must be low fat. The upgraded standards also reduce sodium levels and keep saturated and trans fats to a minimum.

hamburgers, tacos, and pizza, and in some cases, whole-wheat pizza. And the strategy is working—for the adults anyway. It is beefing up lunch sales. And it's also beefing up the profits of fast-food chains whose market shares are plummeting. But it isn't likely to help kids get the recommended number of fruits, vegetables, and whole grains that enhance learning. In fact, the government recently relabeled ketchup as a "vegetable," despite its high sugar content, so school cafeterias could get closer to serving the recommended daily fruits and vegetables.

Building a cafeteria around what tastes good versus what's good for kids, while the nurses down the hall send out letters informing parents that their child's body mass index (BMI) is over the recommended level, is a great contradiction in our education system. It's also a place where parents can make a difference if they advocate effectively. If your school's cafeteria is still serving sweetened beverages, sports drinks, whole chocolate milk, or unhealthy foods and you want to do something about it, begin by getting the facts. Your school district's food service director or business office can supply you with details on the food and beverages sold in the cafeteria and vending machines. Ask for a breakout of the nutritional value of the breakfast, lunch, and snack items served. Lunch is usually regulated under USDA guidelines, but snacks are not. Meet with a parent advisory council at the school or in the district. Every public school must have a health or parent advisory board. Present your concerns using the Power of P3 and begin a dialogue. Parent organizations and websites that advocate for better nutrition in schools are also at www.theparentbackpack.com.

School Gardens to Cafeterias

Some school districts are looking for interesting ways to promote more nutritious lunches and, at the same time, teach kids about healthy eating. This has prompted farm and school garden programs that inspire hands-on project-based learning for kids, reinforce healthy eating, and invite community-wide involvement. Garden-to-cafeteria programs must comply with government regulations under the National School Lunch Program, they often cost more, and they are most logistically feasible in schools with warmer climates. But many resources and success stories exist.

To start a program in your district, find a willing teacher to partner with, get your food service director on board, and check out these websites: kidsgardening.com, farmtoschool.org, gardenabcs.com, edibleschoolyard.org, and healthiergeneration.org (search for the PDF about how to start a school garden).

Birthday and Holiday Celebrations

For the past three decades, birthday and holiday celebrations in elementary schools have ballooned into a heaping competition of sugary treats stacked upon cupcakes for the whole class. Recognizing the negative impact of sugar on kids, many school districts have started to shift the focus of celebrations from sugar to kids. Some states are even banning sweets and treats in schools altogether. If your school hasn't changed its practices yet on birthday celebrations, a few ideas that other schools have adopted include a "celebrate me" book or card where each kid writes one thing that is special about that child; a special school birthday crown and a sash that's worn all day; a visit to the principal's office to get a sticker or a special pencil; being the teacher assistant for the day, the line leader, or the activity chooser. Taking the focus off sugary foods creates a healthier classroom and children who can celebrate all day long. Teachers are often on board with these ideas because they keep kids focused and ready to learn. In fact, a teacher in Illinois took this concept a step further using exercise—with amazing results.

Exercise and Learning

While schools across the country are cutting recess to make more time for academics and testing, a physical education teacher in Illinois decided it was time to try something different. His goal was to get physical education more focused on fitness and real physical activity rather than students spending half their time sitting in the gym waiting their turn or touching a ball every ten minutes. In Naperville School District 203, outside Chicago, Phil Lawler started a revolution by shifting a good part of his curriculum to exercise and cardio work. His kids would run the mile every week and be graded on effort and progress—their personal best. Every day he sent his kids off to class in a state of heightened awareness, significantly more awake with brain neurons fired up and ready to learn. The result? The school district now ranks in the top ten districts of Illinois consistently, though is wasn't even close to a top-tier school before. Naperville students propelled to number one in the world on the science section of the international TIMSS test, even ahead of Singapore. What's good for the body proved to be great for the brain, too. John Ratey, author of *Spark* outlines this and other ideas in his latest book on how to sharpen thinking and supercharge your brain. More information on this can be found at johnratey.typepad.com.

HOW EXERCISE ENHANCES BRAIN POWER

Since that experiment in Naperville began almost a decade ago, scientists have learned much about the effects of physical activity on a child's brain. Just thirty to forty-five minutes of moderate to vigorous physical activity three to five times a week positively impacts memory, concentration, and classroom behavior. Lots of testing showed what other brain researchers are also discovering. The brain is a muscle that grows and expands the more it's used. A key part of learning takes place in an area of the brain called the hippocampus. When your child tries to remember how to spell a word, for example, that triggers one nerve cell to connect to another by way of a synapse. That synapse will naturally weaken unless the word is practiced again. When that synapse is refueled by the glucose in the brain, more signals and neurons are fired, sprouting more branches like a tree. This is also why when kids make more connections to an idea, they learn on a deeper level (as discussed in chapters 3 and 11).

The physiological effects and chemicals released from exercise work like a fertilizer that spreads over the brain's neurons. It increases the synapses to expand and make even stronger connections and associations, thereby improving memory and learning. A brain's hippocampus works like a distribution center with the *prefrontal cortex* (the boss that organizes and releases the neurons to different parts of the brain). While that's a simplified version of how learning works, you hopefully get the idea. Some researchers refer to exercise as "Miracle Grow" for your brain.

So exercise improves your child's learning in three ways. First, it makes your child's mind more alert and more motivated, so it improves concentration. This idea is not new and it's why doctors recommend kids diagnosed with ADHD get regular exercise. Second, exercise triggers more nerve cells to bind together, which encourages more synapse connections and more learning. And third, exercise causes new nerve cells to develop and creates even more connections in the brain. Studies have also shown that processing speed and *cognitive flexibility* (the ability to shift our thinking from one thought or subject to another) is also improved with exercise. Playing a musical instrument and reading music, for example, will fire nerve cells in math and other areas. This brain information paves the way for a more integrated approach to teaching and learning, as discussed in chapter 11. This subject area has become a new field of study called "mind, brain, and education." It's still in its infancy, but it's growing significantly.

EFFECTS OF BREATHING AND GUM CHEWING ON LEARNING

Here are a few other interesting points about the brain and learning. A key idea behind exercise is getting the right amount of oxygen to the brain. This can also be done through breathing exercises. Just taking the time to breathe deeply and slowly for a few minutes before taking a test or before starting homework can have a positive impact on concentration and motivation. This is why it's often a good idea to have your child get some exercise before leaping into homework. Chewing gum is another way to exercise your brain. Studies also show that like exercise, chewing improves blood circulation in the brain, increases memory, and decreases anxiety—as long as the gum doesn't contain a high percentage of sugar. For this reason, some kids with attention issues are given an accommodation to chew gum during school.

So now we understand how nutrition and exercise affect our kids' brains and their learning. Let's turn our attention back to the impact of sleep on the brain and body. Luke's mother's advice to "Eat your best, get plenty of rest; you'll do well on the test," is now rooted in science.

Sleep Needs and Start Times

The latest studies on the connections between sleep, learning, and memory are loud and clear. While earlier findings linked sleep and mood, the latest research suggests that getting the right amount of sleep at the right time leads to better concentration, improved recall, and enhanced new learning. Kids from the ages of three to five need eleven to thirteen hours of sleep a night, according to the National Sleep Foundation. Children ages five to ten need ten to eleven hours, teens (ages eleven to seventeen) need eight and a half to nine and a quarter hours, and adults need from seven to eight hours. The closer we all get to the recommended hours of sleep, the better we function in life, at work, in the classroom, and on the playing fields.

When I was on my child's elementary school council twelve years ago, I volunteered to be part of a district-wide committee on teen sleep needs and school start times. The goal of the group was to determine if sleep and brain research on adolescents was valid enough to warrant a change in school start times. The assumption was that teens needed the extra sleep in the morning because they couldn't get to sleep earlier in the evening. I admit I had a strong opinion going into this committee. I thought, "Are you kidding me? Turn off the screens and the lights and get them to bed earlier. How hard could this be?" As a parent without teens, I was naive. While I went into that committee a skeptic, I came out convinced that sleep needs and start times need to be in sync if we are to provide our kids with an optimal learning environment. Here's why.

SLEEP AND BRAIN BIOLOGY

Do you remember when you used to sleep in forever as a teen? Well, there was a biological reason for that. When kids enter puberty, a shift occurs in their *circadian rhythm*, or their sleep cycle. The sleep hormone, melatonin, begins to release about an hour later as your child moves through puberty. This is called a *delayed sleep phase*. So by the time they reach high school, most teens cannot physically fall asleep before 10:30 or 11:30 p.m. And if they do, it's often because they are sleep deprived from months and years of insufficient sleep—the same kind that you suffered from when your kids were infants. If we do the math on a 7:30 a.m. start time that's typical for most high schools and the nine hours of sleep a teen needs, we end up with a collision course and significant sleep deprivation.

So why are we talking about this when you only have kids in elementary school? Because this sleep deprivation that occurs among teens who start school at 7:30 a.m. impacts their concentration, their learning, their driving, and their mental health at a time when the brain is entering a critical growth stage. Your elementary kids will be adolescents entering middle school sooner than you know, and you'll be faced with this same out-of-sync start time and its repercussions. But the irony is that elementary start times are also out of sync with younger kids' natural wake-up time. While teens are dragging themselves out of bed at 6:00 or 6:30 a.m., five- through eight-year-olds are often awake and ready to go, but are forced to wait two hours before school begins.

IDEAL START TIMES

Ideally, all kids would start school around 8:00 a.m. But the reality is that for budgetary reasons, many school districts run two- and three-tiered bus routes that dictate start times. The result is that school start times continue to collide with the natural sleep cycle of students and parental influence on bedtimes. All this impacts students' ability to focus, concentrate, and learn.

After five years of debate and controversy, our school district changed school start times, giving teens in high school and middle school an extra fifty minutes of sleep. The original 7:25 a.m. bell was moved to 8:15 a.m., for a total of four extra hours of sleep per week or one hundred and fifty additional hours per school year. Within the first year, teachers reported a significant decline in students being tardy as well as students who were much more alert and awake in first block. Accommodations were made in the sports leagues to accommodate later game starts. After the first two years of this start time initiative, SAT scores and high school standardized tests were the highest in the school's history, and we had more winning teams than ever. Meanwhile, the upper elementary school pushed its start times up by forty minutes from 8:25 a.m. to 7:45 a.m. for kids in grades three through five. While this was a difficult shift for many parents and kids, there was no significant change in academic performance based on standardized tests or behavior. And as students enter puberty in middle school, they now will gain an additional thirty minutes of sleep each night rather than lose an hour.

Change is hard for any school district, especially when it impacts family schedules and communities. But schools have an obligation to provide an optimal learning environment for their students in the classroom and on the fields. This means syncing school start times with students' natural biological clocks. More and more schools are exploring or shifting start times now because the results are significant: improved alertness and concentration, more mental acuity, improved memory, more self-confidence, less moodiness, less anxiety, and less depression. If you're interested in advocating for better start times in your district, find some like-minded parents, a couple teachers who see the benefits of a later start time for teens, and a school board member who struggles daily to get her teen(s) out of bed. Then check out nationalsleepfoundation.org and the resources on my website. You'll be a much happier parent of teens.

....

Now that you are clear on how nutrition, exercise, and sleep impact your child's brain and body every day in school, do what you can to change your children's habits at home or at school to maximize their learning environment. If you make just one simple shift in what foods you serve your children, one minor change in your child's exercise habits, and one small variation in their sleep patterns, you are likely to see a change for the better.

In the last and final chapter of *The Parent Backpack for Kindergarten through Grade 5*, I discuss how to help your child get organized and when and how he can begin to advocate for himself.

TOP TEN TAKEAWAYS

TO CONSIDER

- Diet, exercise, and sleep impact your children's brains and their ability to process, learn, and retrieve information in significant ways.

continued

TO CONSIDER

- An overload of simple carbohydrates like sugar cereal, soda, candy, and junk food negatively impacts brain neurons, concentration, thinking, and behavior.

- Chemicals released from exercise work like a fertilizer that spreads over the brain's neurons, improving concentration, motivation, and learning.

- Schools that align their start times with kids' natural sleep cycles have teens with improved focus, memory, mental acuity, self-confidence, and less anxiety.

TO AVOID

- Don't serve your kids junk food, candy, sugary cereals, or soda because they seriously compromise their brains and their ability to focus and think.

TO DO

- Serve your children mostly fresh fruits, vegetables, whole grains, and protein; go easy on processed snacks.

- Teach your children that eating the right foods and getting the right amount of sleep strengthens their brains and bodies.

- Model exercising, eating well, and getting the recommended hours of sleep yourself.

- Encourage your children to exercise at least three times a week to improve their concentration and learning.

- Enforce regular bed times in the elementary ages so kids get the recommended ten to eleven hours of sleep to optimize mood and learning.

CHAPTER 14

Coaching Kids to Organize and Self-Advocate

Tell me and I forget. Show me and I remember.
Involve me and I understand. —CHINESE PROVERB

"Kevin's backpack is filled with crumpled homework, sticky candy wrappers, rotting sandwiches, broken pencils, leaking pens, and lost permission slips," complains Carolyn, the mother of nine-year-old twin boys. "The kid is so disorganized that I don't even know where to begin. He can't seem to get his homework back to class even when I put it in his backpack for him! When he finally does, it's late and gets marked down. His teacher tells me to check his agenda each night, but half the time he either can't find it or he left it at school. His desk is a disaster, and his cubby outside the classroom? Ha! I'm too embarrassed to even look anymore, just like his side of the bedroom. The worst part of it all is I have no idea how to help him!"

....

Carolyn and Kevin are not alone. Many kids in elementary school struggle to keep their backpacks, desks, cubbies, homework, rooms, and themselves organized. This chapter addresses how to help kids who can't organize themselves and how to get kids advocating for themselves by the end of fifth grade. The truth is, organization and self-advocacy are characteristics that some people (kids and adults) have more DNA for than others. Thankfully, these are also learned skills. But in the meantime, the lack of organizational skills can be a very frustrating, painful process for kids, their parents, and teachers. This final chapter of *The Parent Backpack for Kindergarten through Grade 5* gives you strategies that help your kids get organized so by the time they reach sixth grade or middle school, they'll be close to self-reliant when it comes to their schoolwork. The earlier kids can master the skills needed to succeed in school—getting homework done and in on time, initiating and completing projects, managing their time, learning to follow through, maintaining good study skills, keeping their backpacks and desks semiorganized, and monitoring themselves, the more successful they will be in school and beyond.

Executive "Dysfunction"

Organization falls under a cognitive process in the brain known as *executive functioning* (EF). This is the mental capacity we use to visualize multiple steps and know what to do next and to connect past experience to present action. EF includes the skills of planning and organization, impulse control, initiation and flexibility, working memory, and self-motivation. All this takes place in the prefrontal cortex of the brain, an area that is not fully developed until age twenty or twenty-one. Kids who struggle with one of these areas, like Kevin, often have more than one symptom of executive "dysfunction." Most kids who are diagnosed with ADD or ADHD or other learning disabilities also battle executive functioning issues. But not all kids with EF issues are diagnosed with ADHD. Kids with spirited and intense, or slow-to-warm-up temperaments are also more likely to be affected because they are naturally more impulsive or need more time to transition. I also find that kids who are kinesthetic or auditory learners also tend to have more difficulty with executive functioning skills.

WHAT SKILLS WHEN?

Drs. Peg Dawson and Richard Guare, experts in the areas of executive functioning, offer the following list of developmental tasks by grade level that show what behavior should be in place, when. As with the milestones outlined in chapter 1, these tasks need to be viewed as approximations of what a child typically can or cannot do. They are grouped across multiple grades to allow for the range of differences in kids.

Kindergarten to Grade Two (ages five to eight)

- Follow two- to three-step directions (go to your chair, get your book out, open to page three)
- Tidy bedroom or playroom
- Perform simple chores with reminders (make bed, feed dog, or take out recyclables)
- Complete homework assignments in approximately twenty minutes
- Remember to bring papers to and from school
- Decide how to spend money
- Control behavior (follow safety rules, raise hand before speaking, keep hands to self)

Grades Three to Five (ages eight to eleven)

- Follow directions/run errands (remember to do something after school)
- Tidy bedroom or playroom with some vacuuming or dusting
- Perform chores that take fifteen to thirty minutes (dinner cleanup, rake leaves)
- Remember to bring books, papers, and assignments to and from school
- Keep track of belongings when away from home
- Complete homework assignments in less than one hour
- Plan simple school projects (select book, read book, write draft and final report)
- Keep track of changing daily schedule after school
- Save money for desired projects
- Self-regulate behavior (behave when teacher is out of class; refrain from temper tantrums, bad manners, rude comments)

If you're reading this list and laughing (or, maybe you're beyond laughing), your child needs coaching and some built-in structure and supports to get on track and stay there. Sometimes getting children on track is doable; it's the keeping them there that often seems impossible. I'm going to give you a system for doing both, but before we do that, it's important to understand each of the EF skills and how they interact with each other. From there, we'll move into how your child can put these skills to use and advocate for himself.

PLANNING AND ORGANIZING

Planning and organizing is the ability to manage past, current, and future tasks in a systematic way. Kids (and adults) with trouble in this area are usually not able to see what the task looks like when completed or what steps are needed to get there. They have trouble visualizing and identifying the beginning, middle, and end. For example, on a simple homework assignment, Kevin doesn't log in his mind (or on paper) that he has been assigned this homework. Or he does log it in his agenda but it simply says "Do homework" or "Homework due on Tuesday," which does nothing to help him along. (We'll talk more about agendas later in this chapter.) The assignment marks the beginning. The middle is actually doing the homework, and the end, of course, is turning it in; these are the three parts that need to be completed to "do homework." Because Kevin hasn't visualized or identified the three steps, the homework never gets finished. He lacks the trigger he needs to initiate it.

INITIATION AND FLEXIBILITY

Initiation refers to the ability to recognize when it's time to start something or do a task that will spark a response. In short, this means getting things going. Kids who struggle to start their projects, or clean out their backpacks when they're messy, or pick up their toys in the playroom need outside structures that act as cues, or signals, that say "time to do this." *Flexibility* is the ability to adapt and change to a situation, either physically or mentally. These skills are interrelated because most kids need prompts to tell them it's time to go, time to do homework, or time to eat. Most kids don't come to a parent and say "It's time for me to clean my room now." Once a structure has been in place through parent and teacher support for a few years, it should become a natural part of kids' lives. If not, more structures need to be put in place. Kids who are slow to warm up have difficulty transitioning from one activity to the next. They need reminders and visual cues—external structures to help build up their flexibility traits. As the world has become more collaborative and we need to use our right brains more than ever before (as discussed in chapter 11), these skills of initiation and flexibility become even more important.

WORKING MEMORY

Working memory is the ability to temporarily hold information in one part of the brain while retrieving or using other information to complete a task or perform an activity. It's mental juggling or multitasking for the brain. It involves short-term memory and attention, so again, kids with ADHD or other learning disabilities often have deficits in working memory. Third grader Kevin has physical education at the end of the day, so his teacher has the kids pack up their backpacks before they head to the gym. Her instructions include three steps, which most third graders should be able to handle: "It's Wednesday and physical education day, so before we head to the gym, please pack up your backpacks and be bus-ready. If you're changing into your gym shoes, have your other shoes or boots ready to put on when we get back." In this direction, Kevin needs to hold the information about gym while he focuses on getting his backpack and shoes ready. His brain gets tangled up in gym, shoes, backpack, leave, bus, back, and he ends up doing half of the tasks needed. The balls drop because there are too many visuals for him to take in, too much input to follow. Because we have more information bombarding us today than we'd ever begin to use, our working memories are strained more and more.

IMPULSE CONTROL

Impulse control is the ability to stop and think about what you might say or do before acting. Young kids are not expected to completely control themselves and their reactions because, after all, they are kids. But they do need to be building skills in this area with a parent's help. Again, kids who have a spirited or intense temperament or diagnosed disability will need more support and coaching. The immediacy of the world in which our kids live today with social media and texting conditioning kids to expect instant feedback fuels impulsive behavior. Kids with impulse-control problems are more likely to interrupt the teacher or other kids, grab or physically use their bodies to get what they need rather than use their words, struggle to get homework finished, and engage in behavior that is irritating to others, like tapping a pencil, kicking the table leg repeatedly, or overreacting to a situation where someone makes a mistake. It's important first to accept that your child has limitations in this area and recognize that you will need to be part of this process for a while, until your child can recognize his own behavior and self-correct.

SELF-MONITORING

Self-monitoring refers to a person's capacity to step back and observe her own behavior, to see and judge what is working or not working in a social, emotional, or intellectual capacity. This capacity usually works in tandem with one or more EF skills. Kids who have difficulty self-monitoring have trouble learning from past experiences. They misjudge themselves and the impact of their behavior on others. They don't recognize that they irritated another child, spoke out in class four times, or failed to do their fair share in the project, so they are unable to learn from it. They forget to go back and check their math calculations because they are unaware that this is an issue they need to work on, despite lots of discussion. Our role as parents here is to help our kids see themselves, their behavior, and the impact their behavior has on themselves and others. But we can only do this if the right supports and systems are in place.

PAVE the Way to Organization

PAVE is a four-step system I created that supports the five skills of executive functioning and takes into account that most kids are visual or kinesthetic learners. Your ability to PAVE the way and provide the organizational supports your child needs depends, in some part, on your own organization skill level. Think of this section as a series of supports that will help your children and ultimately help you, too. Getting a kid organized is not a process that happens overnight. It doesn't happen quickly for adults either. And organization looks different for every family. The earlier you start this process, the better for your child and you. The first three steps require your child to do the work once you've established the foundation; the last step involves more participation on the parent's part.

Together, they spell out the mnemonic PAVE, a way to remember how to pave the way to an organized child.

P stands for Picture It.

A is for Agenda = Action.

V is for Visual Maps.

E represents External Structures.

PICTURE IT

These are picture prompts—visuals and photos as originally created by EF expert Sarah Ward—of what your child's desk, backpack, bedroom, cubby, bathroom, playroom, or even your child himself looks like in an ideal state. Perfect for kids who struggle with organization, initiation, and working memory issues, these photos are posted to remind kids of what the end goal looks like. Picture it done. This is something they often cannot do without the visual prompt, because many kids literally can't remember what it's supposed to look like. These pictures do the talking so Mom or Dad won't have to constantly nag, badger, or lecture about what needs to be done and when.

Let's take the backpack as an example. Start by teaching your child that any object that helps you organize your life (backpack, cubby, desk, purse, agenda, or closet) is like a pet. It needs to be taken care of, meaning it needs some attention every day. Show your child how to put everything in its place. Let your child decide what goes where, but reiterate that this is its permanent home. It lives there so you can find it again. Pencil case goes in this pocket. Notebooks and folders live here. Agenda's home is this pouch. Lunch money goes in this pocket. Once everything is in its place, take a picture (or a few) of the open backpack and place the photos where they will serve as a reminder. Ideally, wherever your child packs her backpack every night, post the pictures in that place. You can repeat the same process for her cubby, desk, playroom, closet, and so on. Reinforce this at school and ask the teacher if you can take and post a picture of your son's desk and cubby on a good day. Most teachers will be thrilled to support you in this effort.

Another way to use "picture it" is to motivate departures in the morning. Once your child is all dressed and ready to go with shoes on, backpack and lunch in tow on that first day, snap a picture and post it by the door through which he leaves. Since this may be the first day he's ready on time, this serves as a visual reminder of how he looks when he's ready to go and a cue to initiate getting ready. Take the photo by a face clock so your child associates it with the time to be ready. "Do you match your picture yet?" is a low-stress way to ask if he's ready to go. Change the picture with seasons. This technique also works for the morning time. I used to post a laminated "picture it" on the bathroom mirror with visual reminders of make bed, brush teeth, brush hair, get dressed, eat breakfast. Writing on the mirror occasionally with dry-erase markers helps, too: "Yuk! Please brush me!" with an arrow to a visual of teeth being brushed motivates a kid who isn't brushing before school. It works every time, and you the parent never uttered a word! You can also create a "picture it" for bedtime, picking up a playroom, and packing a sports bag, too, so every item gets back in the bag, jacket included.

Now that we've covered how to help your child get out the door in the morning, let's move on to how to stay organized in school.

AGENDA = ACTION

Once your child reaches third grade, most schools suggest that students use an agenda, a weekly calendar notebook that helps kids organize their assignments and homework. It's a best practice in many upper elementary schools today to use these organizers with the teacher involved in the process. If your school doesn't use them, you can buy one at any office supply store, and consider bringing the idea to your PTA, PTO, or parent organization. An agenda is a great tool, but it's only as good as the words and sequence of actions inside it and how it's used. One of the problems I see with how it's used today is kids write down when a project is due, or what day the test is, based on what the teacher says, but they don't always get to the action or steps that need to occur before that due date.

This is where you come in. When you have a child who struggles with organization, it's important for you to assist him with his agenda so he learns good study habits and routines. It needs attention every day, and some teachers give it more attention than others. Checking it every night is key. Be sure to ask and coach your child to look ahead and identify what steps are needed to get to the end goals. If a science test is written down on next Tuesday, what needs to happen in the days before? Show your child how to write these steps down in the agenda using action verbs. This is outlined specifically in chapter 12. The three days before the test might look like this: "Make note cards. Review chapter questions. Study note cards." Once you practice this with your child for a few weeks (yes, it can take that long), he'll get in the habit of doing it himself. Don't forget to send an email to the teacher to let him know that you're working hard on agenda skills with your child—action verbs for each step—and that if the teacher can reinforce and support this effort until it becomes a habit, it would be very helpful. As time goes on, your child will be taking the initiative to do this himself. Remember to praise his effort along the way. This organizing stuff is hard work.

VISUAL MAPS

Inspired by MindMaps used by many corporations today, visual maps are modeled after graphic organizers for writing, as discussed in chapter 6. But they are much more visual with diagrams, icons, timelines, photos, and illustrations included. More importantly, they are an effective way for kids to organize their thoughts and ideas into reports, projects, and presentations. If your child has a report due on Abraham Lincoln, for example, she first reads about and researches Lincoln. Then she can build a visual map with icons and pictures of Lincoln, the White House, Civil War, slavery, assassination, Lincoln Memorial, and so on, each representing a different support point in the paper. The map can be turned in as an outline and used as basis for a first draft. Visual maps can also be used for book reports, practicing math concepts (particularly geometry and algebra), or spelling words (developing compound words off a root word). They are also ideal for developing strengths-based visual maps for a child, creating an easy-to-read visual weekly activity schedule to post on a bulletin board, or as a way to plan summer vacations. Visual maps make initiating projects, outlining and organizing reports, preparing presentations, and organizing schedules fun. A wide range of visual maps can be found at www.inspiration.com/kidspiration.

EXTERNAL STRUCTURES

This final step is the parents' job to initiate and follow through on external structures, or touch points, with your kids. These are verbal supports that encourage your children throughout the school year and keep them motivated to stay on course. If done consistently, they become routine. They include previewing, reviewing, and reminding. Previewing, but not lecturing. Reviewing, but not criticizing. Reminding, but not rescuing. The idea is to set your child up for success, but if she doesn't make it, the consequence falls out naturally.

Preview

Previewing is anticipating and being proactive about what's ahead to save you headaches down the road. It's taking a peek ahead of time at what's coming up and getting a jump-start on it. Teach and model this for your kids. When you work with your child on his agenda on Sunday, you are previewing what's ahead and needed for the week. If you discover from the class newsletter that your child will be choosing a famous scientist for a project next week and you suggest going to the library over the weekend to get a book about scientists before it starts, you are previewing; you are teaching your child to prepare for what's ahead. When you're reading with your child and ask what he thinks might happen in the story, you are previewing the book. Previewing is a great strategy to motivate kids whether they have an EF deficit or not. It models the behavior you want to see in your child. It establishes a healthy habit and a routine. Talk about what you're doing and why it's important.

Review

Reviewing is an integral part of what we do as parents involved in our kids' education. It's important to paving the way to organization and involves revisiting situations, behaviors, and experiences. We review and praise what worked well and praise the effort that was put in or the progress made. We review what he'd like to do differently next time. Ongoing feedback on both ends is important. Review spelling words, material on the test, what you talked about in the parent-teacher conference: it's all part of the process and helps to keep your child on track. It keeps the routine in motion: reviewing what worked well and what didn't work when the group came over to finish the project, reviewing how to ask the teacher for extra help because he didn't understand the lesson yesterday. Reviewing helps create routine. This helps kids learn about their strengths and weaknesses and keeps them focused on doing their best work.

Remind

It will still be necessary to remind our kids of events, homework, activities, and yes, to wear a coat to school when it's twenty degrees, no matter how many systems we have in place or how well we pave the way for them to be organized. The prefrontal cortex of a child's brain, where organization and planning happens, is still developing. This organization thing will be a work in progress for a while. But it will get better if you praise their progress and effort. That propels them closer to the goal. It's still our job, for example, to remind our kids to look at the rubric for the writing assignment so they know what they're graded on. Remind her that her agenda says she needs to review a chapter today for the test on Wednesday. We're not doing, we're reminding. Remind her that the permission slip sitting on the counter needs to get into her backpack or it probably won't make it to school.

All these reminders are part of the process. They are best delivered through questions, especially as our kids get older, or simple statements that lead our children to take action—not demands or criticisms. Point out the fact. Describe what you see or think. State the obvious: "I wonder how that permission slip will get to school tomorrow if it's not in your backpack?" "I noticed your homework is on the table." "I think I see a lunch box on the counter." This way your child can still make the decision and choose to take action or not. You are reminding but not rescuing, reminding but not doing. You are reminding so it becomes routine for your child.

Sometimes reminders won't work and your daughter will call from school looking for her homework that she "left on the orange chair by the door because I forgot to put in in my backpack and I really, really, really need to turn it in so can you pahleeeze drop it off!" Your son will call needing lunch money for the third time this month. How do you handle these, especially if you work from home, within a few miles of the school?

You don't. The kids have to figure it out. The rule we have in our family is that each child gets one "oops" per term—one oops that she decides needs to be delivered to school, but only one. When we first established this rule, one of my daughters called and couldn't believe I wouldn't bring it in after her first oops was used. But once my kids realized they would have to decide if this was their "one," the calls came less and less frequently. They came to focus more on the idea that "I have to remember this so I don't have to use my 'one.'" While "don't want to use my one" may not be the best motivator to remember important papers, it works for us (so far), with just a few consequences as a result. And suffering through the natural consequences is all part of the process. They eventually figure it out and take more ownership next time. While it's tough to let your kid go a day without lunch or get a zero on homework, it's much better for the lesson to be learned now rather than when it really counts in high school.

....

All this previewing, reviewing, and reminding is part of our role as supporters. In doing this, we condition our children to think for themselves in preparation for the time when they go off on their own and take responsibility for their schoolwork. That time usually comes by the end of the elementary years, in fifth or sixth grade. Depending on the child, we can begin teaching them to advocate for themselves as young as first or second grade.

The Path to Self-Advocacy

"Mom," said Sydney gulping down her dinner, "there is no way I can get this math packet done, go to dance practice tonight, and finish my paper for English. And I cannot miss dance or I lose my part. I need you to write a note to my teacher!"

"I understand, Honey," says Sydney's mom, comforting her eleven-year-old daughter. "Why don't you try to finish half the math problems and I'll write a note to Mrs. LaSalle explaining the situation."

"Hold on a minute here," interrupts Sydney's dad. "When is it time for Sydney to start advocating for herself? She's in fifth grade and quite capable of managing her time by this age. I think it's time she explains to her teacher why she couldn't get the homework done. Let her handle this. She's going to middle school next year."

....

It's natural to want your children to succeed and to want to help them out of a jam. In the process of doing that, many parents are guilty of going too far. By age ten or eleven, as children reach their tween years before adolescence, they need to begin advocating for and monitoring themselves around their schoolwork and all that comes with it. Just as parents go to a job every day, a child's responsibility is school. Some kids are capable of self-advocating by their tenth birthday; others may need a little prodding to get there by age eleven. But the sooner they start, and the more you can nudge them toward that goal, the more confident and responsible they will become.

That doesn't mean we stop supporting them, but it does mean that sometime before the end of fifth grade, kids take the lead in organizing and managing their own work with parents checking in to make sure things are on track. When this happens, kids thrive in school and are on track to becoming confident, motivated students in middle school and beyond.

Kids who learn to self-advocate at an early age gain a skill that will benefit them for life. Self-advocacy begins with a healthy dose of self-esteem, and healthy self-esteem comes from a child feeling loved, connected, and confident. All those traits I talk about in chapter 8: catching your children doing things right and genuinely praising the progress they make and the effort they put in fuels their self-esteem. Learning how to set boundaries, stand up for what they need and want, and speak up when they don't understand adds to kids' feelings of competency. This is important so kids can think on their feet. It's also more important in today's classrooms where teachers are juggling more than ever. When teachers see a child who is self-aware enough to ask for what he needs or motivated enough to make a request, they want to help—much more than when parents ask.

If you're not sure where your child stands on the self-advocacy scale, observe him at a playground. Watch her in a group of friends. Does he approach other kids and initiate conversations or offer ideas? Does she express what she wants to do rather than acquiesce to what the other friends want? Observe your children in a store or at the library. Are your kids comfortable asking a store clerk or librarian a question to get more information? This is all part of the process and the earlier they get started, the easier it will be.

THREE STEPS TO SELF-ADVOCACY

The first step to self-advocacy is raising a child's self-awareness level and understanding of her social, emotional, and physical needs. Help your children identify and understand their strengths and challenges. Kids sometimes need help in matching words with their gifts and how they feel. You've been observing your child for years now, so you certainly know his strengths. Be sure to communicate those as much as possible. Talk to your child about temperament and learning styles. If she's an above average kid in intensity or spirit, and likes hands-on learning, knowing this about herself will help her monitor her behaviors and needs. If he knows he tends to be slower to warm up to new situations and that's he's on the reserved side, he can create goals, with your help, that help him become more comfortable—goals like previewing material before he meets as a group or finding out who will be at the birthday party so he can hang with someone he knows. Look back at report cards for other trends. Think about what coaches and teachers say about your child. If geometry in math is consistently a problem, there may be a spatial deficit. No problem, ask the teacher for a little extra help here. A great way to put all this together is to have your child produce a visual map of his strengths, as discussed on page 269. Kids love to do this and will benefit from the boost of self-awareness.

The second step in self-advocacy is to have your child think about goals. What does she want to be better at? What does he want to achieve? This can be in a sport, a class, or an activity. Setting goals is a key part of self-advocacy. If you don't know what you want, it's hard to ask for what you need. It's hard to own it. Help your child come up with SMART goals, to borrow a slice of the corporate world: these are specific, measurable, achievable, relevant, and timely goals in an area that's important to your child. If you child swims, a goal may be to drop two seconds in the fifty free. This is measured by timers each meet, it's achievable if you attend and work hard in every practice, it's relevant to becoming a better swimmer, and timely because the swim meets are scheduled for the next eight weeks. With these goals in mind, your child can ask the coach about what she can do to work harder in practice, shave another second off the turn, and so on. Once these goals are clear, then she's ready to do the asking. The goals can also be added to the child's visual map.

The third step is about asking questions to get what you need. Many kids today are not comfortable talking on the phone or having face-to-face conversations because they text in cryptic code all day with their friends. Sadly, having full conversations is becoming a bit of a lost art. This is all the more reason that we, as parents, need to guide our children in learning how to do this effectively. Role-play what to say. When your child resists having a conversation or says, "I don't know what to say!?" he is looking for guidance. He is afraid of the talk. Without judgment, give your child the words, as if you were doing the asking: "Mr. Binder, I was wondering if you could help me . . ." If they resist, try a different approach: "Ms. Klutch, I'm not getting this geometry stuff. Can I come in after school on Thursday for some extra help?" Keep throwing out different ideas until he feels comfortable with one. Teachers and coaches love when kids advocate for themselves. Chapter 5 and the Power of P3 also helps with language.

Be sure to make your child aware of other existing resources that could answer the question. It's important that they know about these resources and how to tap them. For example, if your child doesn't understand long division in fifth grade, take the extra effort to view a lesson in long division at www.khanacademy.org. Teachers want to help kids who help themselves. Employers want to hire employees who are self-motivated and good problem solvers. Critical thinking and self-advocacy is the means to get there.

Once your children understand their strengths and challenges—once he is comfortable managing his own projects and homework, once she is confident asking for what she needs to reach her goal—they are on the way to self-advocacy. Praise the effort they put in. Praise the progress, even if it's a small step in the right direction. This will motivate them to continue, especially kids who are more reserved.

Now let's return to Sydney, the girl with conflicts between schoolwork and dance practice, whom we met a little earlier. Sydney likes to take a lot on, but her challenge is managing it all. She knows this, but her mom usually helps her out. Now her parents want to help her develop her skills of self-advocacy. Sydney works with her parents to understand what she needs, to come up with some goals, and to find the right words to speak to her teacher the next day. She ends up with this: "I couldn't finish the homework last night, Mrs. LaSalle, because I wasn't managing my time very well. I'm working on getting better at that." Now that she's taken the first step, Sydney is on her way to being a self-confident student who can manage her work and advocate for her own needs. As she moves into adolescence and middle school—a world full of new challenges, new faces, and, no doubt, some rough waters, Sydney will be ready. Her parents will be ready too—still on the banks, waving and cheering her on, as she moves further along her exciting journey of learning and life.

....

Chapter 14 completes the journey of *The Parent Backpack for Kindergarten through Grade 5*. I hope this chapter on organizing and self-advocacy, combined with all the others, has given you some perspective on education today and your role in your children's learning. I hope it's coached you on how to guide, support, and encourage your children along their unique journeys. And I trust it's given you the tools you need to connect with teachers and advocate effectively for what your children need, until that exciting time between ten and twelve when your kids are ready to take on that role themselves. They'll be ready because of a decade of modeling and teaching from you, their first and most important teacher, because you cared enough to be connected to their education in productive, meaningful ways.

TOP TEN TAKEAWAYS

TO CONSIDER

- Organizing skills are part of the brain's executive functioning (EF) process that includes planning and organizing, initiating, working memory, impulse control, and self-monitoring.

- While many children, including kids diagnosed with ADHD, battle organizational issues, these are learned skills that can be improved and mastered.

- The more self-aware your child is, the more likely she will be able to organize herself and self-advocate.

- By fifth grade, your child is usually ready to branch out and advocate for himself, while you continue to guide, support, and encourage him along the way.

TO AVOID

- Remind, but don't rescue your child. Many kids will need to learn lessons by making mistakes a few times before they can take ownership of their schoolwork or their belongings.

- Don't write notes to your child's teacher when your child can handle the issue themselves; some children are ready to advocate for themselves as young as second grade.

TO DO

- PAVE the way for your kids to be organized by creating supports along their journeys as early as possible: "Picture it" photos, Agenda action items, Visual maps, and External structures.

- Set up touch points to keep your kids on course: previewing, reviewing, and reminding helps keep them on course without doing the work for them.

- The better we model goal setting and organization for our kids, the more likely they are to develop strong executive skills.

- Help your children understand their strengths and challenges; give them the words to learn how to self-advocate.

Glossary of Edu-Terms

Asperger's Syndrome
An autism spectrum disorder that is characterized by significant difficulties in social interaction, limited empathy, and restricted, repetitive patterns of behavior. Physical clumsiness and odd use of language are often reported.

Assessment
A measurement of a student's skills or knowledge in a subject area; a test.

Attention-Deficit Disorder or Attention-Deficit/Hyperactivity Disorder (ADD/ADHD)
A condition or disorder characterized by the inability to concentrate or focus. May also lead to impulsivity, disorganization, hyperactivity, hyperfocusing, persistence, creativity, and curiosity.

Authentic Assessment
Gauging students' knowledge in ways other than conventional standardized tests. May include hands-on demonstrations of knowledge, like writing an essay, conducting a science experiment, or creating a portfolio of work. Also called alternative, portfolio, or performance assessment.

Autism Spectrum Disorders (ASDs)
A developmental disability that causes problems in communication, social interaction, and behavior. Symptoms vary from mild to severe. Includes autism, Asperger's Syndrome, Retts Syndrome, and Pervasive Developmental Disorder (PDD).

Average Per Pupil Expenditure (APPE)
(See *Cost Per Pupil*.)

Best Practice
An instructional method, technique, or approach that's been proven through experience and research to be an effective learning tool; it delivers the desired result.

Bilingual Education
A program for nonnative English speakers. Students spend part of the school day receiving instruction in their native language, with a goal of moving them into mainstream English classes, normally within two or three years.

Blue Ribbon School
The National Blue Ribbon Schools Program honors outstanding public and nonpublic elementary, middle, and high schools whose students achieve at very high levels or have made significant progress and helped close gaps in achievement. Run by the U.S. Department of Education.

Charter Schools
Publicly funded schools that have been exempted from certain rules and regulations that apply to other public schools. They are accountable for producing specific results outlined in the schools' charters. Some charter schools are state run; others are run by state-approved private organizations. Many use lottery systems to enroll students.

Child Study Team
A team of people, including teachers, caregivers, school psychologists, and other child development specialists who work together to design an Individualzed Education Program (IEP) or a 504 Plan with the parents to help guide the child's progress.

Children's Internet Protection Act (CIPA)
Federal law mandating that any school receiving discounted rates for Internet access, Internet service, or internal connections must develop an Internet safety policy and use protective measures that block or filter Internet material that is harmful to minors.

Common Core State Standards (CCSS or Common Core)
Educational standards that provide a consistent, clear understanding of what students are expected to learn in K–12. Ensures that students are receiving a high-quality education from school to school and state to state. Began in 2012 with math and English. Expanding to other subjects.

Communication Compact
A written agreement between parents and teachers that clarifies what responsibility families and schools agree to share for student learning.

Conflict Meditation
System of resolving disputes through both sides talking it out. Many schools use variations of this as a way of solving social conflicts. The goal of conflict mediation is to help students communicate clearly, understand one another, and focus on how they can best work together.

Cooperative Learning
Teaching method in which students of varying abilities and interests work together in small groups on a specific task or project. Students complete assignments together and receive a common grade.

Cost Per Pupil (CPP)
Calculated by taking the total expenditures for a school divided by number of students enrolled. Can be analyzed on a state, district, or school level. Also known as average per pupil expenditure (APPE).

Coteaching
Two or more teachers sharing responsibility for instructing some or all of the students assigned to a classroom. Involves distributing responsibility among teachers for planning, instruction, and evaluation of students. Sometimes used in inclusion classrooms (see *Inclusion*) and implemented with a regular education and a special education teacher.

Crisis Management Plan
School's plan for managing an emergency such as a bomb threat, a fire, or a natural disaster. A trained crisis management team—school administrators and other critical staff—implements the crisis management

plan. As part of this plan, schools are required to conduct fire safety and emergency drills.

Criterion-Referenced Tests (CRT)
Assessments that measure a student's performance against a set body of content. Tests that match state standards (standards-based tests) are criterion-referenced tests: they are designed to measure how well a child has learned a specific body of knowledge and skills.

Curriculum
Subject matter that teachers and students cover in class, as well as the educational ends sought for students, usually described as goals or objectives.

DEAR (Drop Everything And Read) Time
An independent reading program in which students consistently take out their books and read for at least fifteen minutes a day in the classroom. Also referred to as Sustained Silent Reading (SSR). Students generally read what they want and keep a reading log, but reading is not tested. It helps to develop a lifelong reading habit.

Due Process
Legal concept ensuring that the government will respect all of a person's legal rights instead of just some or most of them. For example, due process means that children undergoing suspension have the right to know the school's rules ahead of time, to receive adequate notice of the charges, and to challenge the charges.

Education Foundation
Nonprofit, community-based group that raises money for schools. Most education foundations operate independently from the school districts they support.

Elementary and Secondary Education Act (ESEA)
Law first passed in 1965. The law authorizes federally funded education programs that are administered by the states. In 2002, Congress amended ESEA and reauthorized it as the No Child Left Behind Act (NCLB) to establish higher standards and accountability.

Emotional Intelligence
The combination of interpersonal intelligence—the ability to understand the intentions, motivations, and desires of other people—and intrapersonal intelligence, the capacity to understand one's own feelings and motivations. Better known as "people skills."

English as a Second Language (ESL)
Classes for eligible English language learners. Also known as ESOL (English for speakers of other languages) and ELD (English language development).

English Language Learner (ELL)
A student who is still learning English as a new language. Also called LEP (limited-English proficient) and EL (English learner).

Enrichment Program
Education designed to supplement the regular academic curriculum.

Enrollment
Total number of students registered in each school and district. This number is turned into the state and becomes the basis for federal and state funding allotments.

Equity School
Funding approach built on the idea that states are required to distribute resources fairly to all students no matter where they live.

Family Education Rights Protection Act (FERPA)
The education equivalent of HEPPA, a federal law that protects the privacy of student records until the age of eighteen. Parents can review and inspect records and receive a copy for a fee. Allows for disclosure of "directory" information (name, address, and phone number) without consent, providing that a reasonable time period is given for parents to opt their child out.

504 Plan
(See *Section 504*.)

Free Appropriate Public Education (FAPE)

Education is federally guaranteed for any student attending a school that receives public funds. For students with disabilities, this means they may be eligible for special needs education services based on a child's Individualized Education Plan (IEP) at no additional cost to the parents.

Gifted

Term describing students who show high-achievement capability in intellectual, creative, artistic, or leadership capacity, or in specific academic fields, and who need services and activities not ordinarily provided by the school in order to fully develop those capabilities. Defined by some states as top 1 percent; top 5 to 9 percent in others.

Handbook

The main guidebook of a school that outlines school procedures, policies, student behavior expectations, discipline codes, communication, confidentiality, and general school guidelines. Requires parent and student signatures. Usually revised annually; often available online.

High-Stakes Tests

Assessments used by districts and states to make important decisions that affect an individual child or a school. Considered high stakes because scores may be used to determine whether a student graduates or continues on to the next grade, or to determine a school's future, such as replacing the administration.

Inclusion

Education practice based on the philosophy that all children, regardless of their special needs, can and should be educated together in the same classroom. This means students who have an individualized education plan or are part of a special education program stay in general education classes and continue to receive support from the special education teacher or an instructional aide.

Independent Schools

Private, nonprofit schools governed by elected boards of trustees that are funded through tuition payments, charitable contributions, and endowments.

Individualized Education Plan (IEP)

Education plan prepared for each public school child who receives special education and related services. Reviewed annually, with a complete reevaluation every three years, the IEP is a legal document that outlines goals, services, and how the services will be delivered.

Individualized Education Plan Team (IEP Team)

Group of people who come together to create an Individualized Education Plan. Usually comprised of the student's classroom teacher, a school counselor or psychologist, a special education teacher, the principal or assistant principal, and the child's parents or legal guardians.

Individuals with Disabilities Education Act (IDEA)

The federal law reauthorized in 2004 authorizing state and local aid for special education services for children with disabilities, including students with learning disabilities. IDEA governs how states and public agencies provide early intervention, special education, and related services to more than 6.5 million eligible infants, toddlers, children, and youth with disabilities.

Intelligence Quotient (IQ)

Measure of a person's capacity or aptitude for learning. IQ tests measure one facet of intelligent as displayed in verbal and logical thinking; IQ scores alone do not determine a student's academic needs. Current research shows IQ is malleable rather than a fixed quotient.

Learning Disability

Lifelong disorder affecting how individuals with normal or above-average intelligence store, process, or produce information. A learning disability usually reveals itself in a discrepancy between intelligence and academic achievement.

Literacy Coach

A reading specialist who focuses on providing professional development for teachers and the additional support they need to implement instruction; the specialist provides the leadership for a schools literacy program; also assists teachers in developing reading and writing lessons and evaluating student data.

Magnet Schools

Publicly funded special-focus schools designed to bring in students from outside the local neighborhood to reduce or eliminate racial imbalance. They offer programs designed for students with special abilities, interests, or needs.

Media Specialist

Educator who administers the school's library media program, filters and researches online databases, and teaches students how to use the media center, conduct research, and use technology. Formerly, a librarian.

Narrative Report Card

Report that contains written comments by a child's teacher and conveys more detailed information than is possible with a letter or number grade alone.

National Assessment of Educational Progress (NAEP)

The only federal test that provides information about the educational progress of schools in the United States and in specific geographic regions in the country. Also called "The Nation's Report Card," NAEP administers reading and math tests every two years and tests other subjects in alternate years.

No Child Left Behind Act (NCLB)

Most recent reauthorization of the federal government's comprehensive K–12 program, the Elementary and Secondary Education Act (ESEA), which began in 1965. NCLB redefines the federal role in K–12 education in an effort to close the achievement gap between disadvantaged children and their peers, and it is based on four principles: stronger accountability for results, increased flexibility and local control, expanded options for parents, and an emphasis on teaching methods that have been proven to work (also known as "best practices").

Norm-Referenced Tests

Assessments that compare the performance of individual test takers to that of a nationally representative group of test takers. For example, a student in the fourth grade is compared to other fourth graders taking the same test.

Open Enrollment

Policy that allows parents to choose where their child attends school as opposed to being assigned to a school based on where the child lives.

Para Educator

Trained assistant who works with teachers to help deliver classroom instruction and to ensure that individual student needs are being met. Also called educational or instructional aide, classroom assistant, or paraprofessional.

Parent Portal

A secure website that gives parents and guardians access to a student's current assignment grades, report cards, transcripts, class schedule, attendance, and homework. Some portals allow two-way communication with teachers. Usually accessible through the school website with a password.

Parent Revolution

A nonprofit organization that promises to help parents fighting for the schools children deserve through the parent trigger law. Backed by high-profile philanthropic organizations including the Walton Family Foundation and the Bill and Melinda Gates Foundation.

Parent Teacher Association (PTA)

Largest volunteer child advocacy organization in the United States. Local PTA chapters in schools pay dues to the state and national organization. National PTA often takes stands on national education issues and policies, lobbies Washington, and advocates for causes. Local PTAs address school policies, practices, and fund-raising.

Parent Teacher Organization (PTO)

Umbrella organization that represents parent-teacher groups that are independent of the PTA. Groups may take other names such as PCC (Parent Communication Council), PTG (Parent Teacher Group), and HAS (Home and School Association). These are often single-school groups operating under their own bylaws and working for their individual school.

Parent Trigger Law

A law that states a group of parents can take over a poorly performing public school by getting 51 percent of parents in a school to sign a petition to change the administration or transform the school into a charter school. Variations of this law were recently passed in CA, LA, MI, CT, TX, IN, and OH, but so far no school has succeeded in "triggering" a takeover, at this printing. Initially funded by Parent Revolution.

Parochial School

Another name for a Christian-based or religious school that provides both regular and religious education. Usually affiliated with or run by a church.

Partnership for Assessment of Readiness for College and Careers (PARCC)

One of two assessments proposed for the Common Core standards that theoretically measures critical thinking, identifies which students are doing well, which need more help, whether students are college or career ready, and gives students and teachers the information they need to improve. About half the states will use PARCC; half will use SBAC (see *SMARTER Balanced Assessment Consortium*).

Peer Helpers

Students who help other students in academic or social areas. Peer helpers may be paired with new students to help them adjust to the new environment or may serve as tutors for younger students. Also called peer mediators.

Per Pupil Expenditure

(See *Cost Per Pupil*.)

Portfolio

A collection of a student's work that may be used as part of a standardized assessment system or by an individual teacher as part of ongoing classroom grading. It generally includes some sort of self-reflection by the student. Used infrequently as an alternate means of standardized testing.

Private Schools

Term describing nonpublic schools, either independent, religious, or special needs–based, typically nonprofit and tuition driven.

Pull-Out Program
A program that removes a student from the regular classroom setting for one or more sessions a week in order to see an education specialist.

Race to the Top (RTTT)
A program initiated by President Barack Obama and Secretary of Education Arne Duncan that incentivizes schools and supports bold efforts to close the achievement gap by improving college and career readiness standards. Schools must use data that shows improved student performance and teacher evaluations to receive funding.

Religious or Catholic Schools
(See *Parochial School*.)

Response to Intervention (RTI)
Multitiered instruction that allows school districts to provide services and interventions at increasing levels of intensity to students who need them. Student progress is closely monitored at each stage. Results of monitoring are used to make decisions about the need for further research-based instruction and/or intervention in general education, special education, or both.

Rubric
A set of scoring criteria for a project or assignment that the student typically knows in advance. Rubrics help students understand the strengths and weaknesses of their work better than letter grades alone.

School Choice
A public policy that allows a parent/guardian or student to choose a district, charter, or private school, regardless of residence and location. Can also be a tax credit and deduction for expenses related to schooling, vouchers, and homeschooling.

Section 504
A federal law within the Rehabilitation Act of 1973 (Section 504), designed to protect the rights of individuals with disabilities in programs and activities that receive federal financial assistance from

the U.S. Department of Education. The Office of Civil Rights (OCR) enforces Section 504, which ensures that the child with a disability has equal access to a Free Appropriate Public Education (FAPE). The child may receive accommodations and modifications, referred to as a 504 Plan.

SMARTER Balanced Assessment Consortium (SBAC)

One of two assessments proposed for the Common Core standards that theoretically measures critical thinking, identifies which students are doing well, which need more help, whether students are college or career ready, and gives students and teachers the information they need to improve. About half the states in the nation will use SBAC; half will use PARCC (see *Partnership for Assessment of Readiness for College and Careers*).

Social-Emotional Learning (SEL)

A curriculum for learning life skills, including how to deal with oneself, relationships, and work with others in an effective manner; helps students develop the skills to manage their emotions, resolve conflicts nonviolently, and make responsible decisions.

Special Education

Instruction governed under Individuals with Disabilities Education Act (IDEA) that is designed to serve children with emotional, mental, and physical disabilities. Children found eligible for special education are entitled to an Individualized Education Plan (IEP) that spells out the services they need to reach their educational goals. (See *Individuals with Disabilities Education Act* and *Individualized Education Plan*.)

Standardized Tests

Assessments developed using standard procedures and administered and scored in a consistent manner for all test takers. The standardization of tests helps ensure that the test scores are comparable and as unbiased as possible.

Standards

Clear statements about what students should know and be able to do in certain subject areas and at certain stages in their education. Standards can be academic content or performance based.

Standards-Based Report Card

Reflects what children are expected to learn and how they are progressing toward those goals (standards). Designed to assess student performance against a specific and observable set of grade-level skills. A standards-based system measures each student against the identified, concrete standard, instead of measuring how the student performs compared to other students.

Superintendent

The top administrator accountable for a school district; sets and leads district goals and manages the day-to-day operations of a school district. Usually hired by an elected school committee or board. Principals report to the superintendent.

Sustained Silent Reading (SSR)

(See *DEAR Time*.)

Title I

Program evolved from the Elementary and Secondary Education Act (ESEA) of 1965 that provides extra resources to schools and school districts with the highest concentrations of poverty.

Tracking

The term used to define ability grouping over time. Describes the process of separating students into leveled course selections according to academic ability, typically demonstrated by standardized test scores. Critics argue it results in student inequities.

Twice-Exceptional

Term describing young people who are designated as both gifted and having learning or attention disabilities.

Vouchers

Certificates that allow parents to use public funds for their children's educations at a school of their choice, often a private school.

Webmaster

Person responsible for designing, developing, and maintaining a website. Also called Internet director. In a school, typically serves under the director of technology.

Zero Tolerance

Policy under which particular types of misconduct are simply not tolerated and specific consequences or interventions are established and applied in all cases.

Bibliography

CHAPTER 1: UNDERSTANDING YOUR CHILD'S JOURNEY

Calkins, Lucy, *Raising Lifelong Learners* (Reading, MA: Perseus Books, 1997).

Collaborative for Academic, Social, and Emotional Learning, http://casel.org.

Common Core State Standards Initiative, http://www.corestandards.org.

"The Dunn and Dunn Learning Style Model," ILSA, http://www.ilsa-learning-styles
.com/Learning+Styles/The+Dunn+and+Dunn+Learning+Styles+Model.html

Fox, Jennifer, *Your Child's Strengths: A Guide for Parents and Teachers* (New York: Penguin Books, 2008).

Graham, Emily, "What Is Your Child's Learning Style?," School Family, www.school family.com.

Lehrer, Jonah, "Don't! The Secret of Self-Control," *The New Yorker*, May 18, 2009.

Mischel, Walter, Ebbe B. Ebbesen, and Antonette Raskoff Zeiss, "Cognitive and Attentional Mechanisms in Delay of Gratification," *Journal of Personality and Social Psychology* 21, no. 2 (1972): 204-218.

Mogel, Wendy, PhD, *The Blessing of a Skinned Knee* (New York: Scribner, 2001).

Open Circle, http://www.open-circle.org.

"Theories of Learning: Jean Piaget," University of California Berkeley, Teaching Guide for Graduate Student Instructors, http://gsi.berkeley.edu/teachingguide/theories/piaget.html

CHAPTER 2: YOUR ROLE IN A CHANGING SYSTEM

The Annie E. Casey Foundation, *Kids Count Data Book*, www.kidscount.org.

Common Core State Standards Initiative, http://www.corestandards.org.

Hallinan, M. T., "Teacher Influences on Students' Attachment to School," *Sociology of Education* 81, no. 3 (2008): 271–83.

Henderson, Anne T., and Karen L. Mapp, *A New Wave of Evidence: The Impact of School, Family, and Community Connections on Student Achievement* (2002), www.sedl.org.

Marklein, Mary Beth, "SAT, ACT: Most high school kids lack skills for college," *USA Today*, September 25, 2012.

National Center for Education Statistics, Elementary/Secondary Information System, http://nces.ed.gov/ccd/elsi.

National Center for Education Statistics, *Fast Facts: Condition of Public School Facilities* (2007), http://nces.ed.gov.

National Center for Education Statistics, *National Assessment of Educational Progress Reading Assessment*, http://nces.ed.gov/nationsreportcard/reading.

National Research Council, *How People Learn: Brain, Mind, Experience, and School, Expanded Edition* (2000), www.nap.edu.

"No Child Left Behind," *Education Week* (September 19, 2011), http://www.edweek.org/ew/issues/no-child-left-behind.

OECD Programme for International Student Assessment: http://www.oecd.org/pisa.

The Science, Technology, Engineering, and Mathematics (STEM) Education Coalition, http://www.stemedcoalition.org.

Tough, Paul, *Whatever It Takes: Geoffrey Canada's Quest to Change Harlem and America* (New York: Houghton Mifflin, 2008).

21st Century School Fund, *Repair for Success: An Analysis of the Need and Possibilities for a Federal Investment in PK–12 School Maintenance and Repair* (2009), www.21csf.org.

U.S. Department of Education, *A Nation Accountable: Twenty-Five Years after* A Nation at Risk (2008), www.ed.gov.

U.S. Department of Education, *ESEA Reauthorization: A Blueprint for Reform, Supporting Families and Communities* (2010), http://www2.ed.gov/policy/elsec/leg/blueprint/blueprint.pdf.

U.S. Department of Education, United States Education Dashboard, www.dashboard.ed.gov

Weber, Karl, *Waiting for Superman: How We Can Save America's Failing Public Schools* (New York: Participant Media/Perseus Books, 2010).

Weiss, Heather, M. Elena Lopez, and Heidi Rosenberg, *Beyond Random Acts: Family, School, and Community Engagement as an Integral Part of Education Reform* (2010), www.hfrp.org.

CHAPTER 3: BUILDING BRIDGES TO SCHOOL AND LEARNING

The Center for Public Education, "Back to School: How Parent Involvement Affects Student Achievement (At a Glance)," http://www.centerforpubliceducation.org/Main-Menu/Public-education/Parent-Involvement.

Center for Schools and Communities, The PTA Family Engagement in Education Act of 2011 (H.R.1821/S.941), http://www.center-school.org/pa-pirc/documents/FEE-Act-Summary.pdf.

Epstein, Joyce L., PhD, Developing and Sustaining Research-Based Programs of School, Family, and Community Partnerships: Summary of Five Years of NNPS Research (2005), http://www.csos.jhu.edu/p2000/pdf/Research%20Summary.pdf.

GreatSchools, www.greatschools.org.

Henderson, Anne T., and Karen L. Mapp, *A New Wave of Evidence: The Impact of School, Family, and Community Connections on Student Achievement* (2002), www.sedl.org.

Henderson, A. T., K. L. Mapp, V. R. Johnson, and D. Davies, *Beyond the Bake Sale: The Essential Guide to Family–School Partnerships* (New York: The New Press, 2007).

Jeynes, William H., "Parental Involvement and Student Achievement: A Meta-Analysis," *Family Involvement Research Digest* (December 2005), hfrp.org/publications-resources/publications-series/family-involvement-research-digests/parental-involvement-and-student-achievement-a-meta-analysis.

Molland, Judy, *Straight Talk About Schools* (Minneapolis, MN: Free Spirit Press, 2007).

National Center for Community and Education Partnerships, Resources on Parent/Family Engagement in a Child's Education, http://www.edpartnerships.org/Content/NavigationMenu/Resource_Center/Parent_Family_Engagement/Resources.htm.

National Coalition for Parent Involvement in Education, http://www.ncpie.org.

National Parent Teacher Association, www.pta.org.

School Family, www.schoolfamily.com.

Weiss, Heather, M. Elena Lopez, and Heidi Rosenberg, *Beyond Random Acts: Family, School, and Community Engagement as an Integral Part of Education Reform* (2010), www.hfrp.org.

CHAPTER 4: KINDERGARTEN MATTERS

Ackerman, Debra J., and W. Steven Barnett, *Prepared for Kindergarten: What Does "Readiness" Mean?* (March 2005), National Institute for Early Education Research, http://nieer.org/resources/policyreports/report5.pdf.

Clark, Patricia, "Recent Research on All-Day Kindergarten," Education.com, www.education.com.

DeCicca, Philip, and Justin D. Smith, "The Long-Run Impacts of Early Childhood Education: Evidence from a Failed Policy Experiment" (NBER Working Paper No. 17085, May 2011), The National Bureau of Economic Research, www.nber.org/papers/w17085.

Ferrari, Nancy, "Kindergarten Redshirting Is Popular, But Is it Necessary?," March 6, 2012, Harvard Health Publications, www.health.harvard.edu.

Hirsh-Pasek, Kathy, *Einstein Never Used Flashcards: How Our Children Really Learn and Why They Need to Play More and Memorize Less* (Emmaus, PA: Rodale, 2003).

Kelmon, Jessica, "When Should Kids Start Kindergarten?," GreatSchools, www.greatschools.org.

National Education Association, *A Parent's Guide to a Successful Kindergarten Transition*, www.nea.org/assets/docs/HE/44013_NEA_W_L6.pdf.

Pappano, Laura, "Kids Haven't Changed; Kindergarten Has," *Harvard Education Letter* 26, no. 5 (September/October 2010): www.hepg.org/hel/article/479.

Patton, Christine, and Justina Wang, "Ready for Success: Creating Collaborative and Thoughtful Transitions into Kindergarten" (September 20, 2012): www.hfrp.org.

Safer, Morley, "Redshirting: Holding Kids Back from Kindergarten," July 8, 2012, *60 Minutes*, www.cbsnews.com/video/watch/?id=7414212n.

CHAPTER 5: WORDS THAT WORK WITH TEACHERS

Faber, Adele, and Elaine Mazlish, *How to Talk So Kids Can Learn (at Home and in School)* (New York: Scribner, 2003).

Halloran, John, "7 Effective Parent Teacher Communication Tips," TeachHub.com, www.teachhub.com/parent-teacher-communication-tips.

Kaplan, Nochum, "School-Parent Communications: How Open and Honest Should the Lines of Communications Be?" *Educational Pathways* 5, www.chabad.org.

Lightfoot, Sara Lawrence, *The Essential Conversation: What Parents and Teachers Can Learn from Each Other* (New York: Ballantine, 2003).

National PTA, *Parents' Guide to Student Success*, www.pta.org/parents/content.cfm?ItemNumber=2583&navItemNumber=3363.

Stanberry, Kristin, "Making the Most of Your Parent-Teacher Conference," GreatSchools, www.greatschools.org.

CHAPTER 6: WHY JACK *LIKES* TO READ—AND WRITE

Armbruster, B., F. Lehr, and M. B. Osburn, *Proven Ideas from Research for Parents: A Child Becomes a Reader (K–3)*, 2nd ed. (Portsmouth, NH: RMC Research Corporation, 2005-2008).

Calkins, Lucy, *The Art of Teaching Writing* (Portsmouth, NH: Heinemann, 1994).

Calkins, Lucy, *Raising Lifelong Learners* (New York: Perseus Books, 1997).

Codell, Esme Raji, *How to Get Your Child to Love Reading for Ravenous and Reluctant Readers Alike* (Chapel Hill, NC: Algonquin Books, 2003).

Literacy Connections, "Reading Aloud: Tips for Parents and Teachers," http://literacy connections.com/ReadingAloud.php.

Taylor, Melissa, *Book Love: Help Your Child Grow from Reluctant to Enthusiastic Reader* (Colorado: Imagination Soup, 2012).

Trelease, Jim, *The Read-Aloud Handbook,* 6th ed. (New York: Penguin, 2006).

Trelease on Reading, www.trelease-on-reading.com/index.html.

Zimmerman, Susan, *7 Keys to Comprehension: How to Help Your Kids Read and Get It!* (New York: Three Rivers Press, 2003).

CHAPTER 7: IT'S ALL ABOUT THE TEACHING

Chetty, Raj, John N. Friedman, and Jonah E. Rockoff, *The Long-Term Impacts of Teachers: Teacher Value-Added and Student Outcomes in Adulthood* (NBER Working Paper No. 17699, December 2011, revised January 2012), http://obs.rc.fas.harvard.edu/chetty/value_added .html.

Clark, Ron, *The End of Molasses Classes: Getting Our Kids Unstuck—101 Extraordinary Solutions for Parents and Teachers* (New York: Touchstone, 2011).

Gilbert, Francis, "What Makes a Great Teacher?" *The Guardian*, January 18, 2010.

Harmon, Lawrence, "Declaring Peace in Teacher Contract Talks," *The Boston Globe*, December 8, 2012.

"Howard Gardner, Multiple Intelligences and Education," Infed, www.infed.org/thinkers/gardner.htm.

National Council on Teacher Quality, *Best Practices for Teacher Effectiveness: How Districts Nationwide Are Stacking Up*, Bill and Melinda Gates Foundation, http://docs.gatesfoundation.org/united-states/documents/best-practices-teach-effectiveness.pdf.

The New Teacher Project, http://widgeteffect.org.

Rosenberg, Sarah, and Elena Silva with the FDR Group, "Trending Toward Reform: Teachers Speak on Unions and the Future of the Profession," *Education Sector Reports*, http://www.educationsector.org/publications/trending-toward-reform-teachers-speak-unions-and-future-profession.

"What Makes a Teacher Effective?: What Research Says About Teacher Preparation," NCATE, www.ncate.org.

CHAPTER 8: BALANCING ACADEMICS WITH CONNECTION AND CONFIDENCE

Brooks, Robert, and Sam Goldstein, *Raising Resilient Children: Fostering Strength, Hope, and Optimism in Your Child* (New York: McGraw-Hill, 2002).

Brooks, Robert, and Sam Goldstein, *Raising a Self-Disciplined Child: Help Your Child Become More Responsible, Confident, and Resilient* (New York: McGraw-Hill, 2007).

Brooks, Robert, Ph.D., www.drrobertbrooks.com.

Hallowell, Edward M., MD, *The Childhood Roots of Adult Happiness: Five Steps to Help Kids Create and Sustain Lifelong Joy* (New York: Ballantine, 2002).

Hallowell, Edward M., MD, www.drhallowell.com.

Krakovsky, Marina, "The Effort Effect," *Stanford Magazine*, November 2012, http://alumni.stanford.edu/get/page/magazine/article/?article_id=32124.

Tough, Paul, *How Children Succeed: Grit, Curiosity and the Hidden Power of Character* (New York: Houghton Mifflin Harcourt, 2012).

Trei, Lisa, "New Study Yields Instructive Results on How Mindset Affects Learning," *Stanford News*, February 7, 2007, http://news.stanford.edu/news/2007/february7/dweck-020707.html.

CHAPTER 9: WHEN YOUR CHILD NEEDS MORE SUPPORT

"The Hallowell Method: A Positive, Strengths-Based Approach to ADHD," Dr. Hallowell.com, http://www.drhallowell.com/add-adhd/add-adhd-treatment.

Harvard Family Research Project and Jamie Ferrel, *Family Engagement and Children with Disabilities: A Resource Guide for Educators and Parents* (September 2012), www.hfrp.org/publications-resources/browse-our-publications/family-engagement-and-children-with-disabilities-a-resource-guide-for-educators-and-parents.

National Center for Education Statistics, "Fast Facts: Students with Disabilities" (2012), http://nces.ed.gov/fastfacts/display.asp?id=64.

Shah, Nirvi, "On Special Education: The Legal Side of RTI and Students with Learning Disabilities," *Education Week*, September 5, 2012.

Special Education Eligibility/Initial and Reevaluation Determination, www.doe.mass.edu/sped/iep/forms/pdf/ED1.pdf.

U.S. Department of Education, "Protecting Students with Disabilities," www.ed.gov.

Wilmshurst, Linda, and Alan W. Brue, *The Complete Guide to Special Education: Expert Advice on Evaluations, IEPs, and Helping Kids Succeed* (San Francisco: John Wiley and Sons, 2010).

Wright, Peter W. D., and Pamela Darr Wright, *Wrightslaw: From Emotions to Advocacy— The Special Education Survival Guide* (Harbor House Law Press, Inc., 2002).

Wrightslaw, www.wrightslaw.com.

CHAPTER 10: THE SOCIAL AND EMOTIONAL REALITIES OF BULLYING

Coloroso, Barbara, *The Bully, the Bullied, and the Bystander: From Preschool to HighSchool— How Parents and Teachers Can Help Break the Cycle* (New York: HarperCollins, 2008).

Cyberbullying Research Center, "Nice it Forward," http://cyberbullying.us/blog/nice-it-forward.html.

National Education Association's Bully Free: It Starts with Me, www.nea.org/home/neabullyfree.html.

Sheehy, Kelsey, "Parents May Be Teaching Teens to Be Bullies," *U.S. News & World Report*, October 10, 2012, www.usnews.com/education/blogs/high-school-notes/2012/10/10/parents-may-be-teaching-teens-to-be-bullies.

Simmons, Rachel, *Odd Girl Out: The Hidden Culture of Aggression in Girls* (New York: Mariner Books, 2011).

StopBullying, www.stopbullying.gov.

Wiseman, Rosalind, *Queen Bees and Wannabes: Helping Your Daughter Survive Cliques, Gossip, Boyfriends, and the New Realities of Girl World* (New York: Three Rivers Press, 2009).

CHAPTER 11: THINKING, LEARNING, AND TECHNOLOGY

Freedman, Terry, "What Are the Features of a Good ICT Activity?," ICT in Education, September 24, 2012, www.ictineducation.org/home-page/2012/9/24/what-are-the-features-of-a-good-ict-activity.html.

Galinsky, Ellen, *Mind in the Making: The Seven Essential Life Skills Every Child Needs* (New York: Harper Collins, 2010).

"Is the Use of Standardized Tests Improving Education in America?," ProCon.org, http://standardizedtests.procon.org.

Trilling, Bernie, *21st Century Skills: Learning for Life in Our Times* (San Francisco: Jossey-Bass, 2009).

Wagner, Tony, *Creating Innovators: The Making of Young People Who Will Change the World* (New York: Scribner, 2012).

Wagner, Tony, *The Global Achievement Gap: Why Even Our Best Schools Don't Teach the New Survival Skills Our Children Need—and What We Can Do about It* (New York: Perseus Books, 2008).

CHAPTER 12: GUIDING HOMEWORK, PROJECTS, AND STUDYING

Bennett, Sara, and Nancy Kalish, *The Case against Homework: How Homework Is Hurting Children and What Parents Can Do about It* (New York: Three Rivers Press, 2006).

Dawson, Peg, "Homework: A Guide for Parents," NASP Resources, www.nasponline.org/resources/home_school/homework.aspx.

GreatSchools Staff, "How to Help Your Child with Homework," GreatSchools, www.greatschools.org/students/homework-help/3069-cb-1-2-3-help-with-homework.gs.

"Helping with Homework," PBS Parents, www.pbs.org/parents/goingtoschool/helping_homework.html.

"Homework Hub," Scholastic, www.scholastic.com/teachers/lesson-plan/homework-hub.

"Research Spotlight on Homework: NEA Reviews of the Research on Best Practices in Education," National Education Association, www.nea.org/tools/16938.htm.

CHAPTER 13: FUELING YOUR CHILD'S BRAIN AND BODY

ChooseMyPlate, www.choosemyplate.gov.

Cline, John, "Sleepless in America: Do Later School Start Times Really Help High School Students?," *Psychology Today*, February 27, 2011.

Food and Nutrition Information Center, *Role of Nutrition in Learning and Behavior: A Resource List for Professionals*, August 2011, www.nal.usda.gov/fnic/pubs/learning.pdf.

National Sleep Foundation, www.sleepfoundation.org.

Ratey, John J., and Eric Hagerman, *Spark: The Revolutionary New Science of Exercise and the Brain* (New York: Little Brown and Company, 2008).

Tanner, Lindsay, "Junk Foods Widely Available at Elementary Schools, Study Shows," The Huffington Post, February 6, 2012, http://www.huffingtonpost.com/2012/02/06/junk-foods-widely-availab_0_n_1258200.html.

Two Angry Moms, http://angrymoms.org.

U.S. Department of Agriculture and U.S. Department of Health and Human Services, *Dietary Guidelines for Americans 2010*, www.cnpp.usda.gov/Publications/DietaryGuidelines/2010/PolicyDoc/PolicyDoc.pdf.

CHAPTER 14: COACHING KIDS TO ORGANIZE AND SELF-ADVOCATE

Cognitive Connections, http://cognitiveconnectionstherapy.com.

Cooper-Kahn, Joyce, PhD and Laurie C. Dietzel, PhD, *Late, Lost, and Unprepared: A Parents' Guide to Helping Children with Executive Functioning* (Bethesda, MD: Woodbine House, 2008).

Dawson, Peg, EdD and Richard Guare, PhD, *Executive Skills in Children and Adolescents: A Practical Guide to Assessment and Intervention,* 2nd ed., The Guilford Practical Intervention in the Schools Series (New York: Guilford Press, 2010).

Dawson, Peg, *Smart But Scattered: The Revolutionary "Executive Skills" Approach to Helping Kids Reach Their Potential* (New York: Guilford Press, 2009).

Gordon, Merry, "Take Charge! Self-Advocacy in the Classroom," Education.com, www.education.com/magazine/article/charge-advocacy-classroom.

Index